KU-705-713

VICTORIA'S
SPYMASTERS

VICTORIA'S SPYMASTERS

EMPIRE AND ESPIONAGE

S T E P H E N W A D E

The
History
Press

WORCESTERSHIRE COUNTY COUNCIL	
517	
Bertrams	19/06/2009
327.1241	£18.99
KDZ	

First published 2009

The History Press
The Mill, Brimscombe Port
Stroud, Gloucestershire, GL5 2QG
www.thehistorypress.co.uk

© Stephen Wade, 2009

The right of Stephen Wade to be identified as the Author
of this work has been asserted in accordance with the
Copyrights, Designs and Patents Act 1988.

All rights reserved. No part of this book may be reprinted
or reproduced or utilised in any form or by any electronic,
mechanical or other means, now known or hereafter invented,
including photocopying and recording, or in any information
storage or retrieval system, without the permission in writing
from the Publishers.

British Library Cataloguing in Publication Data.
A catalogue record for this book is available from the British Library.

ISBN 978 0 7524 4535 9

Typesetting and origination by The History Press
Printed in Great Britain

Contents

Acknowledgements   7

Introduction   9

1. Intelligence in the Empire, c.1850–1918   25

2. Playing the Game   49

3. Robertson: From Staff College to the First World War   65

4. Wingate, Slatin and Egypt   89

5. Omdurman   101

6. Ardagh and the Anglo-Boer War   111

7. Sir Mark Sykes and the Diplomats   131

8. The Arab Bureau and the Sykes-Picot Agreement   139

9. Robertson and Intelligence after the Boers   149

10. Epilogue: MI5 and Spies   157

Destinations   174

Bibliography   179

Index   188

ACKNOWLEDGEMENTS

Thanks are due to staff at the University of Hull Archives, and to the Sykes family at Sledmere, for permission to use the portrait of Mark Sykes and the illustration of Sykes' Turkish Room. Conversations with staff at Sledmere led to some interesting ideas, so thanks are due to them. Other illustrations are from my own collection. In a broad survey such as this, one has to thank the experts whose work has opened up the questions and some of the answers regarding the story of military intelligence in these years: particularly Andrew Cook, Richard Deacon, Peter Hopkirk and Richard Holmes.

INTRODUCTION

Early in 2007, my book surveying the development of military intelligence in the British Army from the beginnings of the Great Game to the end of the First World War, *Spies in the Empire*, appeared from Anthem Press. That book emerged from my realisation that there was a glaring omission on the military history shelves: intelligence and espionage in the British Empire in those years. The decades between Waterloo and the Indian Mutiny have been traditionally termed 'Years of peace', as if there were an interim period in which nothing of any note happened. But, of course, as Ian Hernon's valuable study, *Britain's Forgotten Wars* (2003) makes clear, British servicemen were busy bolstering the margins of the red areas on the map all the time, in some remote corner or other.

But the gap was a commercial idea, too. The categories were (and still are) 'Napoleonic', 'Empire' and 'First World War,' and even John Keegan's book, *Intelligence in War*, omits the later end of the nineteenth century in England, choosing instead to cover the achievements of Stonewall Jackson. Keegan wanted to focus on theory and influence, so that was understandable, but that lack of any general history made me gather information for this book.

It proved to be a gargantuan task. The sources and records are scattered everywhere, from obscure monographs to memoirs and letters. Those forty years included not only the miserable debacle of the Crimean War but also the under-resourced and terrifying confrontation with the sepoys in India and the arrogance displayed against the Zulu nation. But there was another story beneath the piecemeal assemblage of intelligence in both field and archive: it was a tale of individuals struggling against bias, denigration and confusion as the body of experts and amateurs which gradually became MI5, an intelligence corps per se, stepped into an identity.

Not only did the War Office show scant regard for the proper organisation of intelligence (something they could have learnt from Napoleon) but also for the higher echelons within the power machine, the movers and shakers of war, placing intelligence men on the margins until the hard lesson of the Boer Wars. Most of the time the staff relied in this field on locals and gentlemen scholars, or even farmers and settlers. John Dunn, Zulu general as well as interpreter and guide, epitomises this non-military figure, having achieved marvellous feats in that intractable terrain: he met Queen Victoria and was lionised by the media.

To be fair, some of the great generals had an impact on intelligence work, notably Sir Garnet Wolseley. Paradoxically, some of his best *bon mots* and perceptions are tucked away in his journals, but we do have the well-documented gang of picked men around him in the Ashanti campaign to testify that he was in advance of his time in terms of such topics as local knowledge, astute deployment of field spies and so on. He saw that specialists and scholars had their value.

From that first extended essay in highlighting forgotten figures in this science, then, emerged the germ of a second book. Now I want to tell the stories of some key figures from that period whose names are not household words and who do not figure in the central narratives of popular military history. My aim here is to write their biographies and to explain what they contributed to the growth of intelligence studies and practice. I realise, naturally, that some of these men owe a great deal to their tutors, and there are some secondary figures here such as the strategists and 'brains' working from behind desks or in the classroom. Henderson, of the Boer Wars, is such a person, and also, of course, Baden-Powell, but the latter is all too well known thanks to Tim Jeal's definitive biography.

Who are these men shaded and obscured by the scene-stealers of conflicts across the Empire? The first is Reginald Wingate, most celebrated for his achievements with Kitchener at Omdurman. But later in his life he was Governor General of the Sudan, and then High Commissioner in Egypt. He chose Rudolf Slatin, Austrian adventurer, who had been a prisoner of the Mahdi for years before he came out and won a considerable reputation both as soldier and as writer in the last years of the Victorian period.

Wingate, as we know from that classic of war reportage, *With Kitchener to Khartoum* (1898), by G. W. Steevens, was a man on top form in the march on Khartoum:

Whatever there was to know, Colonel Wingate surely knew it, for he makes it his business to know everything. He is the type of learned soldier in which perhaps our army is not as strong as it is on other sides. If he had not chosen to be Chief of the Intelligence Department of the Egyptian Army, he might have been a professor of oriental languages at Oxford.

Steevens is not above some hero worship, but that assessment is borne out by the evidence of Wingate's character.

Then we have the second-in-command, Rudolf Slatin. Here was a man who did not fit any template or tradition at the time, yet he was invaluable as a source of knowledge about the enemy for Kitchener and his staff. His fascination goes beyond the battlefield, though: he was known by Queen Victoria's court and circles, and he also became a contributor to rather high-class intellectual journals.

As for William Robertson, this man from a Lincolnshire farming family rose to become Chief of the General Staff, and we have pictures of him both reviewing troops and meeting high-ranking diplomats. His autobiography, shamefully out of print, is one of the most informative accounts of the stumbling and uncertain rise of the Intelligence Branch that we have today. Perhaps most valuable of all his contributions is his approach to that writing, because the style and manner are those of a bluff, forthright soldier who tends to think that he has seen a few remarkable things and that it should make a good read. How right he was, but also how he undervalued his own testimony to the men, places and ideas behind the intelligence work done in India in particular.

In John Ardagh we have a man much maligned in the aftermath of the war in South Africa, and here I am attempting a defence of him, as well as providing an account of his earlier career. In many ways, he was the 'fall guy' at a time when defeat and strategic failure were unthinkable in high places.

Finally, there is Mark Sykes, most famous (and infamous) for the Sykes-Picot Agreement of 1916, resolving the Middle East 'Arab Question' in a way that satisfied only Britain and France, and arguably an event which lead to all kinds of later problems. But a study of how Sykes worked in the diplomatic, military and indeed royal circles in the years up to and including the First World War illustrates the workings of intelligence centred on the Arab Bureau in particular. My biography will include his earlier military experience and travels in the East and the Middle East also.

This book has dual aims, however. To bring these people truly into consideration and to create a revisionist look at them, it is necessary to tell their lives more broadly, so I aim to balance the nature and the achievements equally of these characters where possible. It also means that some very major episodes in the colonial conflicts of the Victorian and Edwardian periods will have to be summarised, because above all this book is for the general reader with an interest in military history in the widest sense – from the work done in offices and classrooms to hand-to-hand fighting with the enemy.

The foundations beneath these stories are made of the very meta-narrative of the years 1870 to 1918, and so world scale events in the context of diplomacy have their place too. What stands out when one reviews the intelligence systems in these years is the sheer multiplicity of definitions of what intelligence work constituted and who exactly did it. This is because for the latter decades of the nineteenth century there was a great deal of military and naval information which was accessible to anyone. Tsar Peter of Russia, in the Crimea, said that he learned all he needed to know of British strategy by reading *The Times*. There are stories of academics and politicians from good families visiting boatyards both in Britain and in Germany in the manner of tourists with notebooks.

Baden-Powell has not helped matters either. His influential essay, *My Adventures as a Spy*, highlights a practice of espionage at once ludicrously crass and simple and also very amateur. His account of going butterfly hunting and using nature drawings to hide sketches of gun placements is *Boys' Own* stuff. Nevertheless, espionage had been, for some time before the Fenian movement and the Russian anarchists in the huge metropolis of London, taught some hard lessons in amoral ruthlessness; we had, in a sense, still to grow up in matters of military intelligence. When I was asked about my first book and I said that it was a history of military intelligence, many people replied, 'Oh, and is there any?' The image of the topic as textualised by the *Punch* cartoonist persists. There is also still too much of the *Carry On* pastiche in many people's view of the officer class in the imperial years.

Victoria's Spymasters is a work of discovery and also a plea for a second look at some people who made things happen, and more interestingly stopped even worse things happening (with the exception of Sykes). They all had to take severe criticism and they had to operate in an outmoded system of operations and command at times, but in the end, they were on the sides of the winners.

Along the road to these discoveries we inevitably have undercurrents and parallel stories, some of these relating to some massively important events in their own right. For instance, the impact of the Franco-Prussian War of 1870 was profound in the ranks of the British military establishment.

Students at the Staff College went on battlefield tours to see the landscapes of tactics for themselves. Then there were the personalities: chiefly the diplomats, a body of men whose stories would fill a library with exciting tales and exotic scenarios, midnight intrigues and last-minute escapes. We have a suggestion of this in the life of Sir Howard Elphinstone, whose biography has recently been written by Martyn Downer: *The Queen's Knight* (2007).

Victorian and Edwardian history has a superfluity of eccentric, wayward, egocentric, power-mad, inspired and possessed characters. Many of them were in the ranks of the diplomatists and spies. A few came up from lowly beginnings to positions of power in the security forces and in the new MI5, as Andrew Cook's writings show. I hope that my biographies equally have something of a revisionist element, because I feel that history has dealt unjustly with some of my subjects. In the end, however, their actions will speak louder than any words written about them. If the present work achieves nothing else than helping readers look with fresh eyes at men who were in their time hugely important figures in the British Empire, then I will be satisfied.

A history of military intelligence in those eighty years embraces several major areas of interest and these provide the basis of the following chapters:

(1) The gradual emergence of the military intelligence arm of the military structure of the Empire.
(2) The influential individuals who played a major role in the profession-alisation of intelligence.
(3) The failure of intelligence in several important campaigns, and the lessons learned.
(4) Foreign policy and the men who brought about reform.

Underlying all this, however, there is the undeniable hue of romance colouring the subject. The late Victorian novelists William le Queux, Rider Haggard and Conan Doyle have all played their part in creating this allure. But at the centre of the arena there is a mix of the romance of 'spying' and the straightforward military duties we would term 'intelligence'. This means that the word *espionage* in the context of the Victorian imperial quest covers several elements, all a part of the scene as a whole. The sources of military information available during this period include activities as diverse as map-making and surveying; amateur scholars supplying cultural information; linguists and travellers who learned about the enemy, though in a desultory manner; personnel within the army, for a long period the ranks of the engineers; political officers on missions and, most fundamental of all, native ranks and civilians such as the 'pundits' employed by the administration of the Raj.

In practical terms this means that military intelligence for this seventy years was diverse, piecemeal, chaotic and massively amateur. What was needed was some method of classification and systemic implementation of knowledge. What happened was, until the last few decades of the century, very much a pragmatic process; ad hoc information was gained in any way possible. Of course there are several reasons for this slow and haphazard scale of change: the sheer vastness of the Empire, the pink on the map, was the main feature. In a world map included in a geography textbook published in 1908 the Empire's pink stands out, bold and prominent: the Dominion of Canada; British Guiana; nine African possessions; India, Australasia and another forty islands and smaller places. The central geographical location of the following history, India, is explained in this way:

> Our Indian Empire comprises the central and by far the most important of the three great peninsulas of Southern Asia, together with large territories on the eastern side of the Bay of Bengal. The total area of these vast dominions, most of which are under direct British rule, and the rest subject to British control, is upwards of 1,800,000 square miles, or more than thirty times as large as England and Wales, while the population is (according to the Census of 1901), 294,417,000.

From the early years of Victoria's reign there had been a flowering of all manner of academic disciplines with the intention of listing, filing and describing the nature of the diverse range of peoples within this Empire. It was amateur, random and passionate. Very little in its aims had any link whatsoever with military intelligence. But as the century wore on, the high command was very gradually to see the usefulness of this vast store of knowledge.

Knowledge of language, culture and history was one thing worth attention, but at the basis of the whole enterprise was, before the arguably main turning point of the Crimean War, seldom related to direct information about the opposing armies in a war. In many ways, Britain learned the value of such activities from the Prussians and the French. It seems incredible to note now that the systems of Napoleon in this respect were so little noticed or studied. Napoleon's method was to have a string of local and regional agents who in turn paid a set sum of money to their own agents. In that way, the obvious advantages of having native speakers of the language of the enemy was gained, and also local knowledge of topography, customs and political affairs was already in place to be exploited when the time came. As Edward Whitcomb has explained in the case of Napoleon's information on Russia: 'Bignon was appointed in December 1810 to obtain information on Russia. It was not until August 1811 that he was given 3,000 francs per month for espionage, and not until December 1811 that he was specifically instructed to establish a hierarchy or cell system.'

In other words, Napoleon was well aware of the need to make the diplomatic sources not only more reliable but better organised.

Yet, in spite of the general history involved, the preliminary considerations necessary for this historical survey must begin with the impact of the subject on the individual imagination. In an interview with *The Times* in April 2006, Peter Hopkirk stressed the importance of Rudyard Kipling's novel, *Kim*, in this respect. *Kim* was published in 1901, when the great Mutiny of 1857 was still in the memory but far enough away to be reconsidered. Hopkirk explains the influence of the book in this way: 'I used to dream of being sent on some secret mission by Kim's spymaster, Colonel Creighton…Unfortunately, by the time I was old enough the British had left India.' It is the imaginative pull of the Great Game that persists. The history around it also persists, as Hopkirk said in the same interview: 'It's extraordinary to see how history is repeating itself… Some of the players are different, but the Game goes on. Perhaps my books should be read as cautionary tales. Had the Soviet Union learned from the lessons of history, it would never have invaded Afghanistan.'

The mention of Russia is what completes the picture for the historian of the Victorian Great Game. The principal area of interest in this history has to be the three-edged combat zone of Russia, Afghanistan and British India, but as with all wars, other states and communities were drawn in. It is almost impossible now to imagine the sheer courage and sense of adventure in a political officer such as Captain James Abbott, a man who travelled from Herat to Moscow. His account of this journey, published in 1842, is one of the foundation texts of the military intelligence of that century. But there is more to the origins of the subject in the Indian continent than individuals. There are the families of administrators and their political officers, and these will form the basis of a main section of this book.

The individual imagination, powerful in the case of the lone adventurers, was always subject to the distortions of media representation later on, and so we have an inheritance of falsification; a view of spying within the Raj, for instance, that has generated myths and legends such as we find in the character and career of Sir Richard Burton. His image, as depicted in the brooding melancholic photograph of him in a long cape, taken around 1855, exemplifies this need to see political officers as especially Byronic figures, somehow doomed to be loners in both a physical and a spiritual wilderness. Burton and his personal qualities will recur throughout this history, not only in himself but in his nature as a template for that figure of mystery and intrigue. His biographer, Byron Farwell, crystallises this strange fusion of the eccentric and the rigidly professional in his personality: 'He learned "mantih", or eastern logic, in order to train his mind to think as an oriental. He mixed with Jat camelmen, studying their language and way of life.' But he was capable of another cast of mind entirely: 'Always fascinated by gold, he took up alchemy and tried his hand at producing gold from baser metals.'

There is also a theoretical dimension to this enquiry. The vastly influential classic work, *On War*, by Carl von Clausewitz, was published in 1830, just before his death. But the influence came much later; as Louise Wilmott has noted:

> For some thirty years after his death in 1831, his ideas made little impact. More popular with the general staffs of European armies were contemporaries like Jomini who emphasised formal manoeuvres and rules of conduct, and who forsook the ambiguity and complexity which Clausewitz insisted were an integral part of war. This situation only began to change in the 1860s and 1870s.

The reason why military theory of an adventurous and intellectual turn did not have an impact on the British Army is not hard to find. Even after the triumphs of the war against Napoleon, little changed in the organisation of the structural nature of the army. In many ways, the concise statements made by Clausewitz on 'Information' were exactly what the first intelligence groups were to find out and understand: 'Great part of information obtained in war is contradictory, a still greater part is false, and by far the greatest part is of a doubtful character.'

Basically, at the beginning of the period covered here, military intelligence meant finding out information by the traditional means: scouting, learning basic geography, questioning locals and, most of all, making sure that there were capable linguists in the regiment. At the heart of the whole enterprise was the officer class, and to understand the achievements of the political officers, it is essential to understand the means by which the officer class communicated, bonded and nurtured that special esprit de corps that would pay dividends in battle. One interesting method of gaining an insight into this mindset is to look at the publications of the regiments. For instance, *The Journal of the Household Brigade* of 1871 provides something profoundly important about the army's sense of identity at the time of the Franco-Prussian War in Europe. The journal covers sports reports, lists of brigade masters of hounds, 'the chase and the turf', steeple chasing, pigeon shooting, theatricals, yachting, balls and concerts. Nothing could exemplify the spawning ground of the political officer as well as this: notice that the list of activities represents the enormous gap of time to be filled when an officer was at home, away from the front line of active service. But it was training in disguise: the sport, and other personal developmental activities, helped form an attitude. With all this in him, all the habits of endurance, teamwork and invention, out in India he would go shooting for weeks, and in between the sport there was 'information', and, of course, improvement in spoken Hindi, perhaps.

These officers were to cluster around the more charismatic figures out in the Empire, men such as John Nicholson, hero of the Mutiny, and Henry Lawrence, who had a group of protégés for whom he had a special regard and whose careers he nurtured. Charles Allen has defined this 'band of brothers' very clearly: 'Such close friendships, between lonely men who lived many miles from each other, finding open expression only in the event of the death of one of their company, were very much the order of the day. This was a brotherhood of young men who shared a vocation: they saw themselves very much as a band of brothers, Paladins at the court of their master and mentor, Henry Lawrence.'

It is no accident that the date of 1873 is an important one for the history of military intelligence. As Sir George Aston wrote in his memoirs, 'After 1870 the whole of Europe sat at the feet of the Germans as the most efficient soldiers in the world.' A whole tranche of army reforms in Britain followed that key date, and as Aston notes:

> Once started, the idea that the British Army was maintained, partly at all events, for waging war began to take root, with the obvious corollary that the more that it knew about foreign armies the better. The result was the establishment of an Intelligence Branch (under the adjutant-general of the forces) on a separate basis on the first of April 1873.

The military intelligence existing in the Victorian period has been overlooked in much military history in recent years. It is not an easy matter to explain this. Even John Keegan's book on 'knowledge of the enemy from Napoleon to Al-Qaeda' avoids the British situation in this period and discusses Stonewall Jackson instead. It is tempting to say that the story of the secret services in the year between Victoria's accession in 1837 and the establishment of the Intelligence Branch at Queen Anne's Gate in 1873 is so piecemeal that historians can find no distinctive narrative.

It cannot be denied that from the early nineteenth century, when police informers and *agents provocateurs* were profitably employed by Lord Sidmouth to root out radicals in the working-class movements, to the Crimean War in 1853–56, all the varieties of intelligence gathering were rather ad hoc and rarely well organised. The foundation of the police force in 1829, by Sir Robert Peel, was seen by many as the first step towards a totalitarian regime in Britain, but no-one in the establishment complained when some of Feargus O'Connor's 'Physical Force' Chartists were spied upon and monitored as they drilled on Woodhouse Moor in Leeds.

Throughout the century there was an overlap between military intelligence in the strict sense and all foreign affairs. There was also a blurring of distinctions when it came to understanding what the separate roles of the police were, as opposed to the army personnel, when the Fenians and Anarchists began to infiltrate London from the 1850s onwards. In fact, in much popular writing, police spies were seen as the lowest of the low, often depicted melodramatically as if they were products of the worst excesses of the French Revolution.

But the fact remains that from Waterloo to the Crimea, intelligence available to military commanders was often nothing more than hearsay given by travellers or even newspaper articles. Wellington was asked in 1851 about the Kaffir War, and he replied that he had 'never had any information on the causes of the war… or the objects of the government in carrying it on…'. The Duke relied on newspaper reports during his last years as commander-in-chief, from 1842 to 1852.

Another reason why the subject has not been explored for some time is that the army tended to rely on the reports of English gentlemen who travelled in the dangerous regions where border disputes and potential invasions were always likely. The obvious example is Afghanistan, in the period from 1830 to the end of the century. Most of the intelligence work, when the Russians were seriously engaged in making incursions into India by way of Khiva and Bokhara, was done by bold individuals, either private citizens or young officers out to make a reputation.

In many instances, commanders of British forces would be learning desperately important information as they moved their forces around, hoping that the right characters would be on hand, or that sheer courage and reputation would see them through. One of the direst learning experiences was to be in the Zulu campaigns of 1879, when certain examples of the superiority of the intelligence gained by some of the Zulu *Impis* shamed the British forces, with their reputation for efficiency.

A typical example of the kind of wayward character who tended to figure prominently in intelligence gathering at the time was Charles Masson, a wanderer and scholar who actually travelled on foot across vast areas of Central Asia, and was only found out after many years of random information sourcing by Captain Claude Wade, political agent in Ludhiana. Masson was in reality a deserter from the East India Company called James Lewis. While Liuetenant Alexander Burnes had been cultivating the friendship of Dost Mohammed in Kabul, to maintain a buffer state against Russian designs on northern India, Masson/Lewis had been busy also. When the British government wrote to Dost Mohammed in a tone of haughty disapproval, with no real promises made about backing or supporting him in military terms, it emerged that Burnes's spying and intelligence-gathering had been in vain: the Russians had been in touch with Dost first and alliances made. Masson blamed Burnes.

The affair highlights the failures and dangers of the methods at work at that time: it was desultory and pragmatic. If information was needed, a young officer would be sent to sort it out. The officers in question usually had command of several languages, had diplomatic skills, and preferably had a talent for making rough maps and accurate sketches as they moved along through potentially hostile terrain.

When some kind of system did appear on the table for discussion, it came from a man who was a mere retired major from the Bombay Sappers and Miners. This was Thomas Best Jervis. He had a passion for maps, and worked energetically to persuade the War Office that cartography should be more highly prized. In 1837 he was made surveyor-general of India, and was supposed eventually to succeed Colonel Everest, but he became tired of waiting for this chance and returned home. There he followed all kinds of practical geography, and wrote to Lord Aberdeen to insist that cartography would have helped immeasurably in recent foreign skirmishes.

It took the Crimean War to make heads turn and start listening to Jervis. Lord Raglan, in command of the expedition, was known to comment on his lack of knowledge of the theatre of war he was about to enter. Amazingly, Jervis obtained a detailed map of the Crimea from a contact in Belgium. The map had been made by the Russian general staff. Jervis was going to be listened to after that.

In 1855, the War Office eventually created a specific department for cartography and statistics. The Topographical and Statistical Department (T&S) was to be the first real step towards proper military intelligence within the military establishment.

It has to be asked, however, what kind of intelligence was going to be needed as the Empire expanded and British forces were continually packing up and setting off for distant shores? Clearly, accurate maps were useful, and so was general information about the cultures of the societies who would be hosting their military presence. But what about actual military policy, with some kind of system, in that respect? Britain had learned a hard lesson, and that was from the Prussian Wilhelm Stieber. When he came to the Great Exhibition in 1851, Stieber was seen by many as a 'freelancer'; instead of being dedicated to the Prussian services he was in the pay of Russia. It became clear that Stieber had succeeded in operating as a double agent in many European cities, and when he finally surfaced in Russia after some years of absence, he eventually became the man who did most to initiate the feared *Ochrana*, the Russian secret police in the Tsarist Empire.

It had to be considered: if other powers could do this kind of covert work, why not Britain? Indeed, we were to learn that aspect of the Great Game in such figures as Major Henri le Caron, otherwise known as Thomas Beach from Colchester. Yet still it took twenty years from the creation of the T&S to the first formation of the Intelligence Branch. By that time, it was beginning to dawn on the leaders of the armed forces that military intelligence was a much more complex process than had previously been thought. As John Keegan points out in his book, *Intelligence in War*, the process involves acquisition, delivery, acceptance, interpretation and implementation. It was surely with a sense of shock and alarm that the commanding officers who controlled the British Empire when the Thukela garrison in the Zulu War Eshowe Campaign of 1879 were ready to move, that the Zulus were aware of their intentions. The journal of Lieutenant Hamilton at that time notes that some Zulu spies were captured and gave Colonel Pearson all kinds of startling information, including the fact that the British force was surrounded by 35,000 men.

Obviously, the Zulu had a full understanding of the five stages of intelligence: they had acquired knowledge of the garrison, delivered that information to the *Impis* generals, accepted the facts as true by observation, interpreted the facts and details in the light of what could be seen and counted, and finally implemented their strategy in response by gathering three *Impis* at the right place.

Of course, in 1873, the Intelligence Branch had a massive brief and a whole third of the earth to handle as its province, rather than a stretch of Natal. It seems odd now to read that the first staffing arrangements for the new Branch involved, for instance, two officers and a clerk to cover the Russian empire. The base they operated from consisted of a house in Adelphi Terrace and a shambling old coach house and stables tucked away in Whitehall.

The aims of the new Branch were expressed this way:

> The preparation of information relating to the military defence of the empire and the strategical considerations of schemes of defence; the collection and distribution of all information relating to the military geography, resources and armed forces of foreign countries and the British colonies and possessions; the compilation of maps and the translations of documents.

The two officers and the clerk must have contemplated the map of Russia with a sense of awe and confusion.

By the end of the century, however, when London itself and even the person of the Queen were targets of enemies, there had been an expansion of the responsibilities covered by the Branch, and a sure liaison with the Metropolitan Police. When Sir William Melville, a top policeman in 1896, set to work in defending the capital city, he did so in tandem with the army. This was the man who first recruited the infamous Sidney Reilly, and so began the next age of the spy.

At the beginning of Victoria's reign, the nature and composition of the armies who preserved the Empire is of particular interest with regard to the place of military intelligence. There were two armies, of course, when it came to India, the 'Jewel in the Crown', where most anxieties lay in terms of Russian expansionism. There was a force of a quarter of a million men serving the East India Company, and the 100,000 members of the British Army *per se* with headquarters at the Horse Guards in London. This duality was resolved after the Sepoy Mutiny of 1857 when the direct rule of India passed to the government from the Company. The British Army comprised thirty-two regiments and the engineers. The sappers were, it seems, a floating concept. They were so indefinable in the sense of what duties they performed that at most stages of a campaign they were seen as the home of whatever intelligence personnel might be identified in a particular setting.

As Jan Morris has pointed out, the fact that in most aspects the British Army had not changed attitudes and conduct since Waterloo was never going to help the receptivity needed for anything innovative to be done.

New ideas were not apparent in dress, nor on the parade ground, and not even in marksmanship. Basically, ritual was at the heart of the army, and that had served well as a way of integrating men of all kinds and backgrounds, so why change the whole war machine? It was going to take a major war to highlight the need for proper, respected and effective military intelligence.

The final piece in the mosaic here is the place of the Foreign Secretary and of the general practice of diplomacy and intrigue. How the interests of administrators and military men could clash and cause havoc was seen in the Dost Mohammed affair, when Lord Auckland, in Simla, had failed to understand the relationship between the British buffer zone Sikh leader, Ranjit Singh, and the various aspirants to the government of Afghanistan. But on a more general level, much depended on the Foreign Secretary at home.

The most celebrated example is Lord Palmerston. In the Athenian incident of 1850, when a trader was trying to force some compensation from the Greek government, Palmerston sent a gunboat to sort it out, and his words of explanation are important in our understanding of how military intelligence and diplomatic intrigue were to become so complicated: 'A British subject, in whatever land he may be, shall feel confident that the watchful eye and the strong arm of England will protect him against injustice and wrong.'

Palmerston's statement would prove very difficult to enforce in the distant and dangerous borderland of the Kizilkum Desert and the Emirate of Bokhara, where British agents had been tortured and killed in the 1830s. But Palmerston showed what needed to be done in the role of relating foreign affairs to popular knowledge and support at home: he was skilled in media relations and he knew how to take the pulse of popular feeling about world affairs.

After the fiasco of the Crimea, the importance of the relationship between the implementation of foreign policy and the work done by the War Office on promoting military intelligence was to become increasingly centre stage in imperial politics. With hindsight, and with the sophistication that comes with more complex technological warfare, recent analyses of some of the major battles of the nineteenth century have expended pages of indignant commentary on military incompetence. A publication of 1903 has this comment on a Boer War confrontation: 'In spite of much British bravery, the combat of Lang's Nek was an unquestionable and severe defeat. But many noble deeds were performed.' Now, as Saul David rightly comments on another imperial battle, 'the British commander,

Lord Chelmsford, had made the cardinal error of not according their (the Zulus) capabilities proper respect.' In other words, in an age in which military intelligence is highly regarded and has become an academic and strategic discipline, the wars of the Victorian era, with their amateurish reliance on dash and valour, seem ludicrously simple and defeats are all too easily understood.

As so often in British history, however, the significant advances in intelligence were made in a gentlemanly, inventive way, by individuals. It took a long time for individual men of genius to actually find the right kind of discourse for the subject of 'spying', but when they did it was with a workable mixture of delight and military briskness, as in Baden-Powell's account, *My Adventures as a Spy*, published in an Edwardian compendium of spy stories. Baden-Powell writes lucidly of the three categories of spies as he saw them: strategical and diplomatic agents; tactical, military or naval agents, and field spies. By 1910, the whole subject was open to discussion, established as a part of the scene. Yet this man of extensive knowledge and experience could also 'spin a good yarn', as was the tradition of the gentleman spy, from Abbott to Francis Younghusband, a major player in the later years of the Great Game.

There is also a need to consider the changes in the Russian army throughout this period. After all, the political officers such as Francis Younghusband ventured into the Russian camps and talked with their officers, and this kind of interplay was going on throughout the Great Game. The Russian bear was always loitering on the borderlands and sometimes came into Afghanistan, so to understand the advance of military intelligence, it is necessary to know something of the Russian presence and the nature of their armed forces. After their disastrous Crimean experience, their army was reformed and the composition and background of the Russian officer class was radically changed. Russia was also, naturally, similarly challenged by the formidable geography and people of the India-Afghanistan frontier, and had to slowly build up buffer states before it could trek into Khiva and Bokhara. The similarities with the British problems in tackling the terrain of northern India, and in trying to understand the politics of the tribal cultures, are plain to see when we look at their strategies at this time.

In conclusion, it is hoped that this history will provide a survey of the Victorian period to match the admirable account of the Elizabethan secret services by Alan Haynes, *The Elizabethan Secret Services* (1992). Victorian Britain may not have had a mastermind to match Sir Francis Walsingham, but it did have a large number of courageous (often foolhardy) individual officers who, in carrying on the long tradition of the gentleman soldier/ scholar, made a more streamlined military intelligence establishment possible. Perhaps the most astonishing aspect of the pattern of development in the years between Queen Victoria's accession and the First World War was the slow realisation that a mass of knowledge gathered and not applied tends to create more problems than it solves. The Victorian period may not have the small and more visible population of the Elizabethan scene, and there may not have been a puppet-master to compare with Walsingham, but there was more than enough intrigue out on the frontiers of the Empire to keep the intelligence-gatherers occupied in between their shooting expeditions and Arabic lessons.

CHAPTER 1

INTELLIGENCE IN THE EMPIRE, c.1850–1918

In the first phase of the gradual establishment of a dedicated staff with intelligence duties in the context of administration, there was some uncertainty about how the various aspects of the work could or should be organised. This confusion arose from the fact that the primary areas of field intelligence and general intelligence (such as the accumulation of relevant knowledge) had been managed in Wellington's army by the integration of the various services such as the work of reconnaissance, scouts, and, above all, by dragoon couriers for communications. The most noticeable deficiency was in cartography. Wellington on one occasion even had to write home to request Cassini's map of France in 1806.

To understand the situation in 1880 we must first summarise the development of military intelligence from the early years of the century. So many different kinds of influences made the intelligence department of 1876 one of complexity. Matters are further complicated because the Anglo-Boer Wars proved that the War Office still had not properly thought out the nature of intelligence in an increasingly technology-influenced imperial regime.

Following the Napoleonic War, there was no perceived need for change and it took a major crisis – the Crimean War – to change attitudes. By the late 1850s there was a fresh importance given to maps and mapmakers, and the Topographical and Statistical Department was set up, first conceived in 1855 with the backing of Lord Panmure. Thomas Best Jervis took control and his established knowledge of maps in Europe became invaluable. Yet even that was an uncertain step. The notion of intelligence as a discipline, as well as a principal element in army organisation, was still somewhat overshadowed by traditional officer-class organisation and attitudes. But blame also has to be apportioned to the general feeling on the subject, beyond the army itself. As Sir George Aston wrote about this new T&S: 'The history of its origin is illuminating in connection with the "stupid John Bull" legends. Between the battle of Waterloo and the Crimean War very little interest was taken by the British public in the efficiency of its army.'

To understand how a genuine and effective intelligence department was conceived and created, we need to consider several influences. The changes happened in the 1870s, and the subjects of the following biographies emerged from that period, in the sense that very influential men began to realise how important a body of knowledge was to the commander; Sir Garnet Wolseley is perhaps the clearest example. In his own journals from the Ashanti campaign, and in his creation of a cadre of officers with outstanding intellectual qualities, he demonstrates this concern for a dependable access to any kind of knowledge that might impinge on a specific theatre of war.

In terms of a wider influence, the impact of the Franco-Prussian War of 1870 was significant. When William Robertson went to the Staff College to do further study, he visited some of the battlefields, and his tutors used that context for case studies. The influence of that conflict on the more theoretical element in military intelligence cannot be overlooked. A useful example of this is the contents of *The Journal of the Household Brigade* for the year 1871. This publication always had the usual sports and recreation features, such as amateur dramatics, polo and shooting, but in this year there was a feature on the *Kriegs Spiel* or 'Game of War'. The significance of the piece is that it reflects the burgeoning interest in military education in such a wide sense that our modern concept of 'enrichment' might apply to the thinking behind it. In 1871, Major Roerdanz, military attaché to the German Embassy in London, gave a talk on the Game of War to 'a crowded audience', the journal reports.

Roerdanz had already been on a tour of military establishments on the subject; he had visited London, Aldershot and the Staff College previously. The activity was the precursor of modern war gaming, but in the context of 1871, the important statement is that 'it was not a game that could be played out by cadets, but that it required a considerable knowledge of military science on the part of the commanders.'

The new interest in professionalism within the army is also observable in the increasing number of civilian commentators at this time. Journalists, editors, correspondents and academics all had access to ways of mediating their views on tactics, army reform and the Empire. The 1870s as a whole were arguably the period in which revolutions took place at all levels in the army, most notably in the consequences of the Cardwell reforms of 1868–72. Edward Cardwell was at the War Office at the time and took the whole system of purchasing promotions and other issues into consideration in order to establish wide-sweeping reforms. A two-battalion system was created, and the purchase of commissions was abolished. By 1881 the work of Childers, following Cardwell, made the two-battalion structure of each regiment, with each county base at home and a rota for overseas duties. While such reforms were going on at a practical everyday level, intelligence was also finding a proper place in the structure of the army. This was a stunning contrast to the period of the 1820s when the Senior Division at Woolwich where training was then concentrated, as at that time there was no perceived need in the upper echelons of military thinking for training in such topics as learning languages, studying troop movements or intelligence techniques.

In the field, throughout most of the nineteenth century up to the Zulu War, the limits of intelligence work were seen as controlling spies and using reconnaissance in an ad hoc way. It may be argued that it was in the Ashanti campaign, led by Wolseley in 1873–74, that a mainstream revolution in the applications of intelligence was brought about. Much of this stemmed from Wolseley's belief in gathering the best men around him, and the 'Wolseley Set' of handpicked men who worked closely with him became a celebrated and sometimes criticised group in the army generally. By the time he had experienced war in Africa and Canada, he emerged as a powerful figure in the debate on reorganisation under Cardwell, and he tried to create a new concept of a general staff, for which he found himself in opposition to Queen Victoria's son, the Duke of Cambridge, then commander-in-chief. Wolseley played an important part in the development of the new respect for the 'intellectual' officer, something that had always taken second place to the 'true blue' fighting man and adventurer image of the officer on campaign at the edge of Empire.

Around 1880, before his expedition to Egypt, Wolseley had made the group of officers around him into a breed apart, all devoted to the chief. As Joseph Lehmann wrote in his biography of Wolseley:

> From the first campaign in Burma, Wolseley carefully noted those officers who were able and efficient. Each selection was studied, polished and fitted like a precious stone before it became a permanent part of his 'ring'.

He carefully distinguished between fighting leaders and regular staff officers.
Each had a speciality. One was a scout, another added dash to the attack.
A third was a positive genius when it came to prompt organisation.

An important part of his organisation was the emphasis put on learning
and close study of all cultural features of the places in which an army was
to serve. He liked to be with well-read and articulate peers; he moved
in the literary coteries of poets and novelists, and he valued the writings
of historians and cultural commentators. When he began the Egyptian
campaign against Arabi, he had his team with him, and representative of
the kind of officer he valued for analytical knowledge was Lieutenant
(later General) Sir John Maurice. He, along with others such as Richard
Brackenbury, represented the kind of establishment the Hartington
Commission of 1875 had wanted – a War Office in which there were
departments that would spend their time collecting information.
Innocuous though that sounds, it was absolutely crucial to the growth of a
well organised and respected military intelligence arm in the services.

Before the 1870s, there had been a massive body of cultural and
topographical knowledge of the many states and territories of the British
Empire, but this knowledge was amassed in such things as learned journals
and was often the work of gentlemanly enthusiasts and dilettantes. Many
of these were officers, men who had learned several Indian languages for
instance, and had spent their leisure time gathering information which
would be potentially of real value in a wartime situation. But essays on
anthropology and basic maps of trade routes or drawings of tombs and
temples were not easy to catalogue for military purposes. On the other
hand, it is a simple matter for historians today to look at the numerous
small wars in the nineteenth century, all across the globe wherever the map
was red for Empire, that more knowledge of such people as the Maoris or
Zulus would have helped the situations a great deal. When the Intelligence
Department finally arrived, the priorities were maps and languages. But
it was also recognised that there was latent value in simply gathering
and ordering a huge amount of information, mainly geographical and
geomorphological. It was decided, fifty years after Wellington wrote home
to buy a map, that something should be done to make such desperate
measures obsolete.

In the Crimean War, the work of Charles Cattley had been an object-
lesson in how cartography is integrated into the scheme of things in a
major war. He was commissioned to ascertain details of the topography of
the area. He began to question Russian prisoners and that became one of

the primary information sources for the staff. In addition, Lord Raglan had local spies, of course, but he was never really convinced of their usefulness. Cattley, a man described by some sources as an interpreter working on the Raglan staff, had a profound knowledge of all Russian activities. What became apparent with hindsight was that in such a major campaign, with a massive investment of infantry in vast and vulnerable locations, a store of relevant knowledge, easily and quickly accessed, was extremely valuable to the high command.

Colonial wars ceased to be distant, privately run affairs when the press expanded and it is necessary here to recall how the revolution in printing and production of journal and periodicals changed the knowledge of warfare for the general public. A mass of popular publications felt it was a commercial necessity to engage experts to write about military affairs. There was an interest in the paraphernalia and dress of the army, of course, along with contempt for men in uniform as expressed by Rudyard Kipling in his poem, *Tommy*:

> We aren't no thin red 'eroes, nor we aren't no blackguards too,
> But single men in barracks, most remarkable like you;
> And if sometimes our conduct isn't all your fancy paints,
> Why, single men in barracks don't grow into plaster saints

After all, even the general public back home could read astonishing tales of Russian spies and their tendency to outwit the British (and of course the whole war was totally understood and witnessed by the nation, via Russell of *The Times*), such as this account from the *Illustrated London News* of 1855:

> Spies in the English camp – Some time ago a soldier of the 44th Regiment, a Pole by birth, informed against the keeper of one of the canteens of the 62nd Regiment, as having been employed in the Russian Secret service at Warsaw, and that he suspected him to be engaged at present as a spy. The charge was investigated by a board of officers, but no conclusive evidence to support it could be adduced… He was known to speak the Russian and German languages, and it did not appear very satisfactory that with such attainments he should choose to enlist as a private soldier…

This shows very clearly how different the British were in this business. Russia had had a well established police element working to counteract spies long before the Crimean War. This report made the army seem merely comparative to the new detectives working in London since 1842, men learning their trade of suspicion and investigation merely from common sense. The professionalism was to come later – and the same applies in the army.

It was realised by the new men at the Staff College, and by the young officers coming through to command, that there were two categories of information in terms of what needs to be stored for potential usefulness: there was the known information that was universally applied in a specific place, such as the *lingua franca* in communities or religious beliefs, and then there was the shifting, transient knowledge that changed with new political formations. This is why the often esoteric work of intrepid eccentric travellers such as Sir Richard Burton or Sir Percy Sykes proved to be invaluable later: they had talked to the locals and given comments on customs and traditions. Later, when it was essential to have spies who could merge into the background and pass off as anything but British officers, the precedents were there in the travel books as well as in the learned papers from the academies.

The essentially chaotic and contradictory nature of espionage, as opposed to field intelligence, in this period, opened up an age of heroic explorers and gentleman officers who embodied a phrase applied once to an officer in the British Expeditionary Force of 1915: 'He was the absolute embodiment of dash and pluck.' This statement could be applied to any of the five men whose lives in military intelligence are recounted here. In the thirty years before the attempts to rationalise matters of information and wars, a succession of spies, working in the 'Great Game' against Russia's aspirations to power in India, were likewise described. We only have to consider the life of Sir Richard Francis Burton. His biographer, Edward Rice, explains the modus operandi when Burton travelled the borderlands:

> Burton was now very much immersed in playing out the Great Game, and the surface show of merchant or dervish was a very skilful way of amassing information. As a wandering trader riding camel, Burton – and other agents – had an excellent means of measuring distances. Unlike the horse, whose pace was irregular, the camel had a steady stride, nearly as regular as a metronome, and made an almost predictable number of paces per hour… Thus, distances in previously unknown areas could be mapped.

This happened in the context of the years between the first army travellers eastwards in the 1830s up to the years of the Indian Mutiny. After that, matters gradually changed and the scope of individual spies was limited to a certain extent, though the Great Game continued into the first years of the twentieth century.

In the period under consideration – from the 1870s to around 1916 – that spirit of eccentric individuality and adventure was in decline. The top brass wanted a new age of professionalism in all areas. Therefore, this is a good point at which to summarise the areas of activity and interest under the heading of 'military intelligence'. Arguably, there were three:

First there was field intelligence, which included everything from scouting and reconnaissance to the facts of the basis of strategy. This was increasingly a matter of assimilating whatever cartography was available with local knowledge.

Second, espionage. This entailed the 'knowledge of the enemy' factor, along with the work of gathering information from previous experience if that could be located. Under this heading came a whole range of local spies as well as linguists and travellers, such as Burton, who worked for the army. Burton was an officer in the army of the East India Company, and became so immersed in eastern culture and religion that he could melt into the background very easily and find information by subtle and indirect means when required.

Finally, there was diplomacy and politics. The overlap between diplomats, attachés and army espionage became blurred as the century went on. Basically, as will be seen in the case of Sir Mark Sykes, when contrasted with T.E. Lawrence, they could be a source of mistrust and misinformation. The kind of spying that was directly and recognisably military was very distinct from the work of diplomacy, and, of course, communication between the two is always essential.

Overall, the Great Game set the stage for further professionalisation by teaching the generation of officers coming through in the 1870s the niceties and complexities of spying within enemy areas. In a campaign, of course, the army is always 'playing away', and local knowledge had to start well before the military encounter. This is why, when William Robertson found himself a part of the new intelligence section in 1875, his first task was to amass and classify information.

In addition to the Great Game, there were the two massive events of the Crimean War and the Indian Mutiny in the years just prior to the new organisation. It is useful at this point to summarise these events.

When the writer and traveller A.W. Kinglake visited the holy places of Palestine in 1844, he wrote this about his time in Nazareth:

> I had fasted perhaps too long, for I was fevered with the zeal of insane
> devotion to the Heavenly Queen of Christendom. But I knew the feebleness
> of this gentle malady… let there but come one chilling breath of the outer

world and all this loving piety would cower and fly before the sound of my own bitter laugh.

This is from his book, *Eothen*, and this reflection evokes a strong sense of irony when we recall that later, in the battle of Alma, during the Crimean War, Kinglake would be caught up in a madness largely stemming from the status of that Holy Ground with regard to Europe and Russia.

The Crimean War (1853–56) was known at the time as 'The Russian War', and much of the political substance beneath the conflict relates to our discussion about Russia in the Introduction. But in the history of military intelligence in the nineteenth century, it contains some of the classic exemplars of what went wrong in terms of field knowledge in the attitudes and conduct of war at that time.

It is useful here to recall that military intelligence has the three areas of field, diplomacy and context. That is, the knowledge required to be successful in war in the Victorian period can be easily applied to the theatre of war itself; to the diplomacy of the high society and to the areas of knowledge in geography, surveying and cartography so essential to military information. The Crimean War provides a melancholy template of the nature of all three domains. It started with a great deal of diplomacy and espionage long before a war became inevitable. The war has become attached to notions of military incompetence and intelligence (or lack of it) and has in some ways dominated later interpretations of the conflict.

The focus of attention was Palestine, part of the declining Ottoman Empire; Napoleon III, who had only recently come to power, made it clear that France would have the right to guard the Christian holy places. Tsar Nicholas I thought in much the same way, so, as matters escalated, there was the foundation of the conflict. Nicholas made it clear that he saw Russia as being responsible for the protection of the Christians within the Ottoman Empire, and, naturally, Turkey was suspicious of this. When Sir Hamilton Seymour, Foreign Secretary, reported these words spoken by the Tsar, other reasons for Russia's pressure on Turkey came to light:

Now Turkey has by degrees fallen into such a state of decrepitude that, eager as we are for the continued existence of the Man [Turkey, 'the sick man' of Europe] he may suddenly die upon our hands... if the Turkish Empire falls, it falls to rise no more. It could happen that circumstances put me in apposition of occupying Constantinople.

Gradually, the diplomats of the four nations directly involved negotiated and searched for an agreement over Russian aspirations and Turkish independence. The various visits made by Russian envoys to the Turkish court led to complex and sometimes farcical intrigue, as when Menshikov came to try to exclude Turkey from playing any part in appointing the Greek patriarch, there was a spy hidden in a wardrobe in the Russian Embassy.

Before the outbreak of the war, Colonel Hugh Rose takes centre stage in terms of his principal role of supplying information about Russia to those who were embroiled in the diplomacy. Rose was sure that there was a need for a British squadron in the Dardanelles; he had one eye on the commercial interest in the area and another on the military possibilities. What was to be done about Turkey became the media issue of the day, and, when a partition of that land was suggested, Rose began to see how quickly and effectively European media were absorbed in St Petersburg – something that would later become an important intelligence issue when Russell, of *The Times*, began his reports from the front. But as the talks about the holy places and the position of Turkey went on, everyone knew that really, under the talk, the fear of Russian expansion and her presence in the Middle East was the problem. The British fleet, under Dundas, was ready for entry into the Black Sea at any time, and preparations for war were going on as the verbal wrangling became more heated.

On the surface, Britain and her ally France seemed to have plenty of intelligence regarding Russian power and positions. Seymour sent reports on this, particularly on the size and capabilities of the Russian Baltic fleet. These influenced Admiral James Graham in his future planning regarding the Baltic. But Seymour noted something else of more threatening import, something that would be crucially significant if war broke out. This was that there were Russian forces in the borderland principalities such as Wallachia. Although Nicholas had problems with some rebel leaders in some of these states, generally, he had enough control there for lines of communication to the Black Sea to be easily maintained. The Tsar sent a note to Britain insisting on his right to maintain these forces.

A large part of Nicholas's policies were, arguably, due to the influence of the Pan-Slavists at the time. The French ambassador, in 1853, thought so, and he was aware of these forces in Russia. Basically, the influence here was that the Ottoman Empire and the Austro-Hungarian Empire were ruling over Slavic peoples; Pan-Slavists argued that the foreign states were oppressing the Slavs within their borders. Prominent Pan-Slavists thought that the time had come to liberate Slavs in neighbouring states.

Ivan Aksakov wrote, 'God has assigned a lofty task to the Russians; to serve the liberation and rebirth of their enslaved and oppressed brethren. There is in Russia no desire for usurpation, no thought of political domination… It desires but freedom of life and spirit for those Slav peoples which have remained faithful to the Slav confraternity.'

There was a certain degree of counterbalancing influence with Nicholas though, and that was in the person of Nesselrode, his negotiator in Turkey. He understood the European position. The British diplomats thought that their best hope of avoiding war came with Nesselrode's influence, but it was not to be. War came, and in February 1854 advance contingents sailed for Gallipoli. Britain and France declared war on Russia on 28 March that year, and, after a bright start by the allies, the British forces were encamped at Balaclava by the end of September. The ensuing confrontation, principally involving cavalry, was to steal the limelight from intelligence.

The British leader, Lord Raglan, had been military secretary to Wellington in the Peninsular War, and he was highly rated as a tactician, though his experience had been largely in administration. Part of his attraction with regard to leading men was the amazing tale of his having lost an arm in battle and then asking for it to be returned as the hand had on it a ring given to him by his wife. There were other virtues: he spoke French well, and though he was sixty-five, he was a man who could command respect. One fundamental aspect of the war, however, was the point that the French were then allies, not enemies. Raglan and other senior officers were going to have to work with Leroy de Saint-Arnaud, the French commander, and his officers. The French had recent experience of war; they had been on campaign in Algeria. They had organised their quartermastering systems much better than the British.

But only two of Raglan's six divisional generals had commanded brigades; all his senior men were over sixty, except for the Queen's cousin, the Duke of Cambridge. Whatever was going to happen in that war, Raglan was going to stand where responsibility lay, and he had a great deal of worry there, with so many men under his command and so many allies to work with. Initially, in the broader operations of intelligence, Raglan had plenty of information; some of this came from the embassies in the Balkans and some from agents. These reports were proven correct in the first phase of the war, as Russian troops moved towards Silistria where a Turkish force, with British officers in charge, had been positioned.

With knowledge of Russia and Russian militarism in mind, one of the other mythic names from the war, Lord Lucan, was appointed in charge of the Cavalry Division. He had been a staff officer in 1828 when Turkey had

to work in a war situation, after diplomatic work in St Petersburg and then actually in the Crimea. Therefore his reports, always as far as we know sent directly to Raglan, indicate what methods he saw as easiest to attain given that there was no platform of previous information on which to build. Therefore, information would need to be directly from the Russian ranks. Consequently, Cattley set the cavalry to work on observations and note taking. Prince Menshikov, leading the Russian army in the Crimea, was a prime target for observation; Cattley realised that local spies would need to be used in that locale, and he began a network, much as Napoleon had always done, relying on good pay and rewards for fidelity and courage.

It was an infiltration task for the local spies and a reconnaissance command for the patrols of cavalry. The latter would need to penetrate the Chernaya, a pass on the river Traktir some six miles south of Sebastopol. On one occasion, a patrol of ten men were frighteningly close to a formidably large group of Russians and retreated sharply. Some of the patrol were cornered and killed. Clearly, these risky forays were being noticed by the Russians, and the area involved was not vast, so every brief Cattley gave was a dangerous one.

Cattley shone in the interrogation of prisoners. During the siege of Sevastopol, he reported to Raglan that after questioning two deserters he had very valuable information. That was an understatement. Regarding the long siege, what the two seamen told Cattley was that massive numbers of Russian reinforcements were on their way, and that Menshikov's intention was to send another force to the rear of the British. Again, Raglan decided to ignore Cattley's information. Raglan's stupidity was astounding. There had been an earlier report, from a naval source, saying similar things about Russian movements. On top of that, his reasons for mistrusting the sources of Cattley's report were nonsensical. Because Cattley had talked to two Polish sailors, Raglan concluded that they could not be relied upon. They were from the town, and not taken from the ranks of Menshikov's force, so Raglan took no action. But, as Terry Brighton has pointed out, even Russell, of *The Times*, knew that this information was sound, writing, 'I was told that the Russkies are very strong all over the place, that reports had been sent to headquarters that an attack was imminent.'

Everyone but the commander, it seems, expected a huge Russian attack. He must have been shocked when it came, early in the morning. The Russians had gathered for attack just beyond the Chernaya pass, so no doubt Cattley's outriders would also have confirmed the sailors' reports.

The Crimean War is interesting in the history of Queen Victoria's spies for several reasons. First, it was a chaotic campaign from the very beginning, so the shortcomings of supplies and provisions were sure to have spin-offs into other areas of ineptitude. Second, it was conducted with very little advance knowledge of the terrain. Finally, it was a war on a massive scale involving high-level sharing of command and decision making; that command would be largely foreigners with no local knowledge, so trusting their Turkish allies was essential. Yet Raglan did not do so. The natural conclusion to this thinking is that as a check on Russian imperialism the war had obvious reasons and aims, yet the rationale of how it was to be conducted was done weakly, with too much reliance on men with long-standing reputations from another age. The army that fought that war had not materially changed from the army of Wellington. It still operated on the buying of commissions and flogging. The reliance on *esprit de corps* and personal courage was still at the ideological centre of the army's sense of identity. Nowhere was this more apparent than with the Highlanders and Sir Colin Campbell. One of the collections of war stories written around 1900 stresses the drama of that achievement:

> Whatever resistance was to be made depended on the 'thin, red line'. Sir Colin, as was usual with him, spoke a few words of warning and encouragement. 'Remember men,' he cried as he rode along the line, 'remember there is no retreat from here. You must die where you stand.'

It is difficult to avoid the conclusion that intelligence work, in the eyes of the commander and his staff, was something best left out of the balance of thought until there was an extreme demand or a crisis. But paradoxically when one thinks of Raglan's methods, Wellington's quartermaster-generals had used light cavalry for short-range reconnaissance, cultivated deserters for intelligence information, and in acting on captured despatches. It has to be said, however, that maps were still low on the list of priorities even with Wellington. But Wellington's intelligence systems worked very well on the whole. One soldier wrote that 'If the French army had been in the bowels of the earth Lord Wellington would have found them out.'

The significant fact about Cattley's contribution to the work of the spy is that he taught the staff officers lessons that would improve their performance in the remaining years of the war in the Crimea. His activities meant more sense of security and preparation when men were on the move or preparing for action.

Naturally, Russell's reports on the privations suffered by men in the Crimea had an effect on future thinking, and there was a logical link between the causes of the problems he witnessed and the presence (or lack of it) of a coherent intelligence structure. Raglan had made sure he had a Special Intelligence Branch, but then restricted its use and applications. In some ways, Russell was one of the best witnesses of the state of affairs with regard to Raglan's shortcomings. As Nicolas Bentley has observed:

> In his reports from Gallipoli and Varna, the Bulgarian Black Sea port used by the allies as a springboard for the Crimea, he began to give his readers some idea of the inadequacies and unnecessary hardships from which the army was already suffering. At headquarters these reports created furious resentment. The reaction was understandable, but it was unjust. Russell saw clearly and made it apparent that the conditions of which he complained were … the faults of … the departmental chiefs at home…

What Russell's presence in the Crimean War affirms is that from that point on, intelligence, in its widest military sense and application, would in the future have another dimension, and that would relate in part to propaganda as well as to the mediation of facts. Behind Russell's criticisms was the inescapable fact that the war had cost England 25,000 men and £76 million. Related to Russell's achievement in showing some of the incompetence behind those losses was the element of documentary in relation to warfare and its intelligence systems. In other words, the jokes about the Tsar knowing what the British high command were thinking by reading the papers was in truth a part of something much wider and entrenched in everyday European culture and communication, at one level expressed in the open and free attitudes of Russian officers about troops and ships when talking to British officers, and at another level, the confidences exchanged in diplomatic circles when 'off the record' subjects were broached. This laxity in the ranks of the diplomat had always had its dangers as well as its eccentricities. In the memories of naval administration produced by Sir John Henry Briggs in 1897, covering the years 1827 to 1892, there are some insightful remarks in this context, and these were made by a man who retired in 1870, after joining the Admiralty in 1825. For instance, during the administration of the Earl of Haddington in the years 1841–45, he writes:

> I was consequently placed in personal communications with the French officials, and was not a little surprised to find that a complete register was

kept of every ship in our navy. Her tonnage, armament and complement, when she was launched, upon what station she had served, what repairs she had undergone, and whether she was fit for further service or not.

Briggs goes on to say that the French were so interested in our navy that every scrap of information printed in the *Hampshire Telegraph* was cut out and placed 'under various headings of intelligence.' We can only be glad that, ten years later in the Crimea, the French were allies of Britain. But this highlights something very important in the area of the exchange of information. In the case of Anglo-French naval rivalry at this time – the middle years of the nineteenth century – it was a feature that there was indeed an exchange of information between rivals, and that was the case in all military spheres.

This tendency may be seen more clearly in a maritime context, as scholars have studied the exchange of information in visits to ports. Some dockyard visitors were spies, and that was apparent. At the time of the Crimean War, for instance, a man called Eugene Sweny was a spy for England, being sent to French dockyards on information trips. In 1859 he actually supplied plans of a ship, *La Gloire*. More significant was the case of Lord Clarence Paget, who was a secretary to the Admiralty in 1859. In plain clothes he walked freely into dockyards at Toulon and went onboard a battleship that was being built. He 'began measuring the height of her battery with his umbrella'.

Related to this, and in part very much linked to what Russell was doing, is the fact that the middle years of the nineteenth century involved a print revolution; states would learn of scientific advances that would have a bearing on military affairs by means of the printed word in all kinds of forms and places, often in scientific or technical language. As one historian puts it:

> Here lay one of the reasons for the efforts made in both navies [French and English] to teach the officer to read and speak the rival's tongue. Many officers were thus able to keep up with new publications in both the important naval languages of the time.

The same historian points out that an English translation of *Tactique Maritime* appeared in 1857, and conversely, *Naval Gunnery*, by Sir Howard Douglas, was printed in French in 1853. There is a fascinating paradox at work in this exchange of information, something akin to two lawyers comparing notes: it is related to the concept of the 'officer gentleman' – someone who could barely resist a polite request from a fellow officer from some other nation. By modern standards this is unbelievable, but it has to be remembered that there was always, even back in the Napoleonic War, an unwritten code of honour and also of attitude and receptivity in the officer class. Behind all this was a belief that tactics and armoury were common to all, so why all the *hush hush* behaviour?

The same kind of interchange of information was bound to go on in military matters also. One only has to look at the publications of the Royal Geographical Society, for instance. In the year 1837, not long before the Crimean War, there were such travel features as the *Memoir on the Northern Frontier of Greece*, by Lieutenant-Colonel Baker, 'with a folding map', together with *Notes on a Journey to the Sources of the River Orontes in* Syria, by W. Burchardt-Barker. The sheer pressure of dealing with huge amounts of information in all kinds of places was a problem for the Intelligence Branch of 1873 – but in many ways this was a welcome problem.

In the future news reporters would have a part to play in the nature and functioning of intelligence in war.

In some ways, Russell is a useful link to the events in the Indian Mutiny just a year after the end of the Crimean War. He travelled to India just a year after the Mutiny, and his book, *My Diary in India* (1860), is crammed with insights into the workings of spies, both pundits and lesser figures who merely reported on everyday facts about whoever was in opposition to the army in the uneasy months after the Mutiny. In this work, Russell tells us a great deal about the military actions and initiatives taken in the years immediately after the Mutiny. There is, however, no exploration of why the Mutiny happened.

What interests historians of military intelligence is why it happened. The causes are manifold, but the rebellion is easy to summarise: mutinous native soldiers (sepoys) staged an uprising in northern and central India, and the aftermath of the harsh reprisals and ensuing repression meant that the long-standing power and status of the East India Company in the Indian subcontinent was transferred to the army of India and the British Crown. But with the common practices of the interchange of intelligence being established, why did the revolt take place and consequently escalate into a major problem for the Empire? One of the principal historians of this vent is Saul David, who points out that certain parties were well aware of the coming mutiny:

According to the King's secretary, however, the Red Fort received intelligence that the troops would mutiny at Meerut, a full twenty days before they did.

Three days before the outbreak, he added, the King's personal attendants were predicting that the army would soon revolt….

An active and important spy called Jat Mall, and another spy, Ahsanullah Khan, reported on conversations with sepoys about the revolt that would come if the contentious greased cartridges were forced on them. Ahsanullah even went so far as to note that the sepoys he had talked with had explained that there had been a long-standing correspondence with other native troops across the land, and that a convergence of rebels was planned, focused on Delhi. So the puzzling question is about the lack of any response to this.

Naturally, as with all major events in history, there were several contributory causes to the Mutiny. Fundamentally, there had been a steady process of annexation directed by Lord Dalhousie, and particular local or regional power bases had been threatened and indeed erased, such as the sons of the King of Oudh, the Ranee of Jhansi and Nana Sahib. There were also tax collectors in Oudh, the *talukdars*, and they had lost income and status as land ownership and settlement had been transformed. In a military context, the Bengal army, with a strong presence of Brahmins in its ranks, was disaffected for various reasons, including undoubted inequalities in the treatment of natives as opposed to British troops. Brahmin soldiers also had to mix with lower-caste men in the course of military duty. Sikhs who had joined the ranks also caused a certain amount of jealousy from other native troops.

In the larger picture, there was also the considerable decline of British prestige and self-confidence after the Crimea and also following the Afghan War of 1841–42. Fundamental to the way the army operated was the essential moral strength and power of command in the ranks of the British officers, but not all of these knew the Indian languages nor very much about the culture, beliefs and traditions of the people they lived amongst.

The issue of the greased cartridges became, in effect, the light for the powder keg, with all other factors underlying this final outrage. The word was spread across the military establishment that the new Enfield rifles being issued were greased with a mix of cow fat and pig fat. The former animal was of course sacred to the Hindu and the latter repulsive to the Moslem. As mistrust grew and statements denying the grease were made by the officials, it began to be felt that British ideology was being percolated into the ranks, quashing native faiths within the army. As with all such panics and rumours, suspicions grew, and before long it was being suggested that there were ground human bones in the army flour.

With these various factors in mind, it is not difficult to see why the Mutiny occurred, but in order to understand the basis for the events we need to summarise what the East India Company had been doing, along with a supporting army of India manpower, to acculturate native communities and to influence the powerbase in certain key areas. The Company had taken all kinds of measures to tighten control over the vast subcontinent, mostly by non-military means. They had applied a British administration which was concerned with private property and land, and they linked this to military security. The first wave of control was either military or economic; revenues could be withdrawn and any resistance from small-scale rural chiefs was dealt with by the sword and the cannon.

In addition, the wastelands and forests had been attended to, with the intention of fragmenting any centres of power on the margins of the vast areas of arable land. At the heart of the economic changes brought about by British rule was the increase in security on the major roads and lines of communication. House prices increased notably in Delhi in the decades before the Mutiny, and other smaller but equally valued work was done on making travel and movement of goods easier, such as the efforts made by Britain to repair the ruined rest-houses used in the Mughal system, along the main routes. In all regions in which their control was strong the Company administrators worked hard to stabilise the running of the rural communities.

Knowledge increased with all this administration. As C.A. Bayly has noted:

A vast array of statistical information poured into Calcutta Secretariat. As the Company's charter came up for revision in 1813 new revenue assessments were introduced throughout much of the North Western provinces and Madras. By the mid-1820s almost all districts had revenue survey maps going far beyond the earlier Mughal route maps...

In the decades before the Mutiny, the British rule in India had been basically stable because there had been efforts to use diplomacy, mainly in the second-level bases of power in the states, because these were naturally where the stirrings of rebellion would often start. The administrative focus was always on a flexible method of liaison and control. A case in point that supports the viability of the system in place before 1857 is the 'white mutiny' in Mysore, 1809. This conspiracy was prevented because one man in the balance of power there, Purniya, was ultimately faithful to the Crown. That had been achieved through diplomacy, and in turn much of that process had been attained because there had been some effort to understand the native ideology. The fundamental aim was to neutralise Indian states which might be potentially opposed to British rule.

Yet at times there was confrontation, and from these much should have been learned that would have helped the 1857 regime to see the trouble coming. An instance of this was in Gwalior in 1843. There was a constitutional right of interference in print allowing Britain to intercede in home affairs in that state if there was a call for their help. When an intriguer Dada Walla succeeded in attaining power there, with the expulsion of Mama Sahib, there was a delicate diplomatic and military situation created. In bordering Scind the Maharajah was under British protection. When there was a development involving the succession in Scind, the cooperation of the Gwalior regime was needed along the borders. Britain felt that interference in Scind was needed, and they brought into the debate the Treaty of Burampoor of 1804, which was read as a document supporting British interference.

From this a diplomatic situation emerged in which Britain was defined as a 'guardian' in Scind, and from that situation came an impasse: the governor-general wanted to meet with the Maharajah, but intelligence made it clear to the army command that a British army must not enter Scind until that meeting with the Maharajah had taken place. Advice dictated that the advance of the army across the river Chumbul should be delayed, for that reason. The Company resident, Colonel Sleeman, made the matter of protocol very clear:

> When I mentioned his Lordship's intention to cross the Chumbul on the 22nd, Suchurun Rao, the brother of Ram Rao Phallthea and Bulwunt Rao, who had come to meet me, expressed a very earnest desire that this might not take place, as it was unusual for his highness to pay the first visit to the governor-general on the other side of the river.

Eventually the river was crossed; the British Army entered Scind, and it was disastrous. Some men who had previously been friendly to the British crossed the line into rebellion. The treaty that was supposed to take place never did, and a battle was on the cards. Communication had not been successful, and as a chronicler writing just a decade after the battle tried to explain: 'Despatches like that of the commander-in-chief in this instance, are not written for the information merely of the individual to whom they are addressed; they are framed for the public eye.' In other words, he was questioning the use of the intelligence information, gleaned by diplomats and Company administrators, in the field.

There was a confrontation and it was a bloody one. Of special interest is that of all the various regiments involved in the battle in Scind following this error, the Indian centre was to be attacked by native troops: Brigadeer Stacy's brigade of infantry, consisting mostly of native men, was led by Lieutenant-Colonel Gairdener.

This case study explains how the always delicate balance of administrative logistics and military presence in the native states could lead to major problems if information was not absorbed and used in the right way.

In the build-up to the Mutiny one of the most prominent spies in the story is, again, Jat Mall. He figures in the escalation of the chapatti communications as the mutinous ideas were spread. The chapattis, with their symbolic significance, are still an enigma to historians. One early reaction to their appearance typifies the mystery and unease at their significance. This was a magistrate, Mark Thornhill, based in Mathura, who found four chapattis lying on a table and described them as 'dirty little cakes of the coarsest flour'. But although many people responded tamely to them, the major newspapers considered the cakes to be indicative of something very serious yet to come, a foreboding of a large-scale disaster.

Jat Mall, who lived in Delhi, had several good reasons for their existence, all collected from talk on the streets and in eating-houses. He 'claimed that some people regarded the chapattis as a warning of an impending calamity, others that their purpose was to warn against the government's plot to force Christianity upon the people.' Officers from various parts of the land had also had encounters and conversations which, with hindsight, were far more important than they realised at the time. Colonel George Carmichael-Smyth, for instance, commanded the 3rd Light Cavalry at Meerut. In March, he had been in the Himalayas and there he had conversed with an old Indian soldier who had said to him: 'I have been thirty-six years in the service and am a havildar [a sergeant], but I still would join in a mutiny and what is more I can tell you the whole army will mutiny.'

In the course of the rebellion, the only kind of intelligence of any import was information about how, when and where troops could be moved to the front lines where sepoys and other disaffected men were active, together with despatches concerning small triumphs and disasters. A central concern was the transport of European troops, often being done in small detachments by dak carriages. But in the aftermath, when forces were on the move against remnants of dissent, the intelligence was once more of the kind reliant on well-guarded despatches with information on the size, composition and strength of the enemy. Russell witnessed one such event in this process, when despatches arrived reporting on a scrap with Bailine Madho's sepoys:

This man made his appearance almost about the same time that an emissary arrived from Evelegh, carrying a despatch in a quill concealed about his person, in which the Brigadeer gave an account of an action he had just been fighting with this very Bainie Madhoo's sepoys. Long practice has made the natives very expert in concealing despatches, and we have unfortunately been reduced to many makeshifts to carry our meaning from one part of the country to another without any chance of detection.

Clearly, the subtle devices of Nain Singh and Montgomerie had some parallels in the more directly military arm of military intelligence as practised at various stages in the history of the Raj.

The rebellion began in the Bengal regiments of the East India Company, where only eighteen out of seventy-four regiments stayed loyal. Fortunately, the Mutiny did not move into the Company areas of Bombay and Madras, but it took two years to combat and suppress. In 1860, the Company's regime in India ended.

It is typical, and also ironic, that the years following the suppression of the Mutiny and the re-establishment of British control in India should reflect the massive transformation in the nature of military intelligence begun by Russell. This meant that all kinds of non-military people could have a say about matters of espionage, information-gathering and plain diplomacy. Examples of this are legion, but one man in particular represents this trend towards wider commentary on military matters by journalists, writers, travellers and artists. This is W.G. Steevens, the man best known for his book, *With Kitchener to Khartoum* (1898).

Steevens wrote a short book about India in 1905, published simply as *In India*. In principal, this was an assessment of India written twenty years before, in the 1880s. The Mutiny was not so distant that it was not in most hearts and minds. Steevens assesses the military situation with regard to ensuring no repetition of the Mutiny would happen. He saw the problem as one connected to the logistics of troop movements, and this was true to a large extent, but mutinies had happened before, and sometimes over other, more easily definable things, such as the one at Vellore in 1806. The cause of this trouble was an attempt at trying to compel sepoys to wear round hats and leather stocks. This meant that they could not have their distinctive facial markings and earrings and necklaces, which had religious importance for the men.

But Steevens is eager to put forward a rationale of what is needed so that things do not go wrong in these affairs. He says, 'How can even a proper regimental feeling be maintained when officers and men are forced to grow stranger? What is to become of the senior officers, deprived of their chances of learning to handle a regiment?' He was anxious, after reading that the Royal Warwickshire Regiment had arrived in India after service in Khartoum, only to find that 'it had been sent there by mistake or prematurely.' Steevens also found out (we don't know how or where) that half of the regiment was 'dumped down in Fort George, with no ground for manoeuvring or shooting within miles, and the other half at an obscure place called Bellary.'

What had been happening in the forty years since the Mutiny and the Crimea was that amateurs of all kinds and backgrounds were becoming 'informed commentators' and the comments from the Tsar about learning the allies' tactics from reading *The Times* was becoming a prophecy on the shape of things to come in terms of intelligence and war.

What Steevens did understand, however, was that the largest military problems in the past had been ones exacerbated by profound divisions and oppositions in the mindsets of soldiers. He writes:

> It may be true that a Mussulman may never quite surmount a feeling of antipathy – at any rate strangeness – to a Christian… But it is also true that if the breach between races forbids intimacy, it leaves room in the army for comradeship, and even nurtures the personal devotion of men to officers.

But 'John Company' had gone by 1860, and Queen Victoria had already been proclaimed sovereign of India in 1858, and then Empress of India in 1877. This was all about trying to restore some self-belief and prestige after such shameful loss of face in the Empire. From 1860 onwards, things were to be very different in the advance of the pink on the world map, and the focus, in many ways, was to shift to Africa.

To sum up, first, with regard to the Crimean War, the allies had burned their fingers with poor diplomacy as well as unworkable tactics. It seems odd now, but the main fear in 1856 was that, if Britain followed through and went into Russia across the Baltic, they would be vulnerable at home: the French could take us, to pay back Britain for Trafalgar, and of course, for Waterloo. There was also a feeling in some quarters that Britain's sea power was in decline. Naval intelligence was impressed by the birth of more technology in the French navy. So in many ways, the Crimean War deflected attention from espionage as a part of the picture and led people to consider more maritime matters.

The Indian Mutiny was a very different affair in that respect. Naturally, when the storm was over and reprisals were taken, it was realised that knowledge was power, where an empire was trying to dominate a numerically superior native population. Had we had the right knowledge and had we used our communication systems better to relay this knowledge, it was argued, there would have been no Mutiny.

But by the 1870s, attitudes changed, and we can see what was happening by considering the career of Sir William Robertson. After that, up to the First World War, there was a series of cataclysmic failures in war which taught Britain to rethink the organisation of espionage and field intelligence, from the unthinkable defeat at Isandlwana in the Zulu War (1879) to the failures of the Boer War, 1899–1902. The learning curve was long and hard, and what strikes the modern reader is how many amateurs were involved. All kinds of civilians were keen to express their views on reform and to offer advice as the Boer War in particular highlighted our shortcomings. This can clearly be seen in the responses to the debacle of the First Boer War, in which around 8,000 Boers defeated a much smaller British force, and then in the Second Boer War, in which Britain had a numerical advantage of ten to one, but still had to win by a determined gradualism and victimization of civilians to effect another pyrrhic victory.

The sheer disorganisation and idiocy of much of the Boer War is easily grasped when we consider an episode described by Brough Scott on the life of his grandfather, Jack Seely, who led a company of horse into that war. Scott wrote:

> His gripes are now as much about tactics as about conditions. It's been three months since the official stance was that 'the war is almost over' and yet here he was about to be sent off once again round the Vrede–Reitz–Bethlehem–Harrismith circuit with the situation ever more unhappy and uncertain. 'Still more orders contradictory as to police' he says…

This is from Scott's book, *Galloper Jack*, and Scott sums up the dilemma simply as 'Knowing what was happening and where the enemy was'.

What starts to emerge, then, in these forty years, is how military intelligence emerged into something with a sense of identity and purpose. First, the concept gained esteem and respect, after being identified as a separate arm of the War Office and was given proper establishment; then the realisation broke in among the higher echelons of command that diplomacy and espionage must speak to each other. Finally, it was seen that defence of the homeland was the first priority, and by the early years of the twentieth century, Britain had MI5.

CHAPTER 2

PLAYING THE GAME

Before looking at the Great Game in India, something must be said by way of contrast so that Britain's attitude to espionage may be better understood. The contrast is between what was happening in London compared with the work of one of the founding fathers of military intelligence: Wilhelm Stieber. To know what he achieved in Prussia and elsewhere is to understand how Britain lagged behind for so long.

Stieber was the head of intelligence for Otto von Bismarck, founder of a united Germany in 1870. He was born in 1818 in Saxony and began his career as a lawyer in Berlin. At a time when the *agent provocateur* was the favoured instrument of the state in prising radicals and revolutionaries into view, Stieber operated as a police spy, with a front of being pro-radicals (and this was in the years before the Year of Revolutions, 1848, when radicals were to take to the barricades). First established as an undercover agent, Stieber, after saving the life of King Friedrich Wilhelm IV, was appointed Chief of Police, which afforded a lot more power.

Where Stieber becomes really interesting, however, in the context of the Great Game, is when he begins to work for Russia. He made plenty of enemies in Germany and became something of a freelance, going on to St Petersburg and starting to work for the Russian Foreign Office. When the Tsarist 'Third Section' of secret police was formed, Stieber was given the role of administrating the foreign network of spies. In 1858 he started to influence the Russian community in London, working on potential double agents and assassins, and instated what we would now call 'counter intelligence'. When he returned to Prussia he was instrumental in many of the most prominent actions of *Realpolitik* in the move to war between

France and Germany in 1870. When King Wilhelm entered Paris at the
height of Prussian success, there were an incredible 300 Prussian spies
there to welcome him. Stieber had played a prominent part in the rise of
Bismarck and in the consolidation of his power. As John Hughes-Wilson
has written, Stieber was 'the first national intelligence chief to use agents
to monitor and control the press, the banks, business and industry. His
collection of comprehensive military intelligence ensured Prussia's victory
on the battlefield.'

Contrast this with what Britain was doing at the same time. In the
1860s the Raj was recovering from the Mutiny and trying to rebuild there,
while at the same time fighting small wars all over the Empire. Britain was
learning how to use spies, however. The new police detectives of the 1850s
found that they had to work hard to trace Fenians who were bombing
London. But as an actual intelligence focus within the heart of the Empire,
the reliance was largely on the senior officers and their networks of
younger officers in the field and on the trunk roads north across the Indian
continent. What was not being acheived was the 'secret police' mentality
and ruthlessness of Stieber.

The main reason for this lack of logistics at the heart of things military at the
time of the Crimean War and the treks of the Great Gamers was the massive
scale of operations. Kabul is over 600 miles from Delhi and from Karachi on
the Indian Ocean to Calcutta across the Indian subcontinent is around 1,500
miles. These bare facts alone perhaps explain why surveys came first: the work
of Everest and the surveyors, then the pundits who advanced geographical
and cultural knowledge were doing the 'groundwork' in the metaphorical as
well as in the literal sense. Only with fundamental knowledge of geography
and topography could the adventures begin.

The phrase 'Great Game' invokes gentlemanly adventure and male
romance; the notion that a confrontation of two major world powers in
a vast theatre of espionage and reconnaissance could generate Kipling's
novel *Kim* as a central document would have seemed ludicrous to the
men who explored the far reaches of northern India, Persia and Tibet in
the nineteenth century. But that is the basis of the term and the literature
going with it as a self-contained microcosm in which officers, guides,
interpreters, map makers and native pundits roamed across a vast stretch of
Asia in order to ascertain any kind of knowledge that might contribute to
the military intelligence so essential to London and to St Petersburg.

In terms of the sheer proportion of books and articles relating to military
intelligence in the nineteenth century, those relating to the British Raj
have always dominated. The wars in Africa attracted exceptional men, such

as Baden-Powell in the Matabele wars; the Fenian activities in Canada created their charismatic figures, but the Raj in the years 1840 to 1900 provide the military historian with almost too many narratives of discovery to cope with.

The basis of the whole business was the certainty in Whitehall that Russia had designs on extending power to India via Afghanistan. Although that meant confrontation with a whole range of various tribal and national groups and allies, in intimidating terrain, the fears were well founded. But we have to ask why such intelligence gathering as was achieved by generations of young British officers and colonial staff was so diverse, so apparently random and lacking in a central logistical base until 1873. In some ways, the kinds of enterprises undertaken in this context could be bizarre and eccentric, such as the brief given to the great explorer Sir Richard Burton, when, as a young officer, he was sent by Sir Charles Napier to visit souks and bazaars, and one primary interest at the heart of this was a documentary interest in sexual behaviour. He discovered to what extent British officers visited brothels and the whole affair was glossed over, with the result that Burton was sent elsewhere.

To understand exactly what the 'Game' was all about, we need to grasp the nature of Russian ambition towards India. The core means of the expansion of their empire favoured gradual invasion and absorption of nations contiguous to the Russian heartland. They had thus become accustomed to coping with all kinds of ethnic diversity and were adept at taking in these new subjects of the Tsar. After all, through Britain's eyes, the Russian Empire was vast but was all in one block, unlike the British Empire which spread across the globe in clusters. Russia covered land from the border with Prussia in Europe across to the Kazakhs, and in the second half of the nineteenth century, they were to annexe areas of the Uzbek territory, Kokand, and Karakum together with the Pamirs.

What most irritated Britain though was the Russian desire to take the key locations of Bokhara and Khiva. These places did eventually become Russian domains. Linked to Turkestan, these two khanates were dangerously close to British India, and hence the fear of a Russian army finding its way through into the Punjab. The British Army and the army of the East India Company had coped fairly well with controlling the massive area of India and related states for over a century until the Indian Mutiny of 1857, and that was to be a notable warning of complacency within the Raj. But Russia was going even further afield in the mid-century: Nikolai Muravev, Governor of Eastern Siberia, sent various expeditions to the far east of the continent in the 1850s, and they had control of Vladivostok by 1859.

Britain's sense of holding and being confident in India was severely shaken by the Mutiny, of course, and the thirty years of Great Game activities preceding that event had been largely directed by a rising paranoia about Russia being 'on their patch'.

Naturally, it was also a question of the defence of British India, not merely a fear of expansion. Conolly (eventually murdered in 1842 by the Khan of Bokhara) had shown that it was quite possible for a Russian army to march into India by the infamous Khyber Pass, or even through Persia and Heart. Captain Abbot also explored the latter possibility. What these journeys and their evidence of Russian potential demonstrated to the British above all else was the absolute necessity of having in-depth knowledge of the states involved: their structures, ambitions, temperament, bellicosity and most of all perhaps, their susceptibility to bribes and blandishments.

The Russian threat had been most cogently described and argued in a publication of 1829 under the title *On the Practicability of an Invasion of British India*. This was written by Colonel George de Lacy Evans, and he estimated that it would only take the Russians three months to move from the Caspian to the Oxus, that is from Turkey to the first main river-border on entry to India: the route taken by Alexander the Great in 331 BC. According to Lawrence James in his book *Raj: The Making of British India*, in 1836 there were only 17,000 British troops in India, and of these 1,400 were invalids. Common sense dictated that a revolt would be hard to contain. The Duke of Wellington saw the heart of the problem: the nature of the native troops, the sepoys. If the British were considerate and right-thinking about the way the Empire was organised in a military sense, they would ensure the support and respect for the sepoys was always there.

There were various perceptions of how the Great Game would progress at that crucially important point, *c.* 1840. Some considered that there would be a sudden escalation into warfare: open conflict caused by a Russian army moving into a zone perilously close to the Raj borderland. Others, largely the officers on the spot such as Abbot, Conolly and later Sykes and Burnaby, felt sure that the Game was destined to be a relentlessly steady and uncertain series of moves, like a chess game. Whatever the course of events, one fact was certain: key buffer states would always be prime targets, notably Persia and Turkestan, and in India, the region of Sind. A typical manoeuvre in the intelligence machinations in this context was the Russian attempt to persuade the Shah in the 1830s to make a move on Herat. In the 1830s, Russia not only worked hard to influence the Shah, but also made significant advances into the possession of Kabul. The theories of Lacy Evans must have seemed to be coming true.

Because intelligence in the mid-century, from the Crimean War to the turning point of the early 1870s, was piecemeal and ad hoc, it is difficult to see exactly what was going on. But there are three definite areas of interest in a general history of spies and spying in Victoria's age: the individual officers and the interplay with Russian movements; the work on the pundits and Captain Thomas Montgomerie, and the senior officers and administrators who gathered 'soldier sahibs' around them to form operational units ready to move to any part of India when an assignment occurred.

The doyen of Great Game writers, Peter Hopkirk, selects Lieutenant Arthur Conolly as the most typical Great Game player. Conolly had been on the road for more than a year when he finally arrived in a village on the North West frontier in 1831. He was only twenty-three years old at the time. More than this, though, is the fact that Conolly coined the phrase 'Great Game' in a letter to a friend. His main achievement was observing the Russian army. But in order to take that enterprise to its conclusion, he had to cross the feared Karakum desert, and that challenge exemplifies the nature of the Great Gamer. The defining feature of that person is disguise. The officer going into the intelligence adventure had to become so free from his European identity that he moved, spoke and thought like the natives of wherever he found himself. For this reason, many British officers became authorities on the most obscure cultural habits and traditions of numerous tribal states and kingdoms across the continent.

To find a specific journey for military intelligence purposes to use as a representative one is difficult. Most briefs given to the young men who undertook these missions were pragmatic and often done in reaction to an immediate military necessity. But there is a basic feature here which needs to be understood. The men who figure in the central narrative of the Great Game were mostly officers who clustered around charismatic men in the Raj's military structure, notably those known as 'Henry Lawrence's Young Men' – junior officers in the Bengal Army – and those later political officers who served in the special elite force on the North West Frontier in the next generation.

Henry Lawrence was one of five brothers who went out to serve in India. He became most celebrated for his heroic death in the Mutiny, dying at the siege of the Residency at Lucknow. When Henry's brother John heard the news of his death, he wrote, 'My brother Henry was wounded. He died like a good soldier is discharged of his duty; he has not left an abler or a better soldier behind him; his loss just now will be a national calamity.' Henry had gathered the best young officers around him, and in a letter to a friend he paid tribute to these intelligence gatherers: 'I was very fortunate with my assistants, all of whom were my friends, and almost every one was introduced into the Punjab through me… Men such as you will seldom see anywhere, but when collected under one administration were worth double and treble the number taken at haphazard.'

It appears that the battle of Sobraon in the First Sikh War of 1846 was the occasion for the assembling of the 'young men' and Lawrence. Some of the most prominent officers, destined to distinguish themselves in intelligence work, were on the battlefield: William Hodson, Herbert Edwardes and Harry Lumsden. Any intelligence work done for that battle, however, fades into insignificance when we recall that it was at Sobraon that General Sir Hugh Gough's force advanced on a Sikh artillery position, with the 10th Lincolnshires on the left taking the prominent role, advancing in silence, walking through artillery fire. The British then charged the position and took it.

Lawrence was always on the lookout for recruits for his missions north. He carried a notebook in which he noted names mentioned in conversations, and at one point, when he was at last placed in his office to begin administration work, in Lahore, he began gathering his political agents. One description of Lawrence stresses his knowledge of character: 'The colonel surpasses his brothers by having all their decision, all their experience, but with a refined sensitive nature… He surpasses all men I have seen as a perfect knower of men.'

But intelligence work in the field in India was still a shaky item as late as 1880 when, at the battle of Maiwand, near Kandahar, the brigadier-general's brigade was decimated by Ayub Khan's artillery, and the young Robert Baden-Powell, a man with ambitions to become a top intelligence man, was sent to write a report on what went wrong. He stressed poor reconnaissance, and acted in the same way that many of the political officers of his time would have done, wanting to be noticed and given an exciting brief to perform. Baden-Powell became known to Colonel St John, the chief political officer. That action must have been replayed in a thousand different situations in the history of the Raj: intelligence being something gathered piecemeal, from diverse places, and each event being unique, so that what was needed was a process of collation. Few men had the foresight and perception to see that.

It was clear from the beginning, from de Lacy's book, that Afghanistan and the border were to be the focus for the trial of British imperial design. The military senior ranks and general staff therefore realised that knowledge had to be gained and logged. The young men began to go on their journeys, risking their lives at all times in the perilous far reaches of the continent. The struggle for the mastery of Central Asia was to be, as the Russians dubbed it, a 'tournament of shadows', and the shadows would be made by lonely men who dreamt of adventure, doggedly riding over wastelands and mountains to move unseen among all the participants in the game, large and small.

Summarising every mission in this chronicle would take a lifetime, but certain individuals claim the attention, the first of whom has to be Lieutenant Alexander Burnes, known as 'Bokhara Burnes'. After his visit to the Sikh ruler Ranjit Singh in 1831, Burnes proposed a trip to Kabul to negotiate with Dost Mohammed, and then to cross the Hindu Kush to Bokhara. The notion was to collect military information on the Russians and on Afghanistan. At that time Kabul was the focus, as so often in history, of political rivalry and there were claimants to power in various quarters. But the main fear in Britain was whether or not any Russian delegates had been placed in Kabul. The governor-general supported Burnes's seemingly overambitious plan, and took an English doctor, James Gerard, with him, along with two guides. One of these, Ali, was a former surveyor with the East India Company, and the other, Lal, was a linguist. Everything about Burnes's expedition is informative regarding the perceived aims of intelligence at the time. A priority was simply writing a journal so that all details were recorded. This secretarial duty was given to Lal. The need to be 'native', to avoid suspicion, made languages essential and, like Richard Burton, who is perhaps the best known multi-lingual officer in the Raj's history, Burnes would have had to have learnt Hindi and Arabic from books and conversation, picking up survival vocabulary at first, and then learning to speak (when absolutely necessary), allowing guides to take on most of the conversation as they wandered into places where local dialects or a *lingua franca* would prevail.

However, even with all these precautions, it was still practically impossible to become entirely 'native', so the aim was basically to go undetected. Burnes had letters of introduction and, of course, he had his passport, but ahead of his party lay the Khyber Pass. They avoided this treacherous stretch of mountain by going a long way round, toward Jalalabad. It took six weeks to go from the Indus to Kabul where he was to meet Dost Mohammed; the man who had wrenched the kingdom of Kabul from his brothers as his clan had kicked out Shah Shujah. He had been in command for six years when Burnes arrived. The crux of the matter was that Britain saw the need to take a lead in diplomacy with Dost, as the Russians would most certainly try to do the same. Burnes was a ground-breaker in this respect. As Dost hated Ranjit Singh (friendly to the British), Burnes had to learn to be a diplomat as well as a soldier. He was becoming a skilled intelligence man through sheer hard necessity.

What Burnes and other officers on these missions actually did is a question with multiple answers. Much of their behaviour when in personal contact with important figures in the domains they entered depended on smart survival skills and clever lying. Burnes in Bokhara had prepared the way by writing a letter packed with compliments and praise to the Grand Vizier, and though this gained him an audience with the great man, it was a delicate situation. What Burnes had to be aware of comprises of several layers of knowledge such as facts about where non-Muslims were allowed to go, and more importantly, what to say and how to speak when asked awkward questions. No-one had trained or prepared Burnes for such close-up spycraft. He had to think on his feet, and if there was any doubt then he had to create some kind of safe middle ground of half-truth and diversion to avoid being committed to follow up any statement made.

In this case, Burnes was compared to all other foreigners and infidels; naturally he would be compared with the Russian envoys, and to make matters worse, the Bokharans were a slave-dependent society, so Burnes, as all future agents were to find out, had to adapt his thinking and his emotions to these cultural factors, or he would have made mistakes. But most important of all in these dangerous endeavours was the fact that genuine friendships could be made. The Grand Vizier certainly became friendly; the potentates in such isolated places wanted to know about the distant world in Europe, and Burnes was a skilful storyteller.

What the senior officers wanted, however, was military information, and what strikes the modern reader about this is that the reports written for their superiors by the political officers were naturally going to be interpretations and theories of strategy based on observation and various conversations. In other words, they were prone to errors and invariably subjective. Burnes's report was entirely typical in this regard. His main aim had been to find out about Russian activities in the high borderlands, and to ascertain the attitudes of the buffer states. As he returned to India there was a crisis in Constantinople, as Mohammed Ali, ruler of Egypt, marched on Constantinople and a Russian fleet moored there. This led to an impasse and a delicate situation for the Foreign Office. Never was knowledge of Russian aims and objectives more pressing.

Burnes conjectured that the cities of Herat and Kabul must not be allowed to be taken by Russia. The route from them to India went through the Hindu Kush, and Burnes knew that an army could succeed in negotiating that terrain. He estimated that a Russian army could defeat Afghans in their home base: something we know with the hindsight of history was entirely wrong-headed. But Burnes did see the importance of holding Kabul. What he had realised was that the longitudinal string of locations from Teheran across to the river Indus was the key to control: if the Russians had Persia and then moved along that line, taking Meshed, Balkh, Herat before Kabul, they could, if they consolidated at each point, work towards controlling the regions around Kabul and eventually isolate the Afghans. South of that line were the deserts of Kerman and Helmund. Below that, leading to the Punjab, was a route through Baluchistan, the route Alexander the Great had taken. But from the current Russian territories to that southern route was formidably long with no facilities for sustaining an army.

With these thoughts and conjectures, Burnes presented his military report. British agents had also been directed to some of the other khanates south of the Caspian Sea, and Russia was becoming aware of this. They knew about Burnes as well, and they knew that there was a potential for action by Britain in the lesser states to play a part in preventing Russian expansion. When Burnes asked to go to Kabul on his next trip, St Petersburg decided to act. Nicholas I, Tsar from 1825 to 1855, had witnessed the expansion of his empire to such an extent that it was financially strong; he had reached a point in which trade with China was thriving; the number of working-class people to maintain the daily labour of keeping the empire had trebled. But what the Raj administration did not perhaps fully appreciate was that Peter had his own priorities which did not really include expansion beyond Persia: he wanted to expunge Turkey from the land of Europe. His reign had seen problems with Hungarian and Polish nationalism, and India was not yet a central concern.

Burnes did return to Kabul, and there he met Dost Mohammed. As Nicholas I was being told that Afghanistan deserved some attention, he had an officer called Vitkevich sent in response to a cry for help from Dost, who was also playing the game in keeping British interests sweet and apparently welcome. Dost wanted substantial help from Britain before Vitkevich arrived. In this context we now find that another category of agent is becoming a part of the scene. The East India Company, at this point in somewhat of a decline, had its own team of political agents in the field where there was need for them. Confusion, duplicity and mixed fortunes dogged Burnes, and this situation was no different, because the Company agent (called a 'news writer') had deserted and was a condemned man named Masson. Captain Wade of the British Army found out about Masson and had his death penalty cancelled out. Masson was destined to be extremely opposed to Burnes and his mission, and as a case study in Raj intelligence work, the Burnes–Masson mission at Kabul is highly informative.

Basically, Burnes was caught between two rulers in search of further power: Ranjit Singh in the Punjab had British support, but he was opposed to Dost. Britain had to reassure Dost that he mattered to them. In the middle of this was Burnes. What then happened is that Lord Auckland, the Governor General, wrote a letter to Dost which created massive problems for Burnes and for all intelligence work. Auckland's tone was threatening: Dost would be punished if he allied himself with the Russians. It followed that Dost's ambitions to run Peshawar could never happen. It must have seemed to the court in Kabul that Britain was acting like a schoolmaster in a bad mood, stating in plain terms exactly what would and would not happen.

The intelligence case study now turns to the issue of the individual, working in a military context, being uninvolved in the general diplomacy of a region in the Raj. Burnes was the man on the spot who had to face Dost – not Auckland. What this reveals is the nature of work in the field, so to speak, at any location in the Empire: there might be a threefold layering of activity, all impinging on intelligence work but not working together: diplomacy, general spying by native personnel and Company men, and finally the young officers like Burnes with a specific brief to fulfil.

Dost Mohammed, if he had not until then thought seriously about a deal with the Russians, was thinking seriously now: Captain Vitkevich was in Kabul and unaware of what Auckland had done, but Burnes welcomed him and dined with him on Christmas Day, 1837. Vitkevich won the day, of course: Burnes eventually left, feeling a failure. Vitkevich had given Russia a foothold of diplomacy in the fortress, the Bala Hissar, of Kabul. Masson, ready to criticise Burnes, spent time and energy noting the officer's faults.

The Burnes case is instructive in showing clearly the clash between individuals on intelligence missions and the complex machinations of the Raj administration. It also highlights the limitations of the intelligence network, because Rawlinson, the agent in Persia, had not known, and given notice of, the Russian advance into Afghanistan. As was the case in so many instances, the lone spy was the unknowing victim of this many-layered process of coping with a succession of rulers in the buffer states.

If we now shift our attention to the situation forty years later, the focus moves from Kabul to Khiva, and the outstanding character in intelligence work in the Great Game was then, for many, Frederick Burnaby. Khiva is between Merv in the south of Turkestan and the Aral Sea, about 230 miles west of Bokhara. For the Russians at this time, it was the first town of any size since they began their expedition from Orenburg in the Urals. If they sent an army into Turkestan, it would be 800 miles of formidable country before they saw the walls of Khiva. The place was notoriously barbaric: when the Hungarian linguist Arminius Vambery went there in 1863, in disguise, he saw human heads roll from old sacks and old men having their eyes prised out of their sockets. It was 'the secret city'. Three years before Fred Burnaby published his book, *A Ride to Khiva* (1876), a Russian force, under General Kauffmann, had occupied the town.

Captain Burnaby of the Blues (the Royal Horse Guards) was an adventurer who had already seen much of the world when he took on the task of travelling from Orenburg to Merv. He knew that the Russians were then prominent in the whole area and that he was ostensibly following their main army. Almost twenty years had passed since the end of the Crimean War, and Russia had not only regrouped but had affected major reforms in the army, notably a new attitude towards the officer class. Many new officers were, by the 1870s, not aristocratic but in English terms 'lower middle class'. The emancipation of the serfs had taken place in 1861 and the Russian Empire was being re-energised by a very different outlook to that of Burnes's time. Burnaby, therefore, saw it as his main brief to enquire into the nature of the Russian presence. He did far more than that: his book is a disquisition on Russian character and habits, with a military strategy built into the argument.

In 1864, the Russian Chancellor, Gortchakoff, wrote a memorandum for all the European powers, to make Russia's situation *vis a vis* Central Asia clear. His forces had just taken the town of Chemkent in Turkestan, and he wrote that as Russia had consolidated her control of the border states, she had no ambitions to extend her interests into India. But this meant nothing really. Only a short time after the memorandum, general Tchernayeff besieged Tashkent, capturing it in July 1865. British attitudes towards Russia at the time of Burnaby's ride were mixed and ambivalent. Diehard Tories like Burnaby wanted a tough line on the 'Russian Bear', and while his book appraised the Russian temperament it was clear that he wanted more from the diplomacy of Gladstone, who, after coming to power in 1868, had sent an envoy to agree on keeping Afghanistan as a buffer, neutral and comforting to both powers in its independence. The statesmen agreed that Russian activity and imperial designs should have a limit at the river Oxus, but there was no agreement reached on the North West Frontier. Therefore, after several decades of wrangling and paranoia about the Afghans, nothing changed on that front.

Burnaby's mission consequently had the central aim of finding out just to what extent Russia had advanced into Turkestan. He cast scorn on the idea expressed by some in Britain that there were benefits in Russia and India being neighbours. He wrote, 'People in this country who advocate the two empires touching are not perhaps aware that our Indian army would then have to be increased to three times its present strength, and in spite of that precaution, there would be less security for ourselves.'

Amazingly, Burnaby planned his journey for the winter. His leave of absence from his regiment could only begin in December, and this reminds us that officers engaged in intelligence in the Raj tended to make their contributions in their own time: on official leave for several months, they would often prefer a trek into unknown regions rather than a trip home. After all, many of them had no family back home. The way Burnaby prepared for the trip, throughout November, is informative on the attitudes behind such intelligence. He bought a huge sleeping bag made of sail cloth and two guns: one for wolves and one (a service revolver) for humans. Essential items such as quinine and cooking materials added to the weight of his burden. But the most intriguing feature of this trip, as in all Great Game journeys, was that liaison with the Russian high command was sought. This was still an era in which officers and gentlemen would converse, be civil and indeed cooperate with actions taken by the enemy. Hence the word *game*. Consequently, Burnaby tried to talk to the Russian War Minister, Milutin, until he realised that there had been a breach of etiquette and that Milutin was perturbed:

> I now first learned that General Milutin ... was personally opposed to the idea of an English officer travelling in Central Asia, particularly in that part which lies between the boundaries of British India and Russia ... A Russian traveller, a Mr Pachino, had not been well treated by the authorities in India. This gentleman had not been permitted to enter Afghanistan and in consequence General Milutin did not see why he should allow an Englishman to do what was denied a Russian subject.

By the 1870s, we have to conclude, the Great Game had become a strange concept: on the one hand the military aristocracy still perceived the manoeuvres on both sides in attempting to gain intelligence to be a gentlemanly affair, and on the other hand, with pragmatic diplomacy in mind, there was a new Machiavellian ruthlessness emerging.

But Burnaby developed a report on military affairs of a practical nature, which he incorporated into his book. For instance, at one point he notes about Kirghiz horses:

> We are apt to think very highly of English horses and deservedly, so far as pace is concerned; but if it came to a question of endurance, I much doubt whether our large and well-fed horses could compete with the little half-starved Kirghiz animals. This is a subject which must be borne in mind in the event of future complications in the East.

More seriously, he assessed the Russian officer class and its attitudes toward expansion and open conflict with Britain. The fact was that the officers were often in isolated border areas, with little to do but patrol and observe; they could go hunting to enliven their time on duty, but Burnaby saw that there was more to it than this. He notes:

> You cannot be with Russian officers in Central Asia for half an hour without remarking how they long for a war. It is very natural; and the wonder to my mind is why Russia has not extended herself still farther… and as the only public opinion that is said to exist in the Tsar's Empire is represented by the military class, which in a few years will absorb all the male population of the nation, we ought to be thoroughly prepared and ready for an emergency.

Reading Burnaby's book, the reader is staggered by the apparent availability of statistics. He quotes facts and figures that, if accurate, would have been very valuable to all kinds of people, but he himself is not sure of their accuracy and does not give his sources. He writes that if Russian reserves were called out they could put 1,300,000 men in the field and that there were 33,893 Turkomen males who could conceivably be one day in active service for Russia. But Burnaby writes that these are 'Russian data', and then admits that there is no way of ascertaining their accuracy. This once again leads us to believe that the agents on the Great Game missions relied on hearsay, chance conversations and any ostensibly 'official' data that might be gained – possibly simply from newspapers.

The lackadaisical attitude to the journeys of the officers on these missions is staggering. When Burnaby was planning his trip, he quite sensibly went to see the Military Attache at the British Embassy in Orenburg; Burnaby comments, 'there was no-one at home save the Military Attache and he was so engaged in having a lesson that he had no time to see me.' The only advice he was given was that the Russians would never believe that a British officer would travel to a place like Khiva for mere diversion and interest. It seems astounding that, decades after the work done by Abbott and Burnes, attitudes had not changed, and that policy still relied for its workings on amateurs and officers on vacation.

In 1877 Burnaby published a second book, *On Horseback through Asia Minor*, and here, although the pattern of enquiry and reportage are the same as in his first book, he adds considerable detail in his appendices which show very clearly what the value of his work was going to be: more perhaps in the factual basis of his writing than in his growing Russophobia. For instance, he gives a detailed account of the routes traversing Asia Minor, covering the rivers Euphrates and Tigris. It appears that, as the nineteenth century wore on and gradually the command at the Staff College realised the importance of all the pathfinding work done by men like Burnaby, the mass of facts was seen as something to re-evaluate. Burnaby's notes included just the kind of practical data that would be valued by future military movement and gambits, such as his account of a path from Angora to Sivas, in which he says, 'The road from Angora by Tokat to Sivas is the shortest. It is best provided with provisions... the route from Caesarea to Diarbekir leads eastwards along Melas till that river joins the Euphrates below Malatia. The river is then crossed by a ferry-boat...' He was, in fact, doing the kind of work done by Indian pundits, in concentrating on the topography and the fine details of transport. But Burnaby also dipped into geopolitics as it was now called, writing copious notes on *The military importance of Syria*, for instance, in which he concluded that:

> If Syria is easy to attack she is equally difficult to conquer. Her territory is mountainous. A small army could defend itself for a long time against a large force. In Mesopotamia and in Egypt a single battle won would be sufficient to reduce the entire country. In Syria it would only enable the foe to occupy a more advanced position.

Burnaby was six feet and four inches tall, and weighed fifteen stones. He was destined to die in action, speared to death in the Sudan in 1885, aged forty-two. As Peter Hopkirk has noted, when London learned of Burnaby's death, 'the nation was plunged into a frenzy of grief.' A poet called Burrows-Smith wrote a poetic tribute to the hero with the lines:

> Again he leads his daring band
> With noble mien,

And with them makes one gallant stand
For England's Queen.

James Tissot painted Burnaby reclining on a sofa (now in the National
Portrait Gallery), languidly holding a cigarette and wearing his smartest
mess uniform. This became the abiding image of the man as a heroic
Victorian. The words beneath the image are: 'Frederick Gustavus Burnaby,
1842–85. Soldier, traveller, politician and balloonist. Memorable for his
famous Ride to Khiva in 1875–76. Killed in action in the Sudan.'

Burnaby's ride to Khiva had made him a celebrity – something that
did not happen to the officers around Henry Lawrence. He was invited
to dine at Windsor, and the media wanted him to lecture the world on
the Russian 'menace'. But there is a final irony about the expedition, as
when he fell into conversation with a Russian colonel about his 'seeing
Khiva', and the colonel replied: 'Khiva, that is nothing … Why, one of your
colleagues, Major Wood, an officer in the Engineers, was here last summer;
he could have gone to Khiva any day he liked.'

Burnaby's books received mixed responses and the common criticism
was expressed most neatly by *The Spectator*, with the point that 'It has been
outrageously puffed by party writers and absurdly praised by people in
society'. The book was summed up in the same piece as 'an indictment of
Russia and a panegyric upon the pashas in general.'

Burnaby's adventures remind historians of the Great Game in that it
is always necessary to separate the intelligence work that was an official
brief from those activities taken on as unofficial initiatives. Burnaby falls
into the latter category, and a comparison of the Burnes and Burnaby
expeditions helps to enlighten matters regarding the Victorian ethos of
the time. By the time of Burnaby's books, the Russian question was not
so far from an open conflict, and the Crimean War was still fairly fresh in
the minds of his readers and military colleagues. He was therefore aware
that he was making a contribution to a national paranoia about the Slavic
imperial drive. The propaganda about Pan-Slavism was well entrenched in
the worlds of literature and art. But for men like Burnes and Abbott, the
focus was all on Afghanistan and about control of the key communication
channel between Russia and India.

Chapter 3

Robertson: From Staff College to the First World War

The military career of Sir William Robertson is truly remarkable. He was from a Lincolnshire family at Welbourn, and was destined to work in domestic service, but that was not his plan for life. He was born on 29 January 1860, of Scottish ancestry, and his father was a tailor and also the village postmaster. William liked school and made good progress. But at fifteen, he started out in domestic service, and fittingly, the service was done at Deene, Northamptonshire, the home of the Brudenell family, whose most famous member was the 7th Earl, James Brudenell, of Crimean War fame.

There was William, having come from the company of farmers and small tradesmen, taking in the grandeur of an aristocratic home. He was a footman, and he said at one time that he was 'a damned bad footman'. All we know is that by 1877 he had joined the army. In his memoirs, he wrote:

> I was seventeen and three quarters old when … I took the Queen's shilling from a recruiting sergeant in the city of Worcester on the 13 November 1877. The minimum age for enlistment was eighteen, but as I was tall for my years the sergeant said the deficient three months would involve no difficulty.

He started with the 16th Lancers at Aldershot, and he was in the army just as the Cardwell reforms were having an effect. Purchase of commissions had ended and a soldier's life was then very different from the conditions in the age of Wellington. Robertson's main memories of that early phase were of the barrack room conditions; but the quality of life was steadily improving. The officers generally made attempts to have rewards available for good conduct, provide books and reading rooms, and have more time for education.

As Robertson joined not too long after the Crimean War, he experienced the results of all kinds of reforms: the situation around Robertson's birth was that there was a complicated structure. There were seven separate bodies, mostly rather ignorant of what each other was actually doing, and intelligence was placed in this only loosely, a floating concept. Control of the army was rationalised in 1855; at the centre of the new power base was the Secretary of State for War for general areas, and the commander-in-chief for war itself and all issues relating to combat.

Robertson did his basic training, and as he had joined a few years after the Franco-Prussian War (1870) various influences from that time still affected army life, chiefly in the concept of manoeuvres. The army gained land for combined exercises, and these were held at Aldershot, Colchester and The Curragh. Robertson found himself in the cavalry, and as a ranker he was always busy and had plenty of small matters to complain about. His letters always showed his capacity as a writer of clear and informative English, and his own memoirs are a valuable source of information on the growth of the Intelligence Branch over this period. He had plenty to say on a range of duties, including guarding prisoners and cleaning equipment. But he knew that he had to somehow obtain a commission, such was his ambition and drive.

Robertson was fortunate in that he found an officer who backed him in that aim. As an officer he would need a large sum of money to live the lifestyle of that rank; but naturally, in that class-ridden society, it was Robertson's origins and provenance that went against him. Nevertheless, he had determination and willpower, and he studied hard to make sure that he had the educational attainment necessary for an officer. When a new CO backed him, he finally saw that his best chance of success was to accept a commission in India. In June 1888, he was gazetted second lieutenant in the 3rd Dragoon Guards, and left for Muttra in India. What he had realised was that it was in languages that the highest distinction lay, and he was also aware that a linguist was always going to be in demand, and would stand out in most situations across the Empire. He began the study of Arabic, having already acquired a fluency in French.

Perhaps just as important was his first success in logistics: he organised transport in service at the Kohat frontier, and he overlooked all arrangements for the transport of men at Hassan Abdal and Kushalgargh. When he had orders to report to HQ in the hill country at Simla, it was a moment of destiny. He was to become an intelligence officer. It is important at this point to define exactly what the intelligence units in India and elsewhere would do with their time. Robertson reported to Colonel Elles, director of the Intelligence Branch. On the Indian frontier, there was still the presence of Russia, not too far away, and there was also the uncertainty of the tribal organisations. Therefore, paramount for intelligence work in such multicultural and politically unstable places was the compilation of accurate information, mainly on topography, geography and general statistics. He proved to be very skilful at that task, doing as chosen men working with the great Wolseley did at that time in Egypt.

Robertson worked on the *Gazetteer and Military Report on Afghanistan.* It was an acceleration of what had been a steady but relentless rise for him. It had taken eleven years to move from enlisted man to lieutenant, and then a further four years before his time in intelligence work took off. But such a concept as a gazetteer was entirely typical of the age; the last quarter of the nineteenth century was a time of gathering and codification of facts. The ruling ideology of utilitarianism was dominant from schools to the higher echelons of the Civil Service. Robertson had a penchant for amassing information, and he was also talented when it came to acquiring and disseminating information. There had been an intelligence branch formed within the quartermaster-general's department in India in 1878. It was reorganised when Robertson arrived, with a staff of five officers and four assistants, and later, in 1903, the officer in charge was a brigadier. The defence of the north-west frontier at the time was of paramount importance, and earlier errors, in the time of the first Great Game spies, had taught the officers in command a great deal. Strategic planning to hold and control the tribal areas meant that knowledge of a definite and precise nature was needed. That was where Robertson came in.

There were also, in the years from 1882, Indian Muslim agents based in Afghanistan, based in Kabul. What happened to really effect radical change was the Second Afghan War of 1878–80, and Robertson was in the thick of it. In 1879 the Russians started a forward policy, initially against the Turkomen of the Karakum; they planned to advance as far as Tashkent. British intelligence knew of this, and Sir Frederick Roberts at Simla learned that Afghans were attacking the British residency in Kabul. There followed a massacre on the Bala Hissar in Kabul. General Roberts organised a force to march against the insurgents; he reached Kabul and handed out some punishments, including the hanging of a hundred natives. But the malaise reached further and a full campaign was imminent

against the Afghans. It was generally thought that there was a Russian
force on its way from the north, and so the Afghan force was heartened,
and Roberts expected an attack. He had used his spies to good advantage,
and he also had plenty of technology at his disposal, including Gatling
guns. But there was a determined attack on the Bala Hissar Residency, and
at that encounter, Lieutenant Hamilton led a resolute defence. In the close
fighting, Hamilton and many others died, but the Indians did not surrender
when told to do so by the Afghans, and it has often been pointed out that
there should have been Victoria Crosses won that day. Six hundred of the
Afgans had died.

Then, closer to Robertson's time there, there had been the massacre at
Maiwand, where, in 1880, the Governor of Herat tried to attack Kabul to
stage a coup, and was met by a force under Brigadeer General Burrows.
He was overwhelmed and around a thousand of the British force died.
Baden-Powell went to the battlefield not long after and his biographer
notes that Baden-Powell 'Found that the sand was worse than sodden red.
Over a thousand Britons had died, and not a few Afghans, and many had
been dug up by jackals and dogs. The ground was littered with decaying
half-corpses of men and horses.'

This was the immediate context of Robertson's arrival there, and he was
soon to have his own near-death experience. But he was assigned to the
Intelligence Branch, and he was fortunate in that behind that organisation
was the remarkable Henry Brackenbury. He had been Director of Military
Intelligence at the War Office; he was a bookish soldier, and had been picked
by Sir Garnet Wolseley for the Ashanti expedition fifteen years earlier. He
had been an officer of artillery during the Mutiny, and had established a
reputation as a military theorist. As he had supported the movement to bring
in Cardwell's reforms of army organisation and promotions, Wolseley had
liked him and taken him under his wing. Known to his friends as 'Brock',
Brackenbury created a massive reputation, partly through his writing of a
lengthy history of the Ashanti campaign, but also as a respected teacher. Many
who knew him talked about his ugly appearance and his tendency to talk
with the upper-class accent of the public schools, rather overstressed for effect.
One description of him was that his face was like a squashed strawberry.

But Brackenbury's intellect and vigour were what made the Branch
at Army HQ and Robertson efficient, and this was done in the face of a
chaotic general organisation; at the time, intelligence work was controlled
as part of the quartermaster-general's remit, so topics such as transport,
training and provisions were in that responsibility, along with intelligence.
Basic to the system in India was the tendency for intelligence staff to be

selected based on reasons that were not necessarily related to such abilities and linguistic fluency or good communication skills. There was a degree of favouritism and the canteen culture included liaisons and favours, of course, as that was the way in which things had always been done.

Brackenbury, and others, set out to change all this. Robertson, for instance, found that his 'line manager', Lieutenant Colonel Mason of the Royal Engineers, was a man of great cultural and anthropological knowledge. Consequently, Robertson learned a good deal about the frontier peoples. He wrote of Mason in his memoirs:

> Of a retiring nature, he was slow to confide in new acquaintances, but I gained his confidence fairly soon, and he taught me much about the life, customs and attitudes of the heterogeneous tribes of the north-west frontier, which I could have learned so well from no-one else. It was due to him that within a few weeks of my arrival at Simla, Lord Roberts approved my temporary appointment being made permanent.

Robertson was responsible for territories that covered Afghanistan, Kashmir and Baluchistan, a stretch of land covering 2,000 miles, from Tibet westwards. When Robertson was there, in 1892, the victor of Maiwand and his peers had made an allegiance (with payment) to keep a certain cooperative relationship with India going, rather than entertain Russian envoys. It was a buffer state, and intelligence work therefore had to operate in that dangerous no-man's land in which there was no absolute trust and little certainty about who was a genuine ally. Robertson described Afghanistan as 'a waterless, treeless, foodless, roadless, mountainous country ... in which a large army will starve and a small army be murdered.'

His immediate concern was to understand the boundary questions. There were three routes within the Russian-British line of axis: Pamirs, Kabul and Kandahar. This meant that there were immense distances between the various frontiers held by outsiders. Espionage or even simple tasks such as measurement were always going to be risky. What happened was that Russia very steadily pushed southwards and eastwards, while various pocket tribal areas waged intermittent war. Kafiristan was the one persistent problem area, and a boundary commission of 1884–88 had ostensibly defined the Russian-Afghan border, but the land of the Pamirs was squashed between the important boundary points. Robertson found himself involved in the Pamir question.

Until the Intelligence Branch really gathered a store of information, the reliance was on amateurish sources such as reports written and spoken by individual travellers. The stock of intelligence did grow, however, and Robertson notes that the *Gazetteer* took a year of his life, and that the final volume was 3,000 pages long. But in 1893 the focus was on the Pamirs. His quandary related to two conflicting schools of Empire thinking back home at Whitehall, and indeed in Parliament. The 'forward' school wanted to push aggressively northwards and put pressure on the Russians, whereas the defensive outlook was to hold, consolidate and wait for the right opportunities to act. Of course, the latter is easy to understand; after all, the Great Game had been rolling on for sixty years when Robertson found himself preparing for a trip to the Pamir routes in 1894, and nothing significant had happened. It had all been like an eternal game of chess.

Warfare and military honours were to come his way in 1894. To get out there into dangerous territory was the only sure way of really knowing the terrain and the routes for further progress, so he was sent out to Pamir country, to Chitral. There had been some trouble and the political agent and some troops were placed under siege. The man in charge was to become famous in 1917 when he was in charge at the calamitous Siege of Kut in Mesopotamia: Captain Townsend.

The boundary of Afghanistan at that time extended north of the Hindu Kush, including the Pamir district of Wakhan, between Kashmir and Russian territory. It followed the course of the river Amu Daria, and then turned south-west to Zulfikar. The southern and eastern boundaries touched British territory. The area within these limits covered 250,000 square miles – an area five times that of England and Wales. In June 1894, Robertson found himself on a train to Rawalpindi, and there he was to travel on a 'tonga' – a two-wheeled wagon – until he reached the Muree Hills. He then crossed the Kashmir valley and had to get from there to Gilgit. It was when he reached the country of the Hunza and Nagar that he must have been most worried. He wrote: 'Secure in their mountain strongholds, and having ready access to the passes north to the Yarkand valley, the Kanjutis (Hunza and Nagar) were able to waylay and pillage with impunity the rich caravans travelling by the great trade route between India and Turkestan...'

When it came to trying to fulfil an order to survey a road south from Dir, he had a first taste of real fighting and came close to a bloody death. He left Gilgit with a Ghurka escort, a native guide and a Pathan. This is what happened:

> I gradually forged ahead of the escort and was followed by two guides only. Suddenly I was twice fired at from behind, and could not imagine what

had happened. Looking round I saw the 'Kazi' [the main guide] rising from his knee, in the act of throwing aside the 12-bore breech-loader which he had been carrying, preparatory of achieving with his sword – or rather my sword – what he had failed to accomplish with his gun. He was yelling with the fury of a madman, and I realised that he had become ghazi – a religious fanatic.

Although Robertson could only defend himself with his fist, he still 'floored the fellow', but then, as the man tried to run, he got hold of his revolver and brought him down, though he was not dead. The Ghurka arrived then. The encounter made the news, appearing in *The Daily Graphic*, with images that showed the assassin being shot, and Robertson fighting him. A DSO was awarded to him for that skirmish.

He was then promoted to captain. He concentrated after that on his education, because his sights were set on advancement now that he had found his metier in the army. He got married to Mildred Palin, a daughter of a general in the Indian Army. His immediate objective was to sit the competitive examination for entry to the Staff College. This had been founded at Camberley in 1858, but had gone in decline, largely due to the Duke of Cambridge's opposition. His attitude was that competitive examinations meant very little, and he thought that such things would undermine the regimental *esprit de corps*. By 1870 the situation was that if a junior officer aspired to take the exams, and so do a two-year course at the College, there was a high chance that his aspiration was simply a way of escaping arduous regimental duty, and he may have been seen as a slacker. But by the time Robertson applied, there had been significant changes, largely due to the energy and creativity of Sir Edward Hamley. He opened up the opportunity for Robertson, as he made room for six officers from the Indian Army to apply. One of his most remarkable advances – again something that an intelligence officer would relish – was the introduction of European battlefield tours and arrangement by which English officers met foreign officers. A typical outcome of this attitude is seen in the account of Autumn manoeuvres in the *Journal of the Household Brigade* for 1871:

Conspicuous among the guests was a lieutenant of Prussian infantry. He stood some 6ft 6 or 6ft 7in. tall, and was built in proportion to the strongest horses known. Once he galvanised an officer by saying he had read through the Queen's regulations. He spoke many languages, a grave, serious young man.

It is clear from this that the army was beginning to take note of Prussian militarism: after all, Cardwell's reforms and the notion of reserve forces were linked to Prussian theory and practice. The effect of these wider, more intellectually challenging attitudes was felt in the Staff College that Robertson joined. In 1870 there were forty students there; by 1884 there were sixty-four. The abbreviation p.s.c. next to a name started to gather a certain cache. Wolseley was known to like a man with those initials; in fact, Wolseley's attitudes to decisions in command reflected the impact of the new thinking. As Edward Spiers wrote: 'He looked to his staff to provide administrative support in his headquarters, to furnish information on local intelligence and reconnaissance, and to supervise the vital matters of communications and supply.' He encouraged applications to Staff College. In fact, it was one of Wolseley's main disciples, G.F.R. Henderson, who taught Robertson. He became Professor of Military Art and History, and wrote the seminal book, *Campaign of Fredericksburg*. His teaching was both practical and abstract, as he enjoyed all aspects of learning and was open to constructive debate. One student wrote that his students 'found themselves expected to replace the actors, to work out the operations step by step with map and compass...'.

Robertson had to pass the exam first. He studied when he could grab some time while on service at Simla; not for him the time spent with crammers in London (as Reginald Wingate did briefly). He had to study languages, including German, from scratch. But he also selected Hindustani, something that turned out to be a very wise choice. He finally sat the exam but failed to gain one of the open vacancies by one point. But Sir George White gave a special recommendation and Robertson made some small but significant army history: he became the first ranker officer to go to Staff College. That was in January 1897, and there he came under the influence of Henderson, and also another theorist and skilful teacher, Colonal Hildyard, a man so radical that he did not believe in written exams. The spirit of the place under the new regime is captured by Robertson:

There were five military instructors or professors – one for strategy and tactics, one for artillery and fortifications, one for administrative duties, and two for topography, as well as two for languages – French and German. Topography was the subject students liked least in learning to draw the conventional signs for trees, churches, public houses. This seeming waste of effort was not without excuse, for some officers had but a hazy notion of how to make or read a map, and were not much surer of themselves in regard to the working of a magnetic compass.

A particular influence on Robertson was Henderson. Henderson had written a study of Stonewall Jackson and was very much involved in teaching and encouraging in innovative ways. He had become a close friend of Lord Roberts, later Field Marshall, and Roberts wrote of Henderson:

> The influence of such a man must bear good fruit, and the more widely his writings are read, and the more closely his teachings are followed, the more successful will be our would-be commanders, and the better it will be for England when again she is forced to go to war.

Robertson clearly felt himself to be a special case, having reached the College by recommendation. There is a lot to learn about his character in this episode. He was a very driven, highly motivated man, eager to compete and to excel in everything he attempted. Reflecting on his own progress at this time, he looked at the other officers who had entered by open examination, and was determined not to fall below any standards that they might have. His main focus at first was on languages, and French was a language he knew: now he had a chance to use it and to update his knowledge. It had been more than twenty years since the Franco-Prussian War, but the lessons learned from that conflict by the British forces was considerable in many ways. Robertson passed his French at the end of the year, and much of the success was due to his visit to France to see some of the battlefields of the previous war.

He went to see the fields of Woerth, Spicheren, Vionville and Gravelotte in particular. The influential and charismatic Henderson went as his guide, and this episode clearly illustrates the kind of learning done by intelligence staff at the time of that great but short-lived conflict which served to highlight the military virtues of the Prussians. One notable feature of this was the success of using railways to transport and deploy forces: this was something that was to be important in Egypt when Kitchener went to take on the Khedive in the Sudan, leading to Omdurman (see chapter four).

Robertson saw the virtues of this study at the time, writing in his memoirs of the cultural, international meetings, obviously a part of the educational objective: 'When visiting the battlefield of Woerth, we stayed at Niederbronn, a small spa prettily situated in the Vosges. It was much frequented by Germans in the summer, and by German officers from Bitche and other neighbouring places.'

But little did Robertson know how much his industry and energy had been noticed, until one day while on manoeuvres, he was asked to report to Brackenbury. The general wanted some reformation made to the cavalry arrangements on the manoeuvres. Robertson put things right. This turned out to be something of a test. Brackenbury came to Captain Robertson to thank him and to make it clear that he had not forgotten what had been achieved. It was, as we would say, 'a good career move' to show off the requisite skills.

There was William Robertson, on his way to more promotion, having been reviewed along with other officers at the College by Wolseley himself. His summary of the College was that it did not aspire to make wise men, but it made 'good men better'. He also made the point that all graduates were taught the same methods of administration. He wrote, with hindsight, that he and his friend Maudsley, late commander-in-chief in Mesopotamia (now Iraq) kept in touch over the years, and to mutual advantage. In short, the Wolseley principle of selecting the right men for the job, and then letting each man flower within the range of his talents, was a good way forward. It was to be implemented in intelligence work.

Robertson was now detailed to the Intelligence Division at the War Office. He had not returned to regimental duty, but was sent to work under Sir John Ardagh, whose career is the subject of a later chapter here. But before we look at Robertson's later career, we need to look at the context of the founding of that branch, looking at the wider picture and some colonial confrontations.

In 1903 a special publication, *The Report of His Majesty's Commissioners on the War in South Africa*, criticised the organisation and management of the Anglo-Boer War. Every contributing department of the military machine of the Empire was called into question, with the exception of the Intelligence Branch and its leader. As the historian Correlli Barnet has noted, as early as 1896 the Department of Military Intelligence had informed the general staff that it would take two months for reinforcements to reach troops in South Africa, and that at that time there should have been an increase in manpower in that region. That detail might not sound like such a momentous fact, but it was, and the reason for that was that even after twenty-three years, the Intelligence brains were not necessarily awarded any status or seen as particularly noteworthy by many in positions of power.

Yet over that twenty-three years there had been a quiet revolution. Before the founding of the Intelligence Branch in 1873, the so-called 'Long Peace', between 1815 and the Crimean War, had been largely a matter of complacency and neglect in terms of the growth of intelligence as a respected department of the war ministry and military structure. The Great Game, in one sense, was peripheral, amateur and always overshadowed by the machinations of diplomacy. It is not difficult to see the concerns of the spies and surveyors out in the Raj and the Levant as secondary to the larger question of maintaining a power base near home.

Of course, the Crimea and the Mutiny changed all that. Despite the poor reputation that posterity has given to Lord Raglan, at least he saw the importance of military intelligence. As John Hughes-Wilson has written: 'The fact was, in the long peace, the British Army had forgotten how to collect intelligence. The Great Duke's legacy has much to answer for. Lord Raglan... railed at his lack of intelligence. The truth is that Raglan was a calculating and sophisticated commander.'

By 1870, that type of commander was exactly what was needed. The Franco-Prussian War had taught the rest of Europe a lesson about how to conduct warfare: the Prussians had beaten France because of their short-term service system and their reservist corps. They had seen the value of streamlining provisions, from uniform victualling to transport, and they had highlighted the value of having truly professional soldiers. In Britain in 1870 the army still worked by the system of purchase of commissions. The Empire was ticking over with surprising ease when one considers that most British officers bought their commissions, as they had been doing for as long as there was an Empire. But at the time when the Intelligence Branch was set up, the new theorists and army professionals were beginning to be a presence, and much of this change was down to the Gladstone ministry, and in particular Edward Cardwell who became secretary at war in 1868. In addition to ending flogging, which was common practice in the army, he had Gladstone's help in abolishing the purchase system. When the lords blocked his Army Regulation Bill in 1874, Gladstone went to the Queen and used her power to see the legislation through. Queen Victoria did this because she could not tolerate the terrible row this subject had caused in her government factions.

Cardwell has been called the armourer of Britain. In his Army Enlistment Act of 1870 he introduced short service, and in many ways this was to open up possibilities of radical change in the perception of the place and importance of military intelligence. Prussia had benefited from a large reserve of experienced men who had done a limited-term service and yet were standing by for action when required. Cardwell brought in a six-year term and opened up a more rigid selection procedure. The army had long been defined as the depository of criminals and renegades, the tough types who had won the field at Waterloo, perhaps, but in late Victorian years it was perceived that there was more to being an officer than dash and horsemanship, and there was more to being a squaddy than drilling and hard drinking.

It was during these momentous years between 1870 and 1874 that the Intelligence Branch arrived, and a man whose attitude to the army matched the new thinking came along at the right time, following Sir Richard Brackenbury in 1887: Sir Garnet Wolseley. William Robertson was destined to become an important figure in the new department. In his memoirs he writes of the birth of this branch:

> When first formed in 1873 it was a branch of the quartermaster-general's department; later it was placed under the adjutant-general; and was, when I joined it, more or less under the commander-in-chief, Lord Wolseley. It had a staff of about sixteen officers and, with the 'Mobilisation Section' of three or four officers, was the only semblance of a General Staff then in existence. The mobilisation section had originally been under the director of military intelligence, but was afterwards absorbed by the adjutant-general's department and then, like the Intelligence Branch, came under the commander-in-chief.

Robertson added that the two branches had been 'constantly tossed over from one high official to another.' He noted that intelligence organisation was therefore always going to be influenced by whoever was in charge at any particular time. Clearly, there was a problem in how the department and its work were seen by the top brass. What Stieber had achieved in Prussia was certainly interesting in its outcomes, but the thinking was that there was no way that Britain was going to ape the Prussians in Stieber's own brand of espionage. The bottom line was that the most useful intelligence work that had been done since the war with Napoleon had been done by individuals – by people like Cattley or Abbot – and so it took some time for the new department to have a clear identity. Robertson explains the early work done there, in the office at 29, Queen Anne's Gate, as primarily the collection and collation of information on foreign countries. He also notes that such knowledge was somehow to be processed, taken into the catalogue of current information on every state that might play a part in conflict, and kept for future reference.

Before this new departure, according to Sir George Aston, the prevailing attitudes had been more domestic:

> The military authorities were still under the influence of the Palmerston Royal Commission of the early sixties, which was responsible for the idea that fortifications could do the work of warships, the theory being that the introduction of steam propulsion had rendered obsolete Raleigh's old

principle that it was better to deal with foreign invading armies at sea in those early years, intelligence was mainly devoted to studying how to deal with a foreign invading army.

In the 'long peace' the army had been more interested in tactics than in strategy, but that was going to change. The initiative began with a memo from Stanhope (who was later to be chairman of the central committee) in June 1888. This defined the aims of the new branch according to the three main functions: the support of civil power, the provision of staff for the India garrison and the capability of mobilising corps of regular and auxiliary troops. What was happening behind all this was the emergence of forward planning with regard to geopolitics: the event of a war with a European power or the Raj. The subtext, we might guess, was again something gleaned from Prussian professionalism: to have an intelligence arm of the forces that would have an important status and that would be part of an organic function in times of war.

In 1875 the Hartington Commission recommended a War Office department with a Chief of Staff whose business would be largely that of collecting information. In fact, in the person of Wolseley, this kind of function had begun, as he had already set about creating a fresh breed of officer, and placed intelligence within a generally more forward looking and educated elite of senior staff. However, although the new branch was initially under Sir John Ardagh's command, at the time of its formation Wolseley was in West Africa, leading the expeditionary force against the Ashanti, and this provides an enlightening case study in which we may see the new attitudes at work, particularly as Wolseley was destined to take over the branch later. Wolseley, in the words of one of his biographers, saw that 'War was a serious business and soldiering a profession, not a pastime for dilettantes. The days of playing at soldiers were over. Education in the army, still at a dangerously low ebb, should permeate through all ranks.'

Cardwell and Wolseley were an alliance, and they were not alone. Other officers had been nurtured into supporting roles. Cardwell, when the Ashanti problem became a most urgent one, made sure that Wolseley would lead the force out there, and we have to reflect that both were out to prove something about the new methods and attitudes. The Ashanti king, Kofi, and other warlords, were conducting a brutal and inhuman regime of terror along the west coast and into the territory of the Fanti. Their militaristic structures combined with bloodthirsty acts of murder and repression led to a state of emergency in which the various British administrators of smaller protectorates feared that a very large scale emergency might arise if something were not done.

Wolseley put the emphasis on gathering the right team of officers around him, and then planned to use native fighters, with a request to the high command that regular troops would be on standby if needed. He even gave his superiors a quote for the job of £150,000. Wolseley also involved the navy, for diplomatic reasons, and so the force that eventually arrived and set about marching on Kumasi, the Ashanti main settlement, was a mixed one in which some of the fiercest African warriors were travelling alongside a naval detachment and Fanti people. But Wolseley realised at a later stage of planning that he would need some professionals from Britain, and he had no less a force than the Black Watch with him.

Wolseley had officers whose task it was to survey local conditions and also to collect a viable force of local fighters. Indicative of the new thinking was the nature of the key men in the Wolseley team. There was Lieutenant Maurice who was an instructor from Sandhurst; Captain Buller, Major Colley and the future principal of the Intelligence Branch, the colourful Captain Brackenbury. But perhaps the most significant feature of the early phase of the Ashanti campaign was Garnet Wolseley's own habits: he studied blue books and reports assiduously and worked his way through all the information about the place and people that he could find. As Joseph Lehmann noted:

> For the first time in the history of the British Empire, a general appointed to command an expedition sat down to a table at the War Office with the Secretary for War, the Secretary for the Colonies, the First Lord of the Admiralty and the various heads of military departments to discuss the necessary arrangements.

There was a library of books on topography and history available for the staff to peruse. Not to put too fine a point on it, this was *intelligent* intelligence in war.

One of the heroes of the Ashanti campaign, Sir Henry Brackenbury, took over the Army Intelligence command in the 1880s, and according to Sir George Aston, a significant change occurred:

> It began to be realised that gathering information about foreign armies was only a means to an end. The next step must be to make the best possible use of whatever army Parliament consented to provide, and at last the question of speedy 'mobilisation', which Prussia had taught to the world in 1870, was grasped.

This implies that Robertson's narrative does not make it clear that it took a good ten years for the lessons from Prussia to be learned. In fact, when Robertson talks about his training course at the Staff College, the importance of the Franco-Prussian War to the changes in British intelligence becomes clearer. Robertson was taught at the College by Colonel George Henderson, whom he refers to warmly as 'Hender' – the man who was to be Director of Intelligence with Lord Roberts in the Boer War.

But the new department still needed to be placed somewhere in the structure of the army. By the time of the office of Sir Henry Campbell-Bannerman, in 1892, the Intelligence Department was put, as so often in the past, under the adjutant-general. Since the 1880s the department had been streamlined in many ways, and there is ample evidence to show that its briefs, assignments and staff were busy doing what intelligence outfits have always done when there is too much to cope with: prepare voluminous reports. For instance, in 1882 John Frederick Maurice, secretary to Wolseley, wrote a *History of the Campaigns of 1882 in Egypt*. This was prepared specifically for the branch. Best Jervis's lessons on cartography had been absorbed by this time, as the volume has eleven maps on no fewer than sixteen folding sheets. Maurice even appends a map illustrating the attack on Tel el Kebir.

We have to ask, though, about the other side of intelligence, the one involving people rather than paper. What was happening out in the field of operations at this time? A rare insight is provided by Wolseley himself, writing in his campaign journal while on the relief expedition to Khartoum in 1884. Just before Christmas, when he perhaps had a little more leisure to fill a few pages, he wrote:

> It is always difficult to get information in a country where money is no temptation to its people to betray it, and the cruelties of barbarous people not only to the spy but to all his family make men hesitate before they undertake to give the invader information. In Europe or America of course money will provide the energetic man with any amount of information.

He and his fellow officers were learning in these years that understanding the cultural and ethnic lifestyles and relationships in the localities of warfare was more complex than previously thought. In fact, the Raj in India had become a touchstone, a model of how to do things in this respect. But as with all templates of this kind, the situation there does not necessarily carry across to other contexts. There was no 'John Company' in Africa, and comparisons with European races and traditions, as Wolseley was realising, had no value in places such as the Sudan. In that same journal he assesses the place of the Mahdi, the leader of the Sudanese rebellion, in this respect:

> Of course native rumours are important and generally contain some grains of truth in them but they are apt to frighten those whose nerves are not the strongest. One day I hear the Mahdi is surrounded by thousands of warriors longing to die for him... the rumours and stories I hear seriously repeated by fairly sensible men very often are to me simply ludicrous.

Under two men, Major-General Sir Patrick MacDougall (who had been in charge of the Camberley Staff College) and Captain Wilson, the new branch really went into full throttle by the time of Wolseley's relief assignment in Egypt. That expeditionary army took with it several copies of a massive 400-page volume called the *Handbook on Egypt* which had in its covers almost everything a traveller might need to know about that country, from food to protocol, camels to dervishes. One of the highlights of the branch's early history has to be the part it played in the diplomatic success of the Congress of Berlin, in which Disraeli had faced a potential war with Russia, but came home and made his famous statement that the nation had 'Peace with honour'. Following this, the Secretary for India, Salisbury, wrote that the Intelligence Department of the War Office had played a major part in the success of the 'preceding diplomatic negotiations'.

William Robertson did point out one shortcoming, however, in this period. He wrote that a properly equipped department, led by the adjutant-general, 'could collect all information and place it at the disposal, not of one officer or department alone, but of all the military heads'. But he notes that even by 1895 nothing had been done in that respect: 'although there was a change of government in 1895, nothing was done to introduce the system recommended until the necessity for it was forced upon us by the costly experience of the South African War.'

It is arguably Wolseley's *modus operandi* regarding his staff that formed the most important influence on what eventually turned out to be the efficient central 'engine room' of the new branch. After all, in the 1870s he had Brackenbury with him, as well as Maurice. What Wolseley saw was that side of Brackenbury which has a special talent for articulating the bearing of theory on practice warfare. The man the team called 'Brack' developed into a hard worker and a superbly gifted organiser – very much what we now think of as a 'personal assistant'. But he was not always sitting at a desk or taking notes. He was one of the first men to walk into Esaman in the Ashanti campaign.

The Raj was very much in step with these advances in intelligence as well. In 1878 an intelligence branch was developed in Simla. This initiative was the work of Brackenbury. This was one of the points of real crisis on the North West Frontier. In Robertson's memoirs, he makes a point of noting that it was the quality of the staff running intelligence that needed most attention, exactly as Wolseley had done:

> Apart from the faulty organisation of headquarters as a whole, the Intelligence Branch had suffered because of the inadequacy – and perhaps the inferior quality – of its personnel. Although much had been done by the commander-in-chief, Lord Roberts, to ensure that priority for staff employment should be governed by professional capacity, favouritism and social influence were not yet deemed by the outsider to be extinct.

Robertson is keen to inform the reader that in Simla, up in the hills, life was rather more leisurely. But there was more to the northern Indian town than amateur theatricals and dinners. In 1864, the viceroy, Sir John Lawrence, had made Simla the summer residence of the government of India. Northern India at that particular time was of great strategic importance, and in a more practical sense, the climate was better for getting down to administrative work. This would have been a shock to many residents there, as it had attained the nickname 'Olympus' because of the self-indulgent and languorous Greek gods who ruled from their heights. But Robertson's criticisms were based on his fundamentally serious and ambitious nature. He personally welcomed the fact that the town had a new status and importance.

From that base, Robertson's mission into Pamir territory is very informative about the way that the sheer vastness of India impacted on the work of an intelligence officer. From his reflections on this situation around 1880, it is probably the case that he knew little of the work of men like Younghusband, and all the other loners, and though he was aware that travellers had been to some of the uncharted lands towards the Himalayas, as was mentioned earlier, he was critical of these types of sources:

> When I went to Simla there was no good information available as regards much of the vast area for which the Frontier Section was responsible. We had to rely largely upon the reports of travellers, and these seldom gave the kind

of intelligence that was needed, much of it was many years old, while some of the travellers were themselves more renowned for their powers of graphic description than for the accuracy of their statements.

What this meant for the Simla Frontier Branch was that they had to set to work doing much more than topographical surveys. Robertson was bewailing the lack of directly strategic information, such as assessments of manpower, weaponry and so on. The work being done by the pundits and by individual officers was, by this time, becoming viewed as too marginal in terms of the feared confrontation with Russia on the North West Frontier.

In fact, Robertson's criticisms of the existing information chain in northern India are interesting when we compare what tended to happen when the East India Company had to cope with the Thuggee murders back in the first four decades of the nineteenth century. Counteracting these murderous gangs meant using police informers in a network, with rewards. Finally that had worked, but unfortunately the same methods did not carry over into major international conflicts. Robertson had a sub-text, and this had been made plain to him on his arrival in Simla: there had always been ad hoc decisions and a mindset of mere pragmatism when dealing with intelligence across the vast areas of the northern borders. In the past, various commanders had relied on Abbot, Conolly and Burnes and their ilk; clearly by 1880 that mode of action was being retained, but only marginally. The Great Game, in short, was becoming too leisurely in a military world that had been transformed by the mobilisation and reservist practices of Prussia, combined with Russia's new imperialism that had led them to extend their lands to Vladivostok and the fringes of Manchuria.

The converse was also true. British travellers were writing about those far Russian provinces, the lands which were across the mountains from where the frontier section of the Intelligence Branch found itself. But these were foolhardy and headstrong individuals such as Harry de Windt, who travelled from New York to Paris by land, going by sledge across Siberia. As gentlemen such as Harry were coping with Yakuts and Inuits, gathering all kinds of obscure anthropological data, they were also describing police and officials, so they played a minor part in matters of intelligence. The real work, however, was being done (by the last two decades of the century) by men like Robertson and Younghusband.

The nature of the various armies involved in these power struggles was changing also, along with the political climate in the capitals of the empires involved. Mechanisation and more sophisticated weaponry was having an influence, as was the more advanced technology in communications that would have an impact on the way a war was conducted. As Trevor Fishlock has explained:

> One effect of the Mutiny was to spur the British to forge ahead with building railways over which they could send troops quickly in case of trouble, and stations which could double as fortresses. Lahore railway station was built in 1864 in the form of a medieval castle, with musket loopholes and iron gates.

On paper, at least, the new intelligence work may have appeared to be a structure very much dictated by the attitudes and ambitions of a new breed of officer, and to some extent that was true. Young officers such as Robertson were certainly impressed by the likes of the studious Brackenbury and the meticulous Wolseley. They were receptive to the idea of learning several languages, at least to an everyday functional level, and they were mostly open to the practice of understanding foreign cultures. But when it came to actual warfare, in particular terrain and conditions, the intelligence personnel still had to be there and move with the regiment.

Certainly the new technology applied to transport and communications was beginning to have an influence on the work of men like Robertson, but we still have to consider that the different varieties of intelligence are always there, even as I write this, and Britain is still fighting in Afghanistan. A useful distinction is to separate two basic areas of intelligence work in the nature of a military expedition to an enemy. There is what might be called 'paper and science' work done with maps and field reports, and there is the observation and support for the 'knowledge of the enemy' aspect of a fight.

Again, in Robertson's memoirs we have a case study of this, because he was, as we have seen, a part of the Chitral expedition, in 1895, which was organised after a political assassination in Chitral led to a situation of catastrophic proportions. If we look again at what he did there, it can be seen that his attitude had already won him notice; Brackenbury and Wolseley were learning about him as a promising young officer whose future lay elsewhere than in India.

The area around Chitral had been the focus for a series of coups attempting to wrest power from the inheritors of the throne of the chief (known as a *mehtar*) who had died in 1892. Brothers and an uncle who had been based across the border in Afghanistan were all involved, and an allegiance was formed between the uncle, Sher Afzul, and an ally. Francis

Younghusband was the political officer in Chitral at the time, and there was a brief respite before Afzul took over, by murder. When two chiefs combined forces, they had enough manpower to overthrow the British garrison, and a British force was besieged in the fort. Following that, another British detachment was under siege at Reshun, so things were hotting up when action was decided; there would be a punitive expedition. It is at this point that Robertson becomes involved and we can learn much about the role of intelligence from his actions in that confrontation.

A plan was put together: three separate groups were to converge on Chitral. The main fight was going to involve the Ist Indian Division and the 32nd. Pioneers. The management was in the hands of the quartermaster-general's department, and specifically the Intelligence and Mobilisation Branch. Robertson's part in all this, as appointed by Sir George White, was to collate, with some haste, the various sources of intelligence required. First there was the topography; there was very little available on this except from native sources, so the old problem was there again: how much of that could be trusted? What he did know was that there were four mountain ranges along the route, and that there would be tribal opposition during the march.

The spies' job, as we have seen with Robertson's trek to Chitral, was therefore to obtain knowledge of the three passes referred to earlier in this chapter which would be encountered. The charismatic Chief of Staff, Sir Bindon Blood, made sure that there was an application of false intelligence, as it was vital that the enemy did not know which pass the British Army would take. Everything in these situations depended on surprise and misinformation, even to the extent that officers such as Robertson were deliberately misinformed. But he was beginning to learn the essence of doublethink, and when instructed to prepare for a march to Shakot, Robertson surmised that the real target was Malakand. He writes:

> I laid my plans accordingly, and next morning when the brigade was about to move off, and I was ordered to conduct it to the Malakand and not to the Shakot, I greatly enjoyed seeing the look of surprise on the Brigadier's face at the readiness with which his order was carried out.

What Robertson was engaged in, in terms of the greater scheme of things, was the 'Forward policy' already mentioned in this chapter – that of making punitive expeditions across the border, making Afghanistan (and Russia) aware that Britain was active, not merely sitting pretty in Simla and similar places waiting for others to take the initiative. Winston

Churchill, then a cavalry subaltern and a reporter, formed his conception of what part should be played by Intelligence in imperial conflict after the experience of the Malakand campaign. Churchill learned a great deal from Captain Henry Stanton, who was one of the intelligence officers alongside Robertson in Blood's force. The situation in which Churchill, Robertson and the others learned so much about the nature of spy networks is well described by David Stafford:

> Everything about the Malakand Field Force engaged his [Churchill's] romantic spirit. Here for a brief moment he was to play the Great Game, a world of intrigue where every man was a warrior, every house a fortress, every family waged its vendetta. Agents and informers for the Indian Army, like Kipling's *Kim*, provided eyes and ears throughout the land, and political officers exploited enmities between rival factions to maintain an uneasy imperial peace.

It was Captain Stanton who wrote the official report on the Malakand campaign and the functions of the Intelligence Department in that enterprise. In that, we can learn a lot about the kind of men who were in those ranks of native agents and informers. One such was Abdul Hamid Khan, a man from an Afghan refugee family – a family that had for three generations supplied reliable advice to Britain – and the man's skills were very impressive. Abdul Hamid Khan could speak English, Hindi, Persian and Pushtu. He knew all the frontier tribes and he had learned what kind of information was wanted by the British commanders over the years.

Churchill, in his account of the Malakand campaign, was aware of the achievements of such men and of the ways in which they worked with the Intelligence Branch. He learned that, as Stafford puts it, 'intelligence and operations were intimately linked, and that the former should be firmly controlled by those who had to act on it.'

Reading between the lines with regard to the view of these border events as recalled by Churchill, Robertson and Stanton, there is a valuable insight to be gained from a consideration of the bigger picture. That means the 'Forward School', in particular a cabal of three powerful men in the context of the Great Game and Russian threat on the north-west frontier. These were the foremost British authority on the Indian subcontinent, Sir Henry Rawlinson, Henry Bartle Frere (who is prominent in the next chapter) and Sir Robert Montgomery. In Gladstone's first ministry there had been created the Council of India (1858) as one of the political repercussions of the Mutiny. This was made as a consultative body from the ranks of retired administrators from India, with the main function of studying, evaluating and formulating important despatches in the interchange of information between Britain and India. All three had their attention on Afghanistan. The head of the Political and Secret Department of the India Office was Sir John Kaye, and he clearly had a good working relationship with the cabal of three elder statesmen. It was Kaye's job to handle state draft replies to secret and political letters from India.

What becomes apparent is that this group of men knew all about the content of secret material that other members of the council would never see. Their exercise of powerful information in the context of the border expeditions in the decades preceding Malakand set a precedent for such involvement in the encroachments into Afghanistan that many wanted. Frere, for instance, had pushed hard for the establishment of a British settlement at Quetta, which is in fact 200 miles over the frontier into tribal lands.

This group first worked together in 1869 and at that time it was a unity founded on the Persian policy. As Britain at the time was reliant for information on a scattered band of agents and spies in a vast area (the one travelled later by Percy Sykes) there was a perception that something more solid and permanent should be put in what was, to all effects, a buffer state which Russia was keen to control. The forward policy regarding India, c.1890, was a natural result of this thinking.

It is stunning to contemplate the machinations of the London-based Political and Secret Department alongside the daily work of intelligence officers and regional political officers, not to mention the work of Montgomerie and the pundits. Such a multiplicity of intelligence elements had to work across a vast area of India and bordering states, and had to do so in such a way that when something like the Malakand emergency arose there was a degree of unity, or unified action, which required swift communication. The more historians search for meaningful answers to questions about how these elements work together, the more confusing it becomes. This all helps to explain why the new Intelligence Branch was an expression of the new faith in professionalism in Whitehall.

Sir George Aston sums up this new feeling that there might be something worthwhile in listening to men like Wolseley or Brackenbury; he writes about his work at the new headquarters in Queen Anne's Gate, set up in 1884:

> There, in 1886, I began to spend many profitable hours learning from the Army Intelligence officers, with the gathering force of experience behind them, how to get great government departments to do things, instead of perpetually

discussing them without doing anything. The late Sir Henry Brackenbury, an artillery man equipped with good brains and great administrative capacity, became the head of the department in Queen Anne's Gate.

Aston locates the central reason for success: a combination of new organisation with man–management from officers of both field experience and theoretical ability in terms of warfare and strategy. Yet the new cast of thought about intelligence was to have several shocks in the years between 1870 and the end of the century, making it clear that there was still a long way to go in mastering the effectiveness of field intelligence and local networks of informants.

To summarise, then. What Robertson was now moving into, in 1895, was a position in which he would begin to see the wider picture, and to think like a senior officer, at a time when field intelligence and diplomacy were just beginning to come together. We will meet Robertson again in the Boer War, and the man involved in intelligence then was fully aware of the worldwide nature of the empire and what the task of cohesion of governments entailed, as he put it when he wrote with hindsight: 'Our colonial empire comprised some forty distinct and independent governments, and in addition to these organised states there were a number of dependencies under the dominion of the Sovereign which had formed no ministries.'

The results of this for both diplomacy and theoretical intelligence were massively important. The role of knowledge and communication across the globe, comprising so many cultures and identities, would be a logistical nightmare even in the modern age of technology. Ian Hernon's book on the lesser-known wars of Victoria's empire, *Britain's Forgotten Wars* (2003), for instance, discusses twenty-eight minor conflicts in that period of sixty years. A geography textbook of 1905 says of the Indian Empire at that time:

> Our Indian Empire comprises the central and by far the most important of the three great peninsulas of Southern Asia, together with large territories on the eastern side of the Bay of Bengal. The total area of these vast dominions, most of which are under direct British rule, is upwards of 1,800,000 square miles, or more than thirty times as large as England and Wales, while the population according to the census of 1901 is 294, 417,000 people.

This broader perspective helps us to understand the formidable nature of Robertson's tasks at the War Office, as he notes: 'Between 1896 and 1899 there must have been a dozen or more small wars in these (small) territories ... and not being equipped with personnel to deal with them, the Foreign Office had constantly to ask the Intelligence Branch, as representing the War Office, for advice or information'. Wolseley's penchant for having men around him who could compile massive social and cultural surveys of the theatres of war was suddenly becoming crucially important.

As for William Robertson, he was, by the eve of the Second Boer War, in 1899, a much respected officer of intelligence, taught by Henderson and admired by Brackenbury. His story interweaves with the life of John Ardagh, but before we explore this we must hear the story of Reginald Wingate, Rudolf Slatin and the Egyptian campaign that was going on as Robertson took his seat in his new office in London.

It is a stunning thought to contemplate Robertson's achievements in the ideological context of his time. Here was a man who was born in a small Lincolnshire village, began as a ranker, enlisting in Worcester, and then rising to the Chief of Staff for the Home Defence in the First World War. The boy from a poorish Lincolnshire family rose to become a man who rubbed shoulders and exchanged ideas with the likes of Wolseley, Roberts and Kitchener. It would hardly be believed if it was fiction.

Chapter 4

Wingate, Slatin and Egypt

From the 1870s through to the beginning of the First World War, Britain's Empire extended markedly. In the centre of this expansion there was the political and military rivalry which has become known as the 'scramble for Africa', and in many ways, although expeditions were in progress into the interior of the African continent, the most important focus of attention was Egypt and the Sudan. The main reason for this was the Suez Canal, the 106-mile waterway linking the Red Sea to the Mediterranean. British troop ships bound for India could take this route, rather than the longer and more risky one of rounding the Cape.

The Canal was constructed by the Suez Canal Company, directed by the engineer, Ferdinand de Lesseps, and was opened in 1869. In 1875 Britain won a major interest in the Canal when Benjamin Disraeli obtained a loan from the wealthy Rothschild family so that he could buy a 40 per cent share on Britain's behalf. Between 1883 and 1956 the Canal was a protectorate, with a British military presence there. The British presence began after an appeal for help from the Khedive, who was not only in financial trouble, but had an insurrection to cope with. Once Britain intervened, it was a question of what status the land would have regarding the Empire. This was complicated by the fact that France also had an interest in Egypt, and had done so since Napoleon's invasion in 1798.

At first, Evelyn Baring took over the administration, remaining there for many years, receiving a peerage as Lord Cromer. Time went on, and the world could see that, although there was no British occupancy in the sense of a large standing army, as in India, nevertheless Egypt was a part of the Empire. After the revolt of Arabi was put down in 1882, only a year afterwards there was a serious uprising in the Sudan, as a religious leader, the Mahdi, found that his massive following could take on the Egyptian army, which suffered several defeats as the Mahdi's army grew in size and confidence.

The source of much of the advances in intelligence in this field of the army came from the expedition against the Mahdi's successor at Khartoum, in 1898, at Omdurman. Before that, the placing of General Gordon at Khartoum, in 1884, only complicated matters. When Gordon, who had served with distinction in the East, and was known as 'Chinese Gordon', was made Governor of the Sudan, the Mahdi had different ideas. Gordon had very little military strength behind him, so the result was an inevitable failure, with Gordon being murdered at his residency in the city.

The Mahdi was a tremendously important and significant figure in Sudan history. He was born in 1848 at Dongola, from a family of shipbuilders; he was intelligent and a quick learner, and he was destined to be a religious man and a charismatic preacher. In Reginald Wingate's book on the Sudan, *Mahdism and the Egyptian Sudan* (1891), he explains this very lucidly:

What need of description when he could use denunciation; and when he could stretch forth his long arm and point to the tax gatherer who twice, thrice and yet again carried off the goat, the last bundle of dhurra straw? But now a time was at hand when all this should have an end. The Lord would send a deliverer who would sweep away the veil before their eyes, and strong in the faith of their divine leader, these new-made men, with clear-seeing vision and well-laid plans before them, should go forth and possess the land.

The victories the Mahdi's army won were large-scale and an affront to the might of Britain. The first great triumph he had was against General Hicks. Forty thousand dervishes (the name given to the Mahdi's followers) attacked his force at Shaykan, Kordofan, and the British and Egyptian squares folded at the onslaught. Hicks' men disintegrated and the encounter became a rout, with dervish warriors involved in hand-to-hand fighting with a massive numerical superiority. The force fought to the last man: Hicks died heroically, fighting first with his revolver, and then charging the enemy with his sword drawn. He was decapitated after his death and his head used as a trophy. Slatin's account of the aftermath of the battle concludes with the words:

Nothing could have exceeded the savage grandeur of the Mahdi's triumphal entry into El Obeid after the battle. As he passed along, people threw themselves on the ground and literally worshipped him. There is not the slightest doubt that by his victory at the Shaykan the Mahdi now had the entire Sudan at his feet.

The Mahdi died in 1885, but not long after, as Wolseley's force finally arrived, supposedly to relieve Gordon, it was all too late. In that period, between 1884 and the year before Omdurman, Rudolf Slatin was a prisoner of the Mahdists. He already knew a great deal about the Sudan, and his knowledge of the tribes, history and culture, together with his linguistic prowess, made him an excellent intelligence officer when it came to the Omdurman campaign. But first it is necessary to give an account of Slatin's life and career, as he was to become second in command to the head of intelligence, Reginald Wingate, when Kitchener's force finally came to reclaim the Sudan for Britain.

Slatin went to Egypt long before the events related to the rise of the Mahdi. He had acquired a sound knowledge of most parts of the country, and it was a massive country then, as now. Slatin went there first, in 1878, after an invitation from Gordon to go to join him in working for the Egyptian government. However, four years before that, he had travelled to the Sudan, going to the Nuba Mountains and to Delen. He came to know Austrian missionaries working there and that was to be useful experience for him. When he went to work with Gordon he coped well with the exercising of power in a foreign land, amongst unfamiliar mores and customs. He was made Mudir of Dara, in Darfur. That meant that he had to learn how to control the financial arrangements of the area, including taxation. He also had to adjudicate disputes. In short, he learned the art of diplomacy, at the same time as he was mastering the language.

The area of Kordofan alone, where Hickes ventured, extends for 100,000 miles, forming the Eastern frontier, and El Obeid was the capital at the time. The name Sudan comes from words meaning 'country of the blacks' – a phrase created by the ancient geographers of the Arab world. It covers the entire area between the Sahara and what was, in Slatin's time, the Guinea coast, and included the Congo to the south.

Slatin was born in Vienna in 1857, and his first education was commercial. This led to his first link with Africa in his life, as he acquired a post as an assistant to a bookseller in Cairo, who needed a clerk and tutor. He worked with an explorer for a while and then in Khartoum and the Nuba Mountains. He was gaining a great deal of local knowledge when General Gordon arrived on the scene. Gordon gave Slatin government responsibility: first the work was in financial administration, and later involved inspections of outlying areas. This led to his most powerful position under the Khedive (the ultimate ruler of the Sudan): Governor of Dara in Dar Fur. Gordon, operating under Khedive Ismail, needed Europeans in his management team, so Slatin was a valuable acquisition in that respect. But it was tough for Slatin, who soon found himself acting in a military capacity. He had experience in Austria, as he had served as a sub-lieutenant in the forces of Archduke Rudolf (the 19th Hungarian Infantry). But his troops in Dara were unreliable; though they had fought several battles, eventually his men left and he had to surrender to the Mahdi. The Mahdi was Muhammad Ahmad, a man who had won power and influence leading a jihad against the 'infidels'. The word 'Mahdi' means 'guided by God', and Ahmad managed to convince his followers that he was that man. What could Slatin do to survive and still play a part in the war against this charismatic figure? He converted to Islam.

In a letter to Gordon on this he wrote:

> After several battles, all more or less unsuccessful, the Arabian officers who bore me a grudge and who firmly believed in the victory of Achmet el Arabi over the Europeans, gave out among the soldiers that the cause of my defeat lay in being a Christian. In order to stifle these injurious opinions, I gave out that for some years I had already practised the Mahomedan religion.

Slatin had a very hard time trying to make Gordon see that he had been more sinned against than sinning. His letters, some in French or German, in an attempt to reduce the chances of being read by undesirables, were usually in a begging tone, pleading for a proper understanding of his position. He said, desperately, 'Should you accept my services, I beg your Excellency to write me an answer in French.'

But Slatin began to show his real worth when it came to knowledge of the enemy. In another letter he does have something very important to convey: 'Your scribe has written a dispatch in cipher, half Arabic and half cipher, so badly, that they have been able to decipher it, and so found a key to your despatches and have deciphered your Excellency's despatches to Towfik Pasha.' Throughout Gordon's correspondence, and in his journal, Slatin is, through Gordon's eyes, either a very useful intelligence agent or as a rather eccentric and amusing figure. The great man appears to have been very hard on the Austrian at that time. In one journal entry he writes that Slatin had written a letter to the Austrian Consul saying that if Slatin went over to join Gordon there must be no surrender because he (Slatin) would suffer terrible tortures and death. Gordon comments: 'He evidently is not a Spartan.' Gordon would not consider Slatin coming across to Khartoum, his reason being that he would be breaking a parole, something 'sacred when given to the Mahdi'.

Slatin lived in captivity, having a mud dwelling, and was in chains up to the death of the Mahdi. A drawing exists in which 'Slatin Pasha' is shown staring at the displayed head of Gordon being carried by two Mahdists. But this amazing character began a new role when Khalifa Abdullahi succeeded the Mahdi in 1885. Slatin was very poor but managed to fulfil a role at court, though many thought he was a British spy. He did actually send a number of reports to Cairo over that long period in subjugation.

Between 1884 and 1895 Slatin was a prisoner of the Mahdi, but when the army, under Kitchener, came to the Sudan to retake Khartoum and to crush the Mahdist forces, Rudolf Slatin was, in a sense, reborn. He became the intelligence officer he was always meant to be, and he had an incredible local knowledge. As one early commentator on events wrote, 'He knew the workings of the native mind, and he suggested that the best way to prevent the Dervishes from launching a night attack was to give them the impression that their stronghold would itself be attacked that night.' Kitchener had learned well from Wolseley the value of a ruse, and Slatin was as wily as the enemy. It was the combination of Slatin and Major Reginald Wingate working together that played such a prominent role in the success of Omdurman, as will be seen in the next chapter.

First it is essential to understand how their professional relationship developed. We have ample evidence of this, as their two volumes written after Omdurman explain a great deal. Surprisingly, Slatin has been somewhat eclipsed by historiography. In his lifetime he wrote widely for all kinds of serious journals, and moved in high circles at court. In most reference works on the historical figures important in military intelligence, he barely exists at all. The Oxford Dictionary, *Secret Lives* omits his name but includes Wingate's. After all, here was a man who was in captivity for years, a man who was shown the head of General Gordon, and who figures prominently in the Kitchener story. John Pollock, in his recent biography of Kitchener, notes: 'Even more important to the success of the expedition was Reginald Wingate, Chief Intelligence Officer, with Rudolf Slatin as his deputy.' After that there are a few more references, so he remains a shadowy figure. His own account of his life during this period, *Fire and Sword in the Sudan* (1914), contains several images of him, some in native barb, and some with Wingate, looking every inch the modern officer, stern and professional, a man who liked to dress up and to look impressive.

The general opinion seems to be that he was a soldier of fortune and was therefore marginal. But there were few who could explain the Sudan as well. In 1899, when Omdurman was fresh in the mind of the public, he wrote for a journal explaining what Mahdism was: 'Mohamed Ahmed understood the spirit that was abroad, and understood also how to make use of it. He knew the power of religion in uniting discordant elements, and he declared himself the Mahdi, sent from God.' He was to become a great educator with regard to the county that had filled newspapers for decades, and forced changes in the army – most notably in the nature of military intelligence.

Naturally, as time went on, the Egyptian army had to use spies to infiltrate the Dervish forces, and Slatin, as he was a prisoner for some time, saw what happened to those who were unfortunate enough to be caught. He wrote:

> Khalil's companion, Beshara, was sent back with the letters unanswered, whilst the unfortunate emissary, who was an Egyptian by birth, was thrown into chains under the pretext that he was a spy. Ill-treated, and deprived of nourishment, he became so weak that he could not rise from the ground. His tormentors even refused him water to drink and his death came as a happy release.

Britain was soon to be reminded of the truth of Napoleon's statement on arriving in St Helena, that 'Egypt is the most important country in the world', because the Mahdi was a formidable enemy. When it came to the war against his successor, and the huge armies at his disposal, Britain was going to need Slatin and Reginald Wingate. Slatin's first acquaintance with Wingate came when Slatin's release from prison was planned. He wrote in his autobiography:

> Meanwhile my family had not been idle, and no sacrifice was too great for their love. Living in Vienna, ignorant of the real state of affairs in the Sudan, and not aware of how they could best help me, they continued to put considerable sums of money at the disposal of the Austrian agency in Cairo. His Excellency Baron Heidler did everything in his power to help me escape, and he enlisted the sympathies of Colonel Schaeffer Bey and subsequently Major Wingate.

'Bey' was a term used throughout the Ottoman Empire to describe a provincial governor.

Slatin did manage to escape. His help came at night, and they rode out of the city stealthily on a camel; his guides were two men called Zeki and Hamed, and the escape was itself a lesson is espionage. They had brought Slatin a pistol, and they didn't stop until they were just one day's journey from the Nile, after riding non-stop for twenty-one hours. They then holed up in a quiet spot and waited for more help. That was the riskiest part of the escape, because a few acquaintances of the two guides knew what was happening and it would have brought them great wealth if they had told the Khedive's men of their position. After that they followed a caravan route, while Slatin continued to learn how to move and think like a native. At one point he was told to make a ring of stones when encamped, 'as camel herds do in the winter to protect themselves from the cold.' His guide said, 'You know how to do it. You are just as much an Arab as any one of us.' Slatin was to be found later at Omdurman – with an instinctive knowledge of the enemy he was to face.

Back in Luxor, and with his own kind, Slatin wrote that he was the 'object of a lively demonstration of sympathy from European travellers', and he met various Austrians there, including some high-level diplomats. His career in the Intelligence Division was about to start. He explained the beginning of this when he described his new life, coming from the horrors of the Mahdist prison to the Egyptian army. He stayed, when he so easily could have returned to Austria: 'I had entered the Sudan sixteen years before as a first lieutenant in the Austrian army, and, whilst Governor of Darfur, had been granted the Egyptian military grade of lieutenant-colonel, and now, on my return, I was promoted to the rank of colonel, and posted to the Egyptian Intelligence Department.'

That was the beginning of Slatin's work and friendship with Reginald Wingate. Wingate was born at Port Glasgow in Renfrewshire in 1861. He was the youngest of eleven children, and his father, Andrew, was a cloth merchant. After the father's death, the Wingates moved to Jersey and Reginald went to St James Collegiate School, and was helped by a London crammer to prepare for the exams for the army. He entered the Royal Military Academy at Woolwich at seventeen years of age. In 1880, he was gazetted second lieutenant in the Royal Artillery. First he went to India and began the study of Arabic, and then, in June 1883, he was sent to Egypt. He was to be part of Wolseley's relief force for Gordon – too late to save the day – but there he learned a great deal and was at Korti when the news of the victory at Abu-Klea was received. There, Wolseley had defeated the Mahdists by an early dawn attack, an assault by stealth, when the enemy would not be expected anything.

Wingate was staff officer to Sir Evelyn Wood and he was also busy with his first intelligence work. He was to start his learning curve on the Sudan at that time, arranging transport and being close to where the action was. It was at this time that he began to specialise in the intelligence work and developed the use of native agents and other contacts. Evelyn Wood's HQ was at Debbeh, down the Nile, a short way from Korti, and Wingate's spies, as used in the relief expedition, were met there. He learned about plots by locals to stage an insurrection against the Mudir, and Wingate used all his influence and craft to help. One of his main agents then was Sheikh Ettayib, who was to serve the army for another five years before he was captured. Although Wingate won a Queen's Medal for his work on the relief force, the situation generally in Egypt after Gordon's death and the death of the Mahdi was such that Egypt itself was somewhat stagnant. There was a consolidation of upper-Egypt with a strong Mahdist territory to the south. It was an impasse, and was to remain that way until Kitchener and Omdurman. But of course Britain wanted to keep the Sudan. Wingate was there in the interim period, as his biographer Ronald Wingate wrote: 'Wingate was to spend these years in the Egyptian army based in Cairo, with an occasional desert battle for diversion.' He took part in Cairo life to a certain extent, but he studied hard as well. As Wingate wrote:

> Wingate devoted most of his leisure to languages. Though he spoke Arabic well he continued to study it, and among his papers were found many exercise books which he had filled with translations, in excellent Arabic script. He began to learn Turkish and his official work and society alike kept up his French.

In was in 1887 that he was officially given the special responsibility of the intelligence work. The Khalifa Abdullahi was now in command of the Mahdists in Sudan, and Britain was merely defending Egypt – with the Khalifa broadcasting his aim of invading and taking Egypt for himself. It was a case of military matters being on the cusp between defence and attack, and the old adage that attack is the best method of defence was in the air. In the buffer zone of the Frontier Province, Wingate's task was to provide reports on Dervish positions and plans. Then, in 1889, Wingate dropped other duties and became Director of Military Intelligence. That meant that he was in the middle of a triangle, acting with the War Office, Woodhouse (the commander of the frontier district), and the administration in Cairo.

Ronald Wingate, writing on Reginald's life, stated that he inherited the original order of 1892, creating and defining the Department of Military

1 (Above) The end of the Franco-Prussian War: the reading of the capitulation at Sudan. The war had a profound impact on military thinking. (Graphic, Author's collection)

2 (Left) Sir Garnet Wolseley. His 'ring' of officers showed his thinking about the importance of military intelligence on the Ashanti Campaign of 1874. (Graphic, Author's collection)

3 Bringing Gordon's head to Slatin. (*Fire and Sword in the Sudan*)

4 Slatin in native attire. (*Fire and Sword in the Sudan*)

5 Sir William Robertson taken by an American soldier at Coblenz, 1919. (Taken from his autobiography, *From Private to Field Marshall*)

6 The incident at Dir on the Chitral Campaign where Robertson fought for his life against assassins. (*Daily Graphic*)

7 Robertson, third from the right, at army manoeuvres, 1913.

THE LION'S SHARE
"Gare à qui la touche"

Punch (February 26th, 1876) voices the opinion, accepted by the country, that the acquisition of the Suez Canal Shares secured the safety of "The Key to India".

8 Suez – 'The Lion's Share', taken from *Punch*, February 1876, showing an event at the beginning of the campaign to make Egypt a protectorate.

9 Sir John Ardagh. (Taken from *The Life of John Ardagh*, 1909)

10 The square at Abu-Kru. A pyrrhic victory, bloody but brief, typical of many in the Sudan wars. (Author's collection)

11 Khartoum, from an old engraving. (Author)

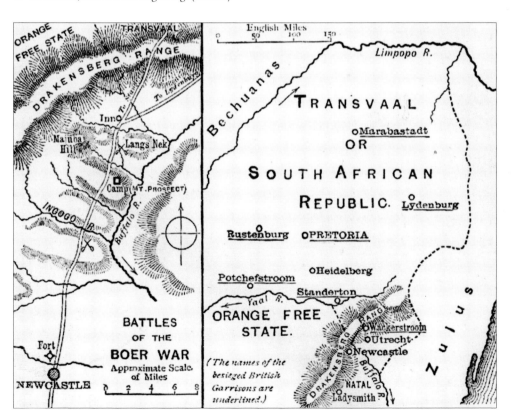

12 Map showing the positions of Majuba and Langs Nek, scenes of heavy defeats for the British.

13 *(Right)* Langs Nek, as depicted in a popular Victorian work on the Anglo-Boer War. (Author)

14 *(Below)* Slaughter at Majuba Hill, during the Anglo-Boer War. (Author)

15 *(Below right)* Sir Mark Sykes. (By kind permission of Sarah Flather, Sledmore House)

16 *(Left)* The memorial to the Wagoners, one of Sykes' own creations from the First World War. (Author)

17 *(Below)* Arab Bulletin No.48. One of Sykes' reports to the War Office, 1917. (Hull University Archives)

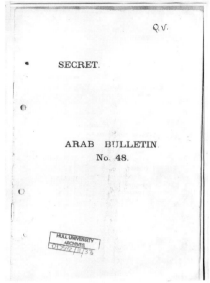

18 Sledmere House, the Sykes family home. (Author)

19 The Turkish Room, Mark Sykes' special place at Sledmere. (By kind permission of Sarah Flather, Sledmere House)

20 A young Mark Sykes with his guide, Isa Kubrusli. (By kind permission of Sarah Flather, Sledmere House)

21 The Sykes tombs, Mark's body having been recently exhumed for medical research. (Author)

Intelligence. Ronald notes that Reginald was the only European officer working in that sphere until Slatin arrived, which might explain their closeness, trust and professional success. Ronald explains that there were four areas of action in intelligence work:

> First, military intelligence regarding the strength, dispositions and intentions of the Khalifa's forces in the Sudan; second, the political and economic position in the Sudan itself; thirdly, the relations of the Sudan with its neighbours; and finally, the fate of those Europeans who had fallen into the Mahdi's hands when the dervishes were overrunning the Sudan.

This is a highly significant brief in the history of Victorian spywork: it suggests a great deal of undercover counter-intelligence being employed to ascertain desired information. Arguably, reading between the lines of this summary, the implication is that it was entirely practical and possible for Wingate to be the puppet-master of the various tribal agents and their own networks. The reality was that the issues were about communication – or the lack of. There was no technological support and the distances were vast. If information was to be taken from A to B then the choice was either a camel or a riverboat.

What Wingate did was establish a network of agents, placed with a certain rationale that would be the best compromise, given the long distances needed to cover, and the increased risk of interception. If the Mahdist movements had to be known, then subversion and the use of the Khalifa's own enemies was a smart move. He used agents operating for pay, of course, across a stretch from Kassala in the east to El Obeid in the west. In other words, it was a case of gradually compiling a full picture as each scrap of information was obtained. The heart of the whole enterprise was danger and risk. Wingate's men were tough, daring and subtle, to say nothing of the necessary subterfuge and performance involved in undercover work. Ronald Wingate points out that one officer reported on an agent's death in this way:

> Bashiri Karrar, Sheikh Khalil's companion, has returned to Cairo, on 1st September. From his statement, of which I enclose a type-written copy, you will see that he made a narrow escape from the Khalifa's dangerous suspicion. Nothing was wanting for Sheikh Khalil's own death. They were placed near the scaffold with their shrouds in their hands for six hours – which looked to them like six centuries – they were prey to despair.

There was a decisive battle at this time which prevented the Khalifa from venturing north: the battle of Toski, in which Sir Francis Grenfell won the day. Wingate was involved, scouting, and was lucky to escape after being seen doing close reconnaissance. Wingate relates that they 'fought all day in the broiling sun' but emerged the victors. This was in August, 1889, and the enemy had been repelled by the usual lines of disciplined fire, with Kitchener a crucial part of the charge.

To Wingate and everyone's advantage, the confidence coming from Toski meant that the army in general was reformed and streamlined. There were British and Egyptian officers, a rooting out of some fringe elements and a proper military academy put in place. This all meant that there was a secure basis for forays south, and also more confidence that the frontier would be more professionally controlled.

At Toski, of 13,000 Dervishes, only around 1,000 warriors made it home. Many were captured; not all were killed or injured. Wingate was given the D.S.O. The stage was set for his major intelligence activity with Kitchener. It has to be said that his years between arrival and the participation in the army going to confront the Khalifa and retake Khartoum, were also the years in which he demonstrated his knowledge and experience by writing the huge tome, *Mahdism and the Sudan*. It runs to over 600 pages and includes maps, statistics and notes that can only be called antiquarian, but which were also useful fodder for intelligence work, as details of coinage and the transcripts of court-martials were included.

Kitchener became the new sirdar (commander of the Egyptian army) in 1892, taking over from Grenfell. He had known Wingate for several years, and both clearly got on very well. As intelligence work at the time was inevitably going to relate to the 'scramble for Africa', both Kitchener and Wingate had a certain involvement in that other 'Great Game', centred in European politics and diplomacy, but having repercussions across the African continent. That scramble stemmed from the Berlin Conference of 1884–85, an event that led to the General Act of 26 February 1885, which stated that there would be 'spheres of influence' for each of the European powers involved, and that the Belgian-controlled Congo Free State would be created. Provisions relating to African possessions were phrased in such a way that future acts of aggression were:

> Any power which henceforth takes possession of a tract of land on the coasts of the African continent outside of its present possessions shall accompany either act with a notification thereof, addressed to other signatory powers, to enable them to protest against the same if grounds exist for them doing so.

In other words, the repercussions of this diplomacy for intelligence work was that most actions in Sudan would have a knock-on effect, partly due to the long traditions of slavery in that area, but also that the southern borders would be close to territory not within the British Empire. Wingate had a taste of this when he met the exiled Zobeir Pasha, formerly someone Gordon wanted to work with but now in Gibraltar. Wingate tried to have him reinstated, and finally persuaded Lord Cromer to let the Pasha back. The fact was that Wingate needed him in Egypt. It was an instance of Wingate going beyond the normal boundaries of his responsibilities.

The friendship between Wingate and Slatin was officially recognised – so much so that they both received high honours from Britain. Such was the dashing and exciting narrative Slatin had to tell that the Queen and her family were entirely captivated. Both men were given the C.B.E. in 1895. It was at this point that Slatin became a national celebrity. Every editor wanted him to write for their publications, and he made an impressive figure in his uniform, being dignified and upright. The Royal Family wanted a photograph of him. With Slatin's popularity came Wingate's. They had both written very successful accounts of the Sudan campaigns, and both their tales were as full of incident and adventure as any popular novel or periodical. Just a few years later, in 1902, A.E.W. Mason, the novelist, was to give the war in the Sudan to the world in the form of a popular male romance, written at a time when this genre was extremely popular (as with Rider Haggard's *King Solomon's Mines* for instance). Mason wrote *The Four Feathers*, a story set in the context of Omdurman, and passages such as this added to the public fascination with Arabs and desert wars:

> For three hours the troops marched across the plateau. It was the month of May, and the sun blazed upon them with an intolerable heat. They had long since lost their alertness. They rode rocking drowsily in their saddles and prayed for the evening and the silver shine of stars.

Slatin and Wingate were now in place, firmly at the reins of the intelligence organisation that would play a prominent part in the forthcoming expedition against the Khalifa, led by Lord Kitchener. Each had learned a whole armoury of intelligence methods and tactics, Slatin through harsh experience and close contact with the enemy, and their culture and language, and Wingate through a successful combination of intellectual rigour and the kind of instinct that makes an officer sense trustworthy and valid perspectives on situations. We might ask where Wingate learned the networking and counter-intelligence discipline.

One answer is that in India there had been certain precedents not long before the Sudan campaigns. The magistrates governing India locally, together with the East India Company administrators, had had to learn how to combat gangs of killers, the 'thuggee', that had been a major problem in the 1830s, notably in the central provinces. Lieutenant William Sleeman had been markedly successful in that action against an enemy who melted into the local population and struck with deadly swiftness helpless travellers. Sleeman cultivated spies, *agents provocateurs*, who infiltrated the gangs. He also adopted the usual ploys of the army political officers who worked across the Indian continent, acting as magistrates, police officers and diplomats.

In addition, on top of the ability to arrange networks of information, undercover work was done with as much planning as possible, and with an acute awareness of the problem of double-agents. Success here depended on interrogation and recruitment, and again, Wingate had the ability to search out truth and dependability with a rare perceptiveness. His energy was phenomenal. He was also, by the mid-1890s, working within a newly reformed army. As Colonel Parr reported to the British High Commission in 1886: 'At this time, after three years, the feeling between all ranks is most satisfactory; as for the English officers, many have become so attached to their new comrades that the matter has become the subject of good-humoured remarks on the part of their brother officers of the army of occupation.'

Wingate and Slatin were about to have their knowledge and experience tested to the full, along with Kitchener, against a huge and confident Dervish army.

CHAPTER 5

OMDURMAN

Herbert Kitchener, surely best known as the stern face on the First World War poster proclaiming, 'Your Country needs you', was a great military leader who seemed to attract controversy as well as hagiography and myth. One early biographer, writing in 1910, expressed the complexity: 'That he wields some strange and subtle power over the crowd is indisputable. The secret of it may lie in the awe inspired by those marvellous successes he never fails to produce by the magic of his patient persistence.' Notice here the words 'awe' and 'magic' placed alongside words that are not directly heroic.

His legendary steely eyes and dignified bearing could instil fear, and he was even seen by some as ruthless. But at the field of Omdurman it was Kitchener who commanded the people of the town to go out and bring in the wounded from the field. Estimates of him vary greatly, but perhaps Richard Holmes' words, in the *Oxford Companion to Military History*, form the best appraisal: 'Kitchener was an indefatigable organizer who understood the absolute necessity of consolidating resources before striking a decisive blow.' On the other hand, Erskine Childers' opinion was that, 'Kitchener was inclined to think too much of propelling and too little of educating his army – to look rather to the quantity rather than the quality of the work done.'

Kitchener was a strategist and a man with a presence on the battlefield. When events were developing in the process of a confrontation, he would appear at just the right time. He was expert in what we might call today the logistics of managing men, supplies and communications. More than anything else, it could be argued, he inspired men; he glowed with confidence, with the assurance that comes from good planning and research. From Wolseley he learned that the time given to finding the right man for the job is the secret of success. When the journalist G.W. Steevens went with the Sudan expedition in 1898, working on what would become the bestselling *With Kitchener to Khartoum* (1898), he wrote that the great general should be a national treasure, or in the words of the time, something that should be exhibited at a national exhibition:

> But it so happens that he has turned himself to the management of war in the Sudan, and he is the complete and only master of that art. Beginning life in the Royal Engineers he early turned to the study of the Levant. He was one of Beaconsfield's military vice-consuls in Asia Minor; he was subsequently director of the Palestine Exploration Fund… The ripe harvest of fifteen years is that he knows everything that is to be learned of his subject. He came at the right hour. He was the right man.

Steevens wrote of Kitchener as 'The Sudan Machine' and that was partly responsible for the hagiography that tended to gather in writing about the man. But when he started out he was an intelligence officer with Wolseley, and that is what formed much of his military attitudes. It is perhaps not too sensible to accept all Steevens's remarks, as he tended to write hagiography, but nevertheless, there is some substance here in his perspective on the men in charge.

Turning to the focus of interest in Kitchener's life; his expedition to Khartoum with his expeditionary force, which first went into action in 1896. The Mahdi had died and the Khedive was now in opposition. True to form, Kitchener assembled his team. Intelligence was under the command of Reginald Wingate, with Rudolf Slatin as his deputy. Wingate, nicknamed 'The White Knight', as he had all kinds of equipment with him, was to be the centre of a spy network, and Slatin's long experience of the country and people would play a large part in this work. Wingate was born in Renfrewshire in 1861; he was the cousin of Orde Wingate's father. His military career began with the rank of second lieutenant in the Royal Artillery, in 1880. He learned Arabic while he was living in Aden and so was the ideal man to start duties in Egypt when the time came. Near the close of Gordon's rule in Egypt, Wingate was given the role of aide-de-camp to Sir Evelyn Wood, sirdar of the Egyptian army (*sirdar* being a Persian word that came into common usage in the Middle East).

Wingate first took the primary role of commanding the intelligence arm of the army in 1889, and then his priority was to keep updated information flowing from the Sudan. It was Wingate who first wrote about Slatin's imprisonment under the Mahdi, and who explained the phenomenon of Mahdism from the standpoint of one who had been living among the cultural and social elements of that rising. Wingate was, in the words of one historian, 'a small, terrier-like man with boundless energy and equally boundless inquisitiveness.' He first met Slatin when the Austrian arrived from imprisonment, and he debriefed the man who would become his most effective and useful spymaster. Wingate's patience and preoccupation with efficiency and minute knowledge were to become fundamental to the success of the network across that vast land. What he had done that was at the heart of his success was to gather a massive bank of information about the Mahdists, and it is truly remarkable that he could place agents in every area that mattered, picking the best men for each place.

Perhaps most remarkable of all, Wingate's early action, before the march south, was the rescue of a Roman Catholic priest, Father Joseph Ohrwalder, and some nuns who were with him. This was naturally a significant piece of spin for the army as it meant that someone had been able to penetrate the heart of the Mahdist territory. Wingate was now so well-informed about the ideology of the Mahdists, as well as of the topography of their land and their social interactions, that he published *Mahdism and the Egyptian Sudan* in 1892.

Now he and Slatin faced the Khedive Abdallahi. When Slatin first arrived he was looked upon with both suspicion and a sense of awe. Here was a man who had been kept imprisoned within the enemy's central caucus of men in power. His letter explaining why he had proclaimed himself a Muslim to Gordon was not generally known, and some thought that he deserved contempt for such an action. But with Khartoum as the objective and Kitchener keen to use the full communication systems available to him, Wingate knew that there was a major role for Slatin to play. After all, here was a man who Wingate knew had a considerable knowledge of the enemy – even the Khedive himself.

What Slatin had to impart was something very important indeed: the fact that within the enemy there was division. In the period since the Mahdi had died, the appointment of Abdallahi had been a focus for dissent and resentment. The reason for this was that the new Khedive was not one of the elite that had been around the Mahdi and his family; he was a nomad, in fact, and not thought to be well educated.

What Slatin and Wingate came to understand was that the followers of Abdallahi were Baggara nomads, and that that class of men were loose canons, likely to follow their own ways rather than be a part of any great fighting machine. Much of the regulation of their affairs was controlled by traditional customs rather than the orders of a leader. Where then, Wingate asked himself, was the evidence of these fighters' loyalty to the Khedive? That point was going to be an Achilles Heel in the coming battles. The combination of Wingate's acumen in gaining and sifting information, Slatin's insider's knowledge and the tactics of Kitchener, things were looking promising at the outset of the expedition.

However, returning to Slatin, it has to be said that there is immense sympathy for the man when we consider his reception in the British camp. Gordon, as we have seen, felt a certain degree of contempt for him and never rated his abilities fairly. Now, here he was with the reputation of having espoused Islam while in captivity – a very un-British thing to do. Neither did he look the part, and that was, in an age when protocol and appearance counted for a great deal in the armed forces, as elsewhere, a great hindrance. When he appeared with the Frontier Force, Slatin did not exactly win friends quickly. He looked seedy, short and unkempt. But there is a story of his walking into the mess and whispering to an officer of the 60th Rifles that he was Slatin (his name was widely known of course); a man who was senior ADC, Jimmy Watson, bought him a beer and made sure that his guest drank it. That was a sure test that the man was really not a Muslim.

The first objective of the expedition was to assemble the right men for each task. Just as the intelligence staff had been handpicked, so the essential camels for use on the journey would be handled by Kitchener's brother, Walter, sent for from India, and an engineer called Girouard was brought in to repair the train line, which had been dismantled after the failure to sort out the rescue of Gordon some years before.

The columns then began their trek into the Sudan; the train was in action and gunboats were moving on the Nile. The first of a sequence of battles was to be fought, leading to the triumph of Omdurman, when the intelligence officers would have their real talents put to full use. As they travelled, spies would join them with reports. Steevens, the journalist, was on hand to observe as the battle of Atbara neared: 'The Intelligence Department only half believes the native stories. The native has no words for distance and number but "near" and "far" and "few" and "many". "Near" may be anything within twenty miles, and "many" ranges from a hundred to a hundred thousand.'

But Steevens had also noticed what Wingate had achieved. He wrote that, 'Nothing is hidden from Colonel Wingate, whether in Cairo or at the court of Menelek, or on the shores of Lake Chad', and 'Whatever there was to know, Colonel Wingate surely knew it, for he makes it his business to know everything.'

On one occasion Steevens saw Wingate in action, using his Arabic and other skills as a communicator. The journalist wrote:

Any day from dawn to dark you might see half-clothed black men squatting before Colonel Wingate. Some were fairly fat; some were bags of bones. But all stated with one consent that they were hungry, and having received refreshment felt that they could do no less than tell Colonel Wingate such tidings as they conceived he would like to hear.

This shows the truth of Wolseley's comments about the unreliability of local intelligence, but it also shows that information given in these circumstances could have been quite certainly verified if the officer in liaison with the natives knew the factual basis of the land in which things happened – and of course, that his Arabic as well as his judgement of men and their speech were up to the task.

It was Omdurman that asserted a testimony to the success of this intelligence work. A few weeks before the battle, Kitchener had seen his last detachments of men arrive. He had a total of around 20,000 men by the time the Grenadier Guards arrived on cattle trucks. He was to have Maxim guns, of course, confirming the poet Hilaire Belloc's couplet, 'Whatever happens we have got / The Maxim gun, and they have not.' This fearsome weapon had been invented by Hiram Maxim, an American who was out to make money and who had been told by advisers that to strike it rich he should invent something that would help the Europeans 'cut each other's throats with greater facility'. He came up with a belt-fed machine gun that could fire 600 rounds in a minute. It was first used just three years before the Khartoum expedition, in the 1893 Matabele War (where Baden-Powell was conspicuous).

The Maxim gun was to play an important part in Omdurman, but Kitchener also had newly equipped gunboats, in sharp contrast to the 21st Lancers. After trying all kinds of approaches to be involved in the war, the young Winston Churchill, rebuffed by Kitchener, managed to use powerful influences to have himself attached to this cavalry regiment, and he was to come face-to-face with Kitchener after the main action.

Kitchener may have had technology and modernity built into his preparations, but there was also the point that he still had to take thousands of men across a massive desert. The engineer who planned the route was also a water-diviner, and somehow that typifies the sirdar's approach: there was always something trusting and instinctive added into his calculations. At Omdurman he actually risked his life several times as the British entered the city and routed out pockets of resistance.

There had been a battle at Atbara some months before this, but Kitchener had rested his troops effectively. Now he had a large force with the addition of technology – all brought up by railway. The gunboats were fitted with new armour and weapons. Omdurman was close to Khartoum, just a little to the north, on the western bank of the river. Next to that was the area of Karari, where open combat was to take place. On 1 September, the army made camp at El Egeiga, on the Nile. The men built a protective banking, a *zariba*. What he had in mind was an advance, not a digging-in, as most enemy forces would expect, because Kitchener was hugely outnumbered (though he had no idea at the time just how much this was the case). This situation echoed recent history – most famously the events of Rorke's Drift, against the Zulu.

The day before the action, the heliograph communicated that a large force of Dervish was on its way to meet the British. The sirdar organised his positions. His army was predominantly Egyptian and Sudanese, and he placed his British to the left and brought his men out in a broad arc. This was going to be the result of his tactics: a small army facing a mass of men 50,000 strong, but with artillery and Maxim guns. The spies had made it clear that Kitchener intended to attack at night, and the ruse worked, because that information prompted the enemy to go on the offensive first.

Here we have different accounts of how this was done. One story is that it was entirely the work of Slatin, and this does seem to be the case because in a biography of Osman Digna, who led one of the Dervish armies, written by H.C. Jackson, we have this account:

> At this point Slatin Pasha, who was on the staff of the Intelligence Department, gained his reward for ten years captivity. He suggested that the best way to prevent the Dervishes from launching a night attack was to give them the impression that their stronghold would be assaulted that night. Slatin took a few of these [spies] aside and told them as a deadly secret that the British meant to attack Omdurman during the night and that they should go at once and warn their families.

Of course, the spies told their own leaders and the news quickly spread throughout the Dervish camp. The Khalifa trusted the rumours and decided to move first. Of the massive force of men who made their morning prayers on the dawn of 2 September, 10,000 were to die in battle.

Later in life, Slatin certainly enjoyed writing about the Sudan, and he became an authority on that episode of recent history. In 1899, for instance, he wrote an account of the campaign for *The Anglo-Saxon Review*, and in this essay he wrote only one paragraph on Omdurman, and in this he simply gave objective facts, concluding that, 'This was the outward and visible sign that it was these two powers [English and Egyptian] in conjunction who had defeated the enemy and taken possession of the country.' The essay was hardly a defensive indulgence in telling the world what a hero he had been. Slatin was writing as a formal expert, not by any means the man who had moved in the dangerous worlds of espionage and imprisonment.

Reginald Wingate edited Jackson's book and wrote an introduction. He must have known that Slatin was named as quoted above. The Khalifa did not begin a guerrilla campaign; he sat and waited, with no more strategy than a direct attack, a brave confrontation against immense firepower. The Mahdist front extended for five miles, and although Kitchener was not aware of the full extent of other forces further back, there were around 20,000 men, some waiting in a *khor* (a dry river bed), and it was these men that would later inflict the worst casualties on the British as they surprised the 21st Lancers. But the main force of the British was confined to their zariba by the Nile, with Gebel Surgham to their left and the Kerreri Heights to their right. It was in the plain between these that Ali Wad Helu attacked. There were gunboats to each side of the British position. Kitchener also had his Camel Corps, with Walter in charge, and these were in the southern parts of the Kerreri Heights. The most visible and therefore vulnerable of all Kitchener's army was Broadwood's cavalry. The sirdar had to use his communications systems well to cover Broadwood.

But the day itself was a slaughter: in the centre of Kitchener's deployment was Maxwell, and Macdonald, who was for many the real hero of the day, was foremost on the right. It was a case of rapid fire at a densely-packed advance. To some, it must have been anachronistic – the kind of battle one might expect in the mid-eighteenth century when blocks of infantry advanced against cannon. There was terrible loss of life. However, Macdonald and his 3,000 Sudanese were facing 17,000 men and they had a tough time. He reported that his guns and Maxims had saved the day: 'Their advance was very rapid and determined and though they appeared to be mowed down by the artillery and Maxims they pressed on.'

The principal design on Kitchener's part was to march into Khartoum. In spite of the fact that there was still a force to his rear; he kept to the plan, trusting in Macdonald to win the rear-guard action. That was the case, but it may not have worked out that way – it was a calculated risk. The fact was that Kitchener had learned from Wolseley the art of the use of the climate in this theatre of war. Wolseley had won Tel-El-Kebir by attacking at dawn, when his troops were fresh and cool. Though Kitchener's men did not have to move very much (except for the lancers), and they had superior firepower, the crucial factor was the hour at which the battle began. The sirdar had not wanted an attack at night from Abdellahi. The Khalifa may well have won had he done that, with the British still in the zariba.

The verdict was, for many, that Omdurman was 'noble, but it is not war' (first said about the charge of the Light Brigade, and now reversed to pay compliment to the noble enemy). As Michael Asher has written: 'Whole families, whole clans of tribesmen were swept away like chaff. Men fell, their bodies torn and shattered. The warriors closed the gaps and stormed forward shoulder to shoulder towards the fearsome dragon of fire.'

It had been a victory won by a combination of good intelligence work and the power of a very great leader in battle. As for Rudolf Slatin and Reginald Wingate, they went on to other things. Slatin certainly did not retire; he came back to the Sudan in 1900, leading a group working for the Sudan Territories Exploration Syndicate. They were looking for gold, and found nothing: something that could be taken as a strong metaphor. By September 1900, Slatin was inspector-general of the Sudan; but he did renew his links with his family and native land, going to Austria every summer. He was destined to move in high places. He could have worked for the Turks or the Germans, but would not work in any capacity against Britain. His last work was for the Red Cross, and he refused the post of ambassador in London for Austria. Rudolf Slatin died in 1932, after one last visit to the Sudan as a guest of the government.

Reginald Wingate became governor-general of the Sudan and stayed there for seventeen years. In this period there was the abolition of the slave trade, curtailing inland raids for slaves. The country was prepared for a new existence as a modern state. Wingate was even involved in the development of the Gezira irrigation plan. In 1916 Wingate took control of Darfur. But he was to have problems again when there was an Arab revolt in Hejaz in which he supported Sharif Hussain. Wingate extended his skills from intelligence operations to quartermaster and diplomat. He made a special trip to Paris to argue that the European powers should talk to an Egyptian delegation. But the case was that Lord Curzon refused, and the consequences were anarchical. Wingate had not been listened to. This is understandable when we recall Curzon's basic attitude to imperialism. As one of his biographers noted: 'His attitude towards the common people was that of a benevolent patrician. He did not even believe that Englishmen, let alone Scotsmen, Welsh and Irish and other lesser breeds, had earned the right to equality with those who had spent their lives and their brains in learning to rule them.'

Wingate became a general but moved out of the foreground; he became a company director, commandant of the Royal Artillery and a governor of the Gordon College in Khartoum, which had been Kitchener's dream from the start, and which had been founded after huge amounts of money were put his way on his triumphant return home. Wingate died in Dunbar on 28 January 1953.

The best tribute to this remarkably able and inspirational man was made by Lord Cromer in 1916: 'It is to my mind the most remarkable compliment that could possibly be paid to British rule that the Sudan should have remained quiet: and this is mainly due to your wise government.' In terms of the control of spies in active operation, he and Slatin had the insight to know when to ground and retrain the men in their network. Key men in that capacity who might be double-agents were restrained and watched. Cavalry patrols were active in keeping Arab reconnaissance in the dark as well, whenever Kitchener had something important in the planning stage. This practical side to Wingate was the reason for his success.

Omdurman was undoubtedly a major triumph. But only a year later, the Anglo-Boer War was to teach lessons with regard to intelligence just as much as to military technology. This war, along with the Russo-Turkish War of 1877–78, made it clear to the high command that infantry who were in defensible positions were potentially capable of easily inflicting serious damage on large forces of attack, whether cavalry or infantry. A writer called Ivan Bloch wrote *La Guerre Future* in the year of Omdurman, and predicted that soon war as it was conceived would be unnecessary and outmoded. But the last years of the nineteenth century and the early Edwardian years were a period of expanding militarism in Britain as in Germany. Arguably, the victories in the Sudan would soon appear to be the last template version of the typical colonial redcoat conflict, a version of battle emanating from the same ideological source as the adventurers of the Great Game and the literary romances of the *fin de siecle*.

As for intelligence in its widest applications, by the 1890s it was to be a case of more comprehensive knowledge of broader issues in the field and more complex diplomacy. Between 1896 and 1899 Wingate still had to assemble forces for the re-conquest of the Sudan, and it is important to note that his expertise and insights were still important in the diplomatic manoeuvres of Mark Sykes and his peers as they networked and liaised with dozens of interested parties in order to bring a settlement to the Middle East.

CHAPTER 6

ARDAGH AND THE ANGLO-BOER WAR

Sir John Ardagh, through the 1870s, mixed with most of the officers and diplomats mentioned so far, as he travelled a great deal (even when on leave), and made a name for himself as a cartographer and military attaché. His career in intelligence runs parallel to that of William Robertson, and they attended Staff College at the same time. But as Ardagh was an expert at cultivating the right kinds of contacts, and at thinking ahead in terms of his career, his experience was much more diverse than Robertson's.

He was born on 9 August 1840, at Comragh House, County Waterford. His father was the hunting-vicar type, and his mother was originally from Ipswich. She died when John was very young. Ardagh was always studious. As he grew up it emerged that he was a skilled artist, which was to prove very useful in his army career. But he was by no means limited to intellectual pursuits, being a very good horseman. He forms another sharp contrast with Robertson, his contemporary, in that from an early age he was aware of good neighbourhood connections, such as the Beresfords, a wealthy and influential local family. His academic abilities meant that he entered Trinity College, Dublin, aged only seventeen, and won a prize in Hebrew.

Ardagh joined a class that was being groomed for entry to the Royal Military Academy at Woolwich, and, in 1859, he was gazetted second lieutenant in the Royal Engineers. His first work was on various docks, including Pembroke and Portsmouth, but after toying with a career in the Indian Army, he decided to stay where he was and focus on increasing his knowledge and experience through travel. We have a description of him when he was around twenty, given by Miss Kinglake, a London friend:

'Mr Ardagh was about the middle height, with a slight and graceful figure, light moustache and hair, both kept very short. Altogether he was very attractive, with a low, harmonious voice and laugh. He did not speak much but what he said was always to the point.'

He joined the Intelligence Department after touring Europe at the end of the 1870 Franco-Prussian War, and was yet another solider who was intrigued by the battlefields there. He realized that it was a useful acquirement to be informed about the success of Germany in that conflict, and he made acquaintances in the German staff.

At the Staff College, in 1872, he was made captain and adjutant to Colonel Leahy. Passing his final examination in 1874, he was commended for his geological studies, and was also qualified in German. The following year he was put in the Intelligence Branch, working with Major-General MacDougall. Then, between 1876 and 1881, he was prominent in the Balkans during and after the crisis of 1878 when Britain and Russia were on the verge of war. What happened was that Serbia declared war on Turkey, and Russia backed Serbia. A major concern for Britain at this point was that if Russia took Turkey they could more easily expand eastwards and have better supply routes into the buffer states between the Middle East and the India frontier. At a meeting Russia did not co-operate in the diplomatic decisions, and Britain called out a massive portion of the Indian Army to stand ready at the border. For two months a war seemed imminent. Then, at the Congress of Berlin in June 1878, matters were settled.

Ardagh was assigned to Turkey for surveying and diplomatic work. It was clear that the War Office saw him as more suited to the intelligence work of an attaché than a man in the field. But that is not to say that he did not travel in demanding and uncomfortable terrain. He journeyed across Turkey to report on the nature of the Turkish army and topography in less known areas of the country. The Morava Valley was the main concern: that had been the focus for the hostilities. But more important for Ardagh's career was his meeting with Sir Arnold Kemball, the British Military Attaché in Turkey, along with other officers in that post. Ardagh then returned to Nisch, where he was in the thick of the action, dodging Serbian bullets. After that it was Constantinople, because Russia was more directly aggressive towards Turkey, and Britain wanted details of defence surveys urgently. Ardagh had been meticulous in this, and this work very likely built the foundation of his reputation. He reported on the state of Bulgaria, and having crossed the Shipka Pass, made notes on that too. It was a job well done.

He took some leave to familiarise himself with Cairo, and he saw the Egyptian army at the time before its reorganization, noting: 'The Khedive's cavalry seem very unhappy at a trot. The infantry are far better, but they march badly and seem badly officered and drilled. They are docile and obedient but are slow to learn. Can they ever make good soldiers?' This is very informative with regard to Ardagh's habits and interests. He took notice of everything, however trivial, looking for significance in minor details. With hindsight, the historian can see the element in him that was eager to have statistics and accurate descriptions and definitions. This is a crucial aspect of intelligence gathering, of course. His superiors saw that when it came to maps and topography, Ardagh was the man for the job. After a brief return to London, he was sent to Bulgaria to make maps. He and his team worked steadily, taking a specific area at a time. He seems to have led the boundary commission. Each day meant a survey of around thirty kilometres and then a ride back to base of the same distance. By November 1878 the map was complete. But he noted in his journal on 30 November that he still had to trace eight copies of the frontier, on a tight deadline, and in December the various parties met and there was a 'stormy debate' before everyone signed agreement except the Russian envoy.

Until 1882 Ardagh continued this kind of work, the scope being extended to include the Greek frontier. By 1882 he was an expert on the geography and geomorphology of the borderlands with Turkey, including that area of northern Greece than called Roumelia. But this account of Victorian intelligence now includes a confluence: Ardagh was assigned to the Egyptian expedition of 1882 led by Sir Garnet Wolseley. The latter could not fail to be impressed by a scholarly, reserved man who had evidence of his expertise on paper and also a long list of recommendations from respected staff. In London he was given a particular assignment by Wolseley, and lost no time in boarding the HMS *Salamis*. Ardagh was going to be an important figure in the campaign against Arabi, the man who wanted to take control of Egypt. Ardagh was assigned defence and reconnaissance duties. His track record working in English ports gave him just the experience Wolseley needed. He was involved in skirmishes too, including one in which nine of Arabi's troops were captured.

Arabi was a soldier who saw his chance and gathered support for an armed insurrection. At the time, Egypt was a part of the Ottoman Empire. Both the economists and the diplomats saw brilliant opportunities coming their way when the Khedive, Ismail, made a mess of his government and failed to control his state. Egypt became subject to a commission for debt, and that meant that creditors had the first claim on income from Egypt and the Sudan. When the humiliation of this European control became too much to bear, the Khedive, Tewfik, who had taken power from Ismail, was ousted by a military nationalist party led by Arabi Pasha (also known as Ahmed Arabi).

What Arabi fronted was no less than a rampant rebellion with the aim of killing, or at least terrifying, all foreigners. He was one of the fellahin – a manual worker – and eventually made his name and gained high status in the army despite his lower-class origins. There had to be British military involvement; apart from the canal and the passage through to India, there were almost 100,000 foreigners in the country, all in danger from Arabi.

The decisive battle was at Tel-el-Kebir. Ardagh had the important task of surveying the country around that place, and he was in the fight, being placed with the Highland Brigade. Ardagh had come to the battle by train – a sign of things to come. The victory at Tel-el-Kebir was swift and thorough. It lasted half an hour. Wolseley planned his advance in the half-light of dawn, and rampaged through the enemy camp. The total British loss was just fifty-four killed and 340 wounded. The Highland Brigade bore the brunt of the fight, so Ardagh saw the epicentre of the battle. As their regimental historian wrote: 'Behind their point of attack the dead lay thickest. The cavalry, led by Drury Lowe, followed the enemy as they fled and cut down large numbers of them.'

Ardagh stayed on at the battle location, given the task of commanding the railway links. It was his role, as intelligence officer, to write reports whenever possible, and on everything. On the railway difficulties, he reported: 'height and the numerical inadequacy of the railway staff was most felt; his sound judgement, good advice, readiness of resource in difficulties and above all his indomitable energy and good example, were of the greatest value.' Ardagh then spent time in Cairo but he was always immersed in theories regarding the part of the world he knew best – the Balkans. He wrote that some kind of war there was inevitable.

Ardagh was involved in other battles as the operations in Sudan continued. The most notable one was against Osman Digna. In 1883 Osman was the Mahdi's agent in the eastern Sudan, and he was a man descended from a Kurdish soldier. He had an influence over the Haddendowa tribe although they appeared not to admire him. He was really an adventurer and trader who led the Beja people. He allied himself with the Mahdi and was made emir of the eastern Sudan. Tamai was Osman's HQ, and the British had found out that the main force of Osman's men were in a limited space and vulnerable if action was quick and decisive. The British, under General

Graham, were in a protective *zariba*, an enclosure made of mimosa bushes, when Ardagh was told to reconnoitre. He found the main force of the enemy and immediately reported back to Graham. By the time the British moved, the Arabs had also moved, and Graham took his whole force forward in a square. But the general knew that he had to attack first, and did so, and although at one point some Arabs broke through the line and did some slaughter, the general onslaught by the various British forces was successful in a long and bloody close-fighting encounter. A retreat action, disciplined troops firing at oncoming Dervishes, continued the success in dragging victory from a desperate situation.

Ardagh wrote in his account that Osman looked from a distance and was disappointed in his expectations. Ardagh wrote: 'Of the 10,000 or 12,000 who were with him … there remained, when he mustered at Tamanib a couple of days afterwards, less than 500.'

Ardagh continued on the Nile, and in other duties, for some years, until in 1887 his career took the turn that led him to the phase of military achievement for which he is chiefly remembered. He was appointed assistant adjutant general, Intelligence Department – a newly created post mainly linked to the notion of mobilization, yet another repercussion of the Franco-Prussian War. Not until 1904 was mobilization transferred to Military Training, and then Intelligence was called 'Operations with extended duties'. Mobilisation was seen as important because at that time the British Army had no plans in place for mobilizing the forces based at home. Again, the Prussians had efficiently mobilized in 1870, and that was a lesson to be leaned by all, but it had not yet been absorbed in England. In 1886, an analysis of what mobilization entailed was done by Brackenbury, who was by then a major-general.

Once again, our biographical subjects cross. Brackenbbury was working with Ardagh. The Secretary of State for War in 1887, Edward Stanhope, saw that what Brackenbury wanted to do was quite manageable. Several other areas of the army were reformed at this time, as mobilization took centre stage, including the Pay Corps and the Remount Department, which meant that new horses for cavalry would be centrally purchased. By the time of the 1888 National Defence Act the government could requisition horses in times of emergency. All these measures were founded on the precept of Prussia. The army was learning slowly, and John Ardagh was on the forefront of this, as he went to work with Brackenbury to reorganize and rationalize the home forces of the Crown.

It is now necessary to consider the whole framework of intelligence as it stood in 1896 when Ardagh took over full control, being made Director of

Military Intelligence, taking over from Lieutenant Chapman. Sir George Aston, in his 1933 book, *Secret Service*, points out that the journey to the department Ardagh led in 1896 was long and slow, and one reason for that was bureaucracy and prevarication. He writes about learning how to get government departments to do things rather than just talk about doing things. He points out that in the Anglo-Boer War of 1899–1902 field intelligence staff began to be prominent. But he adds that 'There I found that the new intelligence officer was looked upon as a sort of handyman, expected to undertake odd jobs of every description.'

What Aston says regarding the war in South Africa is central to the story of Ardagh in his war. He notes that he found himself at times being deployed as something akin to a 'town mayor'. He explains that he should have been concentrating on providing maps, guides and interpreters, and nothing that was irrelevant to intelligence work, but he was not. In short, he was a dogsbody.

In the years between 1896 and the outbreak of the war against the Boers, though, Ardagh had been profoundly involved in the intricate web of theoretical intelligence as well as in giving thought to field intelligence and the defence of the homeland – all part of his remit. One of the most influential factors in those years was the growth of the German navy, a force whom Britain had essentially advised and trained. Now it was causing defensive thinking, and that is where mobilization came into the picture. Ardagh put his ideas regarding his role on paper, including the comment that the work entails considerations of as many different scenarios are there were colonies, and that most places on the red map of empire had multiple frontiers. In addition, he accepted that the naval perspective was vital too. A summary of the growth of the British Empire during the eighteenth and nineteenth centuries makes it clear that the naval command and participation in all parts of the globe had been the support and foundation of everything else. He had experienced that first hand on the Nile. Consequently he saw the navy as an organic part of the intelligence structure.

At the heart of what the intelligence officer was to do in this new establishment was the need to acquire information in all forms, and then to adapt that to each unique application in context. Added to this was the necessary piecemeal nature of the material that would be the basis of the briefing and communiqués in a war situation: that, even the densest chunk of information, copiously written, would still inevitably be merely a piece in some massive jigsaw of pieces that made the whole picture. This is illustrated vividly in the case of Mark Sykes in Cairo, as recounted in the next chapter.

The earlier history of intelligence as it was defined in the army in general illustrates the slow journey to the professionalism now demanded in the department Ardagh headed in 1896. The establishment had come from the topographical and statistical department under Jervis, which was a focus on cartography, to a new world of incredibly complicated Realpolitik, studied diplomacy and military theory. In her biography of her husband, Susan, Countess of Malmesbury points out that Ardagh needed a vast amount of information in order to fulfil his role properly: 'Of all the headquarters staff the director of intelligence was therefore the man most needed to be in close touch with the commander-in-chief and at his call for reference at a moment's notice.'

The new department had seven sections from its inception to the last days of the war in South Africa: the colonial section, imperial defence and home defence, alongside four foreign sections which covered every conceivable issue across the globe from the Russian Empire to the Congo Free State. The records indicate that the department was composed of only a few officers, but their resources were full and in some areas comprehensive. But the total supervision of all this was done by Ardagh and just one adjutant. Much of Ardagh's time was spent on committees and then on writing reports. It is hard not to see the naval and military committees as being extraordinarily important at that time: the naval lord and the Director of Military Intelligence had to be in constant touch. Being based at Queen Anne's Gate, intelligence was close to Downing Street, and as the intelligence staff's main duty was to update information, changing with current events, that nearness was important. But all this will not fully function unless the D.M.I. is a skilled communicator.

Ardagh's early life makes it absolutely clear that he was a natural for the business of communication and lucid explanation. A part of his role was to explain difficult issues to people who were only knowledgeable on matters in their own limited sphere of activity. He was adept at that. Before the Anglo-Boer War brought these matters into the arena for scrutiny and reform, Ardagh's past experience on boundary work came into its own. He was very well informed on such matters, and he could advise the Foreign Office when required, in all kinds of contexts. When the modern reader reflects on all this responsibility it is not surprising that, when the war in South Africa went wrong and blame had to be apportioned by some people, Ardagh and his colleagues were the targets. With hindsight, that was grossly unfair, and we need to recall the war and the workings of intelligence there.

In the Anglo-Boer War of 1899–1902 there were mercenaries and volunteers as well as the official fighting men of the opposing armies.

Many Russians went to fight for the Boers, and one of these, Yevgeny Augustus, wrote in his diary an account of what happened to a captured spy: he was badly beaten by those men led by Lucas Meyer, who treated him abysmally, as was always the way with spies. This one was a Kaffir who had been caught in a nearby kraal. Assistant-General Kock took over:

> 'This is not the first time that we have caught Kaffir spies,' Kock explained
> to the Russians. 'They deliver the most exact data about our positions to the
> British. These rogues have almost established postal communication between
> Buller and White for a handful of gold.' 'Shoot him.' He said casually to the
> Boers. The African was shot instantly on the spot, rather to the Russians'
> embarrassment.

In this way we can learn a great deal about several aspects of the Boer War. First, Kock told the volunteers that his own father and two brothers had been killed by the British. He was out for vengeance. It was a dirty, ruthless and desperate war with high loss of life. It was also a war in which such duties as intelligence were partly the business of a mixed range of characters of all kinds and backgrounds. The army was using traditional methods of allowing the locals the knife-edge of risk, of course. The episode also hints at just how important the war became as a focus of all kinds of discontentment and imperial rivalry. There were plenty of Germans in Africa by this time, as we have noted. There were also a number of other locations throughout the British Empire which were still highly volatile. In some ways the Boer War was to introduce new strategies and attitudes of mind in the British high command, and intelligence work was a vital part of that.

It was destined to be a rough, difficult war in all respects: the phases of the conflict were first a direct series of battles with Sir Redvers Buller being the principal military leader for Britain. Gold mining had transformed the Transvaal, and a massive influx of foreigners (uitlanders) had settled there. Repression followed, with the Boer head, Kruger, enforcing police control. But, of course, gold gave the Boers immense wealth, and that meant they could buy huge stocks of weaponry. By 1900 the Boers had won a series of victories and they held several defensive positions. Second, after Buller was replaced by Lord Roberts, there were 50,000 British troops there. But Buller, at Spion Kop, won a victory with heavy losses and besieged towns were gradually relieved. This led to a retreat by the Boers, who fought a guerrilla campaign in the last phase. They moved north into Natal.

South Africa had been the scene of a long-standing conflict. From 1880–81 there had been a small war in which the Dutch Boers had won at Majuba Hill. Britain had no real worries about giving independence to the insignificant states of Transvaal and the Orange Free State as they were then, but after the gold rush, things were different. By 1898 it was clear that the Boers' power could be a genuine threat to British supremacy in that part of the Empire. Of course, there was support from Germany for the Boers, and Germany made sure that it openly congratulated the Boers after they crushed the strange and wrong-headed Jameson Raid in which the Rhodes-backed Dr Jameson (2 January 1895) led a small army into the Transvaal, ostensibly to stage a coup. The result was that, by 1899, the Boers were becoming a formidable military force.

The turning point was around May and June 1900. After Mafeking was relieved, Roberts went into Johannesburg and the Orange Free State was annexed. In October that year the Transvaal was annexed. It was from that point on that British intelligence involvement was to be particularly important. It was a lesson to be learned, as was the case with all major aspects of that war. As the Boer 'commandos' started their sabotage and skirmishing campaigns, they were fated to go up against Kitchener and his ruthlessly efficient knowledge of defensive positions, internment camps, and his liaisons with Colonel Henderson and Lord Roberts in intelligence work. The scouting and reconnaissance work that went on was destined to be chaotic and dangerous. As Craig Wilcox has said, 'Mounted scouts combed the countryside and quasi-military intelligence officers ran spy-rings to track down resisters.' There were atrocities, such as the episode in which Harry Morant, of an irregular band of volunteers called the Bushveldt Carabineers, was involved in the killing of unarmed men.

The significance of the intelligence section in this bloody and frustrating war begins, however, with the work of Sir John Ardagh. There had been massive preparations for war. Roberts had been active in large-scale manoeuvres in Ireland, and there had been endless diplomatic negotiations. But when war was inevitable, it fell to Ardagh, as head of the Intelligence Branch, to prepare a report on the potential enemy and on all military factors. Ardagh made it clear to Lord Lansdowne, the Secretary of State for War, that there would be need for a force of 200,000 men to take on the Boer army. Winston Churchill, at that time preparing himself for work as a war correspondent for the *Morning Post*, noted that 'Mr George Wyndham, under-secretary of state, alone seemed to appreciate the difficulties and magnitude of the task. The Boers, he said, were thoroughly prepared and acting on definite plans.' It transpired that the enemy would have a new Maxim model of the fearsome machine gun.

Ardagh was always to be found where there was open discussion of innovation and efficiency. A typical example is the Durr light lamp. In 1895 a lamp invented by a German engineer, Ludwig Durr, was given some night time trials. The idea was that this instrument would shed light when there was no gas or electric source. Ardagh directed that a reservoir be filled with petrol as the Durr lamp burned. The lamp worked well and as *The Times* commented: 'In the embarkation or disembarkation of troops and the loading or unloading of store ships or transport wagons at night it would be of the greatest possible service.' Ardagh was the man who would write the report for the War Office. This small example tells us so much about the man: his meticulous attention to detail and his utter reliability in a position of responsibility. It persuades us today that his estimations regarding the Boer War were very likely correct.

For six years Ardagh served in India as a private secretary to Lord Lansdowne before moving, after a brief time in the School of Engineering, into the work he will always be associated with – being Director of the Military Intelligence Branch (1896–1901). He had only just settled into that responsibility when the war in South Africa became imminent. He knew that his main priority was to prepare information relevant to the Transvaal. He had a small staff and very poor resources, but Ardagh's report, *Military Notes on the Dutch Republics of South Africa*, was produced. This document was later the subject of some controversy, and opinions were divided, but it is apparent that the facts in that report were astoundingly accurate. His advice that almost a quarter of a million men would be needed was almost certainly not taken seriously. There was the usual underestimation of the enemy. After all, they were thought to be essentially farmers, not soldiers. It was a fatal error of judgement. In fact, in a short letter to *The Times* in November 1899, a certain P.S.C. wrote:

Sir, some doubt has been expressed as to the accuracy of the information possessed by the Intelligence Department of the War Office with regard to the Transvaal armaments. I have reason to know, and on the most unimpeachable authority, that in the report rendered by Sir John Ardagh on the armed strength of the Boers, the number of their guns given, with their character and calibre, corresponds exactly with our recently ascertained knowledge of what the enemy has put into the field. Moreover, as to the numerical strength, the Intelligence Department's estimate was rather over than under the totals said to be now arrayed against us.

The equivalent number of German staff in intelligence at this time was around 250. Ardagh had twenty men under him. It was observed at this time that in the Transvaal £90,000 was spent every year on financing the equivalent office to Ardagh's, whereas Ardagh himself had a budget of £20,000. Nevertheless, the new Chief of the Intelligence Branch was consulted by the Foreign Office and the Colonial Office for assistance in a range of matters. Ardagh did not keep his mouth closed on the matter of resources, though. He clearly fought a battle with the hierarchy. When he gave evidence before the War Commission, he expressed the problems he had encountered in trying to explain why intelligence work needed more staff and finance. He always gave total commitment to every duty he was given. Ardagh was always attached to any scheme generated by the new department and indeed, as all staff involved in espionage have had to do, he had a wider remit than field intelligence, and, in fact, as was learned after the war, even had agents particularly linked to diplomacy, something that had been the case since the beginnings of the Empire. This had become more difficult as time went on, and particularly in the case of reliable maps when war should arise. He needed a network of agents *in situ* in South Africa, but had none. One of the foremost historians of the Boer War makes it clear what Ardagh's problem was in this respect:

> But Ardagh was a shy, cautious man, known for his alarming silences. Moreover, Ardagh had been given only a shoestring budget for the Intelligence Department – £20,000 to cover the whole world. He had no professional intelligence agents in either the Free State or the Transvaal, so his forecasts were hesitant or conflicting. Where they were to prove accurate – and to favour Wolseley – it was easy for Lansdowne to brush them aside.

We can see from this that opinions as to Ardagh's achievements vary. But the central question is about how the military thinkers anticipated that the Boers would act. It was essential to know not merely what the Boer strength was but whether or not they had the capabilities to conduct a conventional land war, or whether they would be raiders. Ardagh considered that the latter was the most likely. His report had a thesis related to this at the heart of its assessment. First, he thought that the two states would join together (and they did). This would mean that they had almost 40,000 fighting men. He also reckoned that they would have Mauser guns and no more than sixteen 'Long Toms'. The kernel of the thinking behind all this was that the Boers would raid.

The assumption underlying the report was that the organisational powers of the Boer leaders would be limited, and that they had no experience of warfare to compare with the generals who would be leading the British forces. The artillery they possessed was thought to be inferior to the British Armstrongs, and practical topics such as these made sense at the time, in the perspective of previous engagements. But one entrenched attitude produced a line of thought that added to the miscalculations, not so much in those written by Ardagh but by the military minds that extended his initial thinking: and that was the reliance on the established reputation of the British imperial armies. This led to the certainty that the Boers would not be able to stage an invasion and that, indeed, the British could take the offensive and defeat the enemy in the field, forcing them to use raiding tactics. With these thoughts in mind, Buller wanted a 'forward policy' – an offensive to capitalise on these perceived features of British superiority. It was assumed that one sizeable confrontation would put paid to the 'farmers'. It is not difficult to see, with hindsight, the difficulty of Ardagh's situation. He had been given a major responsibility, and his natural sense and caution restricted him to estimations and assumptions based on the limited information he could gather from his sources.

One of Ardagh's more interesting achievements came in this way, and illustrates the spy's best friend – sheer serendipity. We know this tale of the acquisition of Transvaal maps because an account was written by the famous military historian, Brigadier-General J.E. Edmonds, in 1922. His account was from the standpoint of a man who was actually Ardagh's agent in this minor triumph. His story was that in December 1899, the British minister in Berne, Sir Francis St John, noticed a large-scale map on a wall in an ante chamber of the federal building there. It was a map of the Transvaal, and the creator of this very useful item was an inhabitant of Zurich, so the diplomat noted the name, and then contacted him. Sir Henry Angst, a senior diplomat, saw to it that knowledge was gained about other copies of the maps. It was discovered that 3,000 of them could be bought for £3,000. Edmonds then completes the saga: 'Sir Francis St John communicated with London and a high officer of the Foreign Office brought his telegram to the old Intelligence Offices at 18, Queen Anne's Gate. Sir John Ardagh instructed me to go to the War Office in Pall Mall, see the permanent under-secretary, Sir Ralph Knox, and stay there until I got the authority for the money.' Edmonds obtained what he wanted and travelled to Berne immediately. He was taken by Angst to Winterthur where the maps were all packed and ready for movement. He notes that 'The production of the proof-sheet settled the matter. I took as many maps as I could carry back with me, arriving in England on Christmas Eve. Mr Angst dispatched the cases of maps to my private address, where they arrived safely.' In other words, although one case of maps had been sent to South Africa already, before all this took place, the fact was that the map was found by chance, and Ardagh only obtained copies because of a chance sighting by a man walking through a room on other business.

What begins to emerge, then, when we look at the military intelligence of the Anglo-Boer War, in the early stages and in the pre-war days, is a series of actions all disparate, some linked to mere opportunity and chance; in the actual mainstream information, with Ardagh at the centre, is a mix of system, caution and theoretical thinking that was uneven in its results. But as there was no network of agents in place, it became clear that the actual field operations of spies was going to be (as can be seen in the shooting of the 'Kaffir spy') the use of native personnel along with anyone else (military or civilian) who could be included in specific *ad hoc* actions. Of course, for the most perilous and frustrating phase of the war, the guerrilla war from 1900 to 1902, with Kitchener in pursuit, and a method of gradual and patient blockading in progress, spy activity was certain to be dangerous, adventurous and pragmatic. Hence we have, for instance, a proliferation of correspondence between officers concerning piecemeal information, handled as it comes along. For example, a telegram sent by staff at Colonel Ian Hamilton's field force in July 1900 to the Director of Military Intelligence shows estimates and the disposition of Boer forces, notably commando forces at Boekenhoutskloof, and communicates worries about the standard of ability among the officers working under Colonel Hickman. In other words, the larger picture is difficult to perceive. It is useful to recall that a powerful influence on the thinking leading to the Boer War decisions was the 1888 Stanhope memorandum, in which the policy of sending two corps out into the Empire after the reserve was mobilized was laid down. With massive basic concerns such as troop mobilization at the heart of plans, intelligence took a back seat.

The issue of cartography, as highlighted by the story told by Edmonds, was important. The existing maps were unsatisfactory because, according to some estimates, the acquisition of maps through survey work would have required massive amounts of investment and years of survey work. Major E.H. Hills, who was in charge of cartography in 1902, reported to the Elgin Commission that it was a question of lack of money, but also of a long-standing neglect of mapping in several areas of strategic importance. Baden-Powell had done survey work in Cyprus and Palestine, for instance; such duties in marginal areas had been considered to be the task of junior officers who needed some experience as extensions to their general training.

In all matters of spycraft the Boer War has particular interest because it was used as a stage for innovation and experiment. The Playfair Cipher, for instance, was first used in that war, secretly taken up by the War Office along with so many other things. This was a system of coding in which pairs of letters in a plain text are replaced by another sequence of paired-letters. This is entirely typical of the marginalisation of espionage, placed in situations in which success is less important than experimentation. After all, from the beginning, the War Office had done some puzzling things in terms of using intelligence in that war. In July, 1899, as Christopher Andrew has explained, ten men with experience of field intelligence were sent to South Africa. Their role was to gather information and then, at a later date, to assemble and collate these findings. But as Tammy Proctor writes, 'By November, 1899, several of the original ten male officers were unavailable, having been besieged in settlements such as Mafeking and Kimberley.' It was only after Lord Roberts took command that the well-organised Field Intelligence Corps was put in place, with 132 officers and a massive body of agents. It was at that point, when communication became the key issue to combat the commando raiders and the dispersed enemy, that other ancillary aspects of intelligence were employed, such as signalling and cables, pigeon post and press censorship.

It was clear by the end of the war in 1902 that the army needed a revisionary study and some radical changes to be made from the inside. When Sir William Robertson was based at the War Office, from 1902–07, he was once again assigned to intelligence duties. His work was to exist as part of the changes brought about by the 1903 War Office reorganisation committee, led by Lord Fisher and Sir George Sydenham Clarke. Their proposals were that the aim of the War Office must be to prepare the military forces for a state of war, and that there should be a defence committee in the cabinet. They also made an Army Council which was developed from the template of the Board of Admiralty. All actions of primary importance should be made to the Crown by the first lord, as with the Admiralty. The Intelligence Department was to be fused with the general staff. It was one of the members of the Army Council who was to have responsibility for intelligence: William Robertson was a major player in this new scheme of things.

Robertson was given the task of controlling intelligence in all foreign countries, collecting and preparing details on all the main aspects of that work, embracing such topics as geography, resources and armed forces in a range of locations. He also had to liaise with military attaches and work closely with the director of military operations. There were three sub-divisions of the new intelligence section: strategic and colonial defence, foreign and Indian, and executive and telegraphy/special duties. There were forty-three staff members in the new directorate of military operations, and these were led by Major-General J.M. Grierson.

We can learn something of the changes that took place by summarising what Robertson did with his time. He was mainly concerned with work relating to Russia and France. As it was being accepted that there was a shift in the centre of power in Central Asia, with Russia becoming more influential, it was becoming more important to bring about a closer connection with Russia, at least diplomatically. Robertson concentrated on the study of what part intelligence and diplomacy could play in the fundamental situation of being a state with an army ready for war at any time.

What happened after the lessons of the Boer War was that Britain had become a more forthright military state. Militarism was something that was expressed in a variety of ways, and the concepts of espionage, or of field intelligence, were notions that were to be changed and transmuted in many ways as more profound aspects of the *Zeitgeist* found expression. With reference particularly to the growth of the intelligence initiatives in the establishment, the war against the Boers made it clear that there had never been a master plan regarding responses to emergency situations within the Empire. Furthermore, the significance of the contributions made by an intelligence department became clearer. One expression of the lesson learned was put strongly by one historian: 'It was not until December 1899, some months after the war had begun, that any thought was given to the question of security intelligence; then a new section under Major Edmonds was created, H section.' This was a wholly new conception, and Edmonds was vastly experienced in all kinds of organisational leadership and, indeed, in covert work (note his work over the Kruger maps). H section was, in fact, the forerunner of MI5. Security intelligence was something new, and this was where Robertson fitted in best, along with other experienced men. What was new was that this was a more intellectual, comprehensive view of intelligence in matters of war and national security.

One comment at the time about this reform was that 'The days when the War Office was fit for a gentleman came to an end with the Boer War.' Obviously, the man to be consulted regarding staffing the new structures of command was Lord Roberts. In 1899, before the emergence of the later version of the control of the intelligence work at the War Office, the key man was the Director-General of Mobilization and Intelligence, and that went to Sir William Nicholson, on Roberts' advice. An Order of Council of 1901 made it clear that Nicholson's first duty was to prepare and maintain detailed plans for the defence of the Empire. Nicholson's energetic application to that task paved the way for the later successes, when that first plan was refined and took account of liaisons with other organisations. At the heart of the changes was a closer attention to strategy and theoretical perspectives on war. The classic theorists, such as Clausewitz, were once again compulsory reading, though opinions divided on him. E.A. Altham, mentioned in Robertson's memoirs, was a deeply influential figure here, and the team as a whole had a leader who was prepared to fight to obtain more finance. Staff were becoming aware, as the shortcomings of intelligence in the Transvaal became more known, that Britain's directorate in that regard were under-financed.

Nicholson began his series of requests for more money and resources in 1901 when he consulted the Treasury on the topic of the size of his domain. He wanted eight more officers for a start, and the salaries required for that amounted to over £4,000. This request was modified rather, but the next ploy to use against the man with the money, Hicks Beach, was that Germany was well in advance of Britain in this matter. In the end, the support of Lord Roberts proved to be essential when, in 1902, Nicholson asked for a more ambitious increment – the development of his department into a team with eleven more officers, thus being even more costly. This shook the top brass to the core, so much so that they set up a committee to report on exactly what this Intelligence Division was all about.

There was a clash of opinion: some thought that intelligence work in the field was always dependent on specific circumstances, and therefore no blueprint could cover every eventuality; others considered that if a commander in the field put together his own plan for how intelligence should integrate or even operate within his scheme of things, then that would be too whimsical and individual, not relating to any grand plan. It was a confrontation between practical men (some of the advisers fresh from the war in South Africa, and therefore not exactly open to theoretical discussion) and officers with a more abstract, comprehensive frame of mind. But in March 1903 a decision was made and Nicholson's department was given three more officers and four civilians, along with a great deal of official language in which directions were given as to the use and application of resources. Nicholson made it clear that he still thought the higher echelons of power had not understood the concept behind the linking of intelligence and mobilization: 'Unless matters of this nature are carefully studied at the War Office in peacetime it is extremely improbable that a right decision will be given under high pressure.'

In other words, it was an issue of forethought and preparation, together with a perception that all arms of military might should be integrated. It was the old lesson of Prussia, still there on the table waiting for action to be taken, rather than mere talk of action. To make matters worse, after the Boer War the notion of having a Director-General of Military Training was revived. So once again there was going to be dissension and crossovers of influence. Much of Nicholson's work came to little, due to arguments and jealousies within those corridors of power. Even the King interfered at times. The seat of this confusion and dissent was the wounded pride at the failures in South Africa and, of course, the status and prestige of Lord Roberts was a factor there. The result was that, by the time Robertson was involved, from 1902–07, he and other fellow officers were carrying on regardless of these machinations at the highest level. In practical terms, though, it meant that by 1902 nothing had happened to give a permanent footing to any new status and size of the Intelligence Department. Committee followed committee, and discussion followed discussion; only when a document was eventually produced, called *Field Service Regulations Part II*, created by Rawlinson, Lieutenant Colonel Wilson and Hildyard, was something definite achieved: the manual would provide the basis for mobilization, when that actually happened, and there was at least a measure of understanding as to what part intelligence staff would play in that.

Regarding the Boer War, then, intelligence in terms of the more office-based, paperwork kind of knowledge, as exhibited by Ardagh in his report, was often seen as superfluous, hence its low regard in many quarters. It has been commented that Redvers Buller, when he was given a copy of the report, swiftly returned it with a comment that he already knew everything there was to know. But several important and powerful people were learning that intelligence reports on both security and enemy assessments were going to matter more and more. One of these was Churchill. It has often been remarked that, after hearing the announcement that Austria (and its empire) had given an ultimatum to Serbia after the assassination of Franz Ferdinand, Churchill went to his office and wrote a list of items for attention, with the aim of preparations for war – the main focus of the new War Office, of course. On his list he wrote, 'K. espionage'. He was thinking of Vernon Kell, the 'founding father' of MI5.

But Churchill, ever since his own youthful adventures as a spy/observer in Cuba and with the lancers in the Sudan, had been more aware than most of the pitiful state of British intelligence and the types of communities that sort of network normally depend on. Since returning from South Africa, he had given talks on the subject. One of his key references was to the Boer War, specifically to Spion Kop, a fight that makes an excellent case study in this respect. British forces were crushed there, and one main reason for that was the lack of maps. The battle took place on 23–24 January 1900. The essence of that defeat was that Spion Kop ('Lookout Hill') was occupied by a small force of infantry under the command of General Edward Woodgate, but having done so, they found themselves under merciless fire from several quarters. The troops were totally exposed for a long time and casualties were very high. Churchill himself was there that day, and wrote later:

> One thing was quite clear – unless good and efficient cover could be made during the night, and unless guns could be dragged to the summit of the hill to match the Boer artillery, the infantry could not, perhaps would not, endure another day. The human machine will not stand certain strains for long.

Woodgate, who was killed, was succeeded by Colonel Thorneycroft, who retreated from the position. Buller lost the fight, and the statistics make grim reading: 300 men dead and 1,000 wounded. In addition, 200 were captured. In some places the corpses lay piled three deep. The central fact of the misery of the whole experience was that riflemen had been firing down at a vulnerable position. That was something very rarely encountered before that date. It was one more example of how failings in battle in the history of the Empire were often down to underestimation of the enemy or to inadequate attention given to intelligence. The basic fact that British troops were 'playing away from home' – as at Isandlwana in the Zulu War of 1879 – was seldom noted and acted on in terms of using intelligence in all its forms. We can see with hindsight that simple cartography would have been the answer in this case.

Ardagh took extreme criticism over his supposed shortcomings. His wife later wrote of him at that time:

> Anxiety for the issue, sympathy with his many comrades at the front, grief at the army, the stress of all this Ardagh had to share with many another Englishman. But to these anxieties and griefs was added, for him, the

harder task of going on steadily with the daily work of his office, silent and unmoved, whilst the press of England were ringing with the charge that this time of trial, with its humiliations and losses, had befallen an unprepared nation and Government, because the Intelligence Department had failed in its duty.

As George Aston said in his account of the growth of the Intelligence Department, the South African experience caused the British public to take an interest in army reform. The Intelligence Department was strengthened and its staff increased. Once again, what the fiasco of the maps and the armaments proved was that the long history of the army's pragmatic approach to both field and resource intelligence was just not acceptable. One obvious, if simplistic explanation of the failures in the campaign is that there was an attitude of assuming that one good, disciplined British soldier was worth six amateurs. The records show very clearly how wrong that proved to be.

CHAPTER 7

SIR MARK SYKES
AND THE DIPLOMATS

In March 2007, the newspapers were busy with a sensational story concerning bird flu. A court gave scientists permission to exhume the body of Sir Mark Sykes, whose body was laid to rest at St Mary's Church, Sledmere, his country seat in North Yorkshire. He had been buried in a lead coffin, and Professor John Oxford, a virologist, argued that the flu virus would have been preserved in the coffin. Mark had sailed from Syria to France, and he died in Paris on 16 February 1919. The world suddenly knew the name of one of the most remarkable men of his generation, whose career in politics was tragically cut short. He was only thirty-nine at his death.

Mark Sykes is usually remembered as 'Soldier, politician, diplomat'. The exhumation took place, with family permission, and the writer and grandchild of Mark, Christopher Sykes, told the press that 'It's rather fascinating that, maybe even as a corpse, he may be helping others, as it were.' The study will go ahead, and we eagerly await the results. But this strange business shone the light of knowledge on a man who, in his short life, had been MP for Hull, top-flight diplomat in the Middle East, cartoonist and raconteur, soldier and entertainer. The history reference books have his name under 'The Sykes-Picot Agreement.' Yet he was much more than the sum of these parts. His companion in diplomacy, Ronald Storrs, was a man who moved in all possible circles around Egypt and the surrounding states, and he was an excellent judge of men. Here is Storrs' appraisal of Sykes:

He was one of those few for whom the House of Commons fills, and he could hardly have failed to become an under-secretary, perhaps a secretary of state. As a caricaturist and political cartoonist he could have imposed his own terms upon the evening press; as may be seen from 'Foreign Office Attitudes'. The same vein of artistry would transform him into a first-class music hall comedian; holding a chance gathering spell-bound by swift and complete changes of character with matter as well as the manner of Lloyd George, F.E. Smith, John Redmond.

This is a portrait of a man who had talent as well as charm. Naturally, as his career began in the army, and he always took a deep interest in all matters concerned with foreign campaigns, he was destined to be a diplomat. In fact, the main concern of the present is with his work as a key member of the agents based in Cairo. From an early age he was a traveller in the Middle East and elsewhere, and his knowledge of the cultures and beliefs of various peoples around what was then known as the Levant was immense and erudite. He knew such luminaries as T.E. Lawrence and Lord Kitchener. He sat at cabinet meetings with Lloyd George and Winston Churchill. But equally he was a Catholic family man with a deep concern for social justice and local politics.

For present purposes, we begin with a biographical account of his life up to his work on the Sykes-Picot Agreement – the final chapter will focus on that important document and its complex genesis. He was the son of Sir Tatton Sykes, and it was perhaps his father who first led Mark to stand in wonderment at Eastern belief and culture, as he took his son to see the Jebel Druse, a religious community, three times when Mark was a young boy. That experience was perhaps the beginning of Mark Sykes' future as a commentator on those societies and people, as in *Dar-ul-Islam* and *The Caliph's Last Heritage*. He saw service in the Anglo-Boer War, was elected to Parliament representing Central Hull, and was involved in the Council for Imperial Defence.

Mark Sykes was born at Sledmere in 1879, and was educated in Monaco, Belgium and then Jesus College, Cambridge. But the pull of the Middle East was irresistible; even as a student he took time out to travel there. As his obituary in *The Times* put it, this journey was not merely a tourist trip: 'This tour was not the casual trip of the sightseer, but was devoted to a close study of the people, languages and customs, and to the development of that faculty which enabled him to approach local questions and to understand local ideals from the native point of view.' This point illuminates the aspect of Sykes which puts him in the long and illustrious tradition of intelligence gatherers in the Great Game, such as Percy Sykes, Richard Burton and Francis Younghusband. These were all officers who had a need to do far more than the minimum required of officers serving in the Empire. Not for them the shooting trips when they had time off: they wanted to move around as natives and truly understand the places and beliefs in the context of war.

Much has been written about Mark Sykes' early life, as in Shane Leslie's *Mark Sykes, His Life and Letters*, written in 1923, and more recently in Roger Adelson's *Mark Sykes, Portrait of an Amateur* (1975). Christopher Simon Sykes, grandson of Mark, wrote the whole family story in *The Big House* (2004). As there is a substantial amount of material in print on education and family influences, the main areas to explain here are concerned with how Mark emerged as a soldier and an agent in Cairo. In summaries of his life, his first years in the army are often passed over, but his short time in South Africa was very important; in spite of his first comment in 1899: 'Now I have to go to South Africa, which is a most infernal nuisance.' His army career had started in the Yorkshire Regiment, but in 1898 he was attached to the 3rd Connaught Rangers and joined them for manoeuvres in Ireland. He had first applied for a commission in 1897, and he wanted to be in a militia battalion. He was soon a part of the Princess of Wales's own Yorkshire Regiment.

His guide on his travels, Isa, had made a start with Mark in his wish to speak Arabic, but by the time he was back at Cambridge he realised that his Arabic would need more attention. Professor E.G. Browne, another well-versed traveller of Mark's favourite places, was a good contact. At the centre of the ideology Mark Sykes was immersed in at this time was the notion that the British Empire was there to secure and protect the cultural heartland of the Middle East: one of the directing principles of the imperial theme in Victoria's realm. His Arabic steadily improved; and on further travels he even went to more dangerous and uncertain places than most: he even went to the Russian border via Damascus and Baghdad. Later, he was to write of 'greasy, leather-clad Cossacks' who did not exactly welcome him. But he was a man of action, and always had in him the spirit of the man who would later be a major player in the politics of the Middle East. At Cambridge, with the war with the Boers looming, he was ready for action. As Roger Adelson wrote of him: 'The contrast between life in a tent as a soldier or Eastern explorer was too great for Mark to find congenial the civilized comfort of Cambridge.' His regiment was called up in November 1899. His involvement was at first fairly marginal as there were domestic problems at home, and he took leave based on the fact that he was very depressed. But finally, when matters were settled, off he went to war.

His regiment was assigned to Barkly Bridge, near Port Elizabeth, and there his small command kept him busy. Disappointingly he was then laid low with malaria, and could not experience the front line until later when sent to Pretoria. He led a small militia command and events flattened out into a dull routine. He found communication with ordinary soldiers very hard, as he had little respect for them in that context. Reading between the lines, it is clear that deep down he was longing for some action. Finally, the third battalion of his regiment left for Rhenoster Bridge and he had his first taste of the field intelligence shortcomings in that war. There were no maps available for the immediate area, and although he was busy with entrenchment and making blockhouses, there was a certain level of uncertainty about the enemy, and this was confirmed when an offensive was decided. The war was at a turning point then, with Kitchener's tactics of a Fabian, steady blocking of movement and holding civilians: Sykes was to be very critical of the mistakes made at the highest level. But again, he saw poor intelligence at work when he set out from Rhenoster Bridge to find the enemy and surprise them. That was the plan, but in truth they were based in a part of the country that guerrilla leader Piet De Wet knew well. It was close to his home in fact. De Wet knew that there was a massive ammunition dump and lots of provisions exactly where Sykes's men had dug in at the Bridge. On 6 June he sent his men into the area in three groups. It was one of these detachments that ran into Sykes and his column.

Sykes and his men set up camp, but were then attacked the next morning, shortly after moving out. Luckily, other men from other forces came to help, but not before some of Sykes' men were shot and killed. The main lesson he learnt regarding the sorry state of field intelligence came a little later. What he found was that De Wet's spy system had been more efficient than its British counterpart. Kaffirs (the term at the time for black South Africans) in his detachment had been sending information to De Wet, and Sykes found out. By the standards of 1900 his reaction was quite restrained: he ordered them to be lashed by a rope-end by one of his men, an ex-prison warder who was handy with a whip. It might have worked in terms of gaining respect, but in fact many officers would have had them shot. Boers often had Kaffir spies working for the British shot, as recounted in chapter five. But his overall attitude to the Kaffirs was most enlightened. Sykes concentrated on what was possible – reinforcing the position of the bridge and digging in. It was 1901, and Kitchener had been winning the war by slow attrition and desperate methods, fighting guerrillas with such actions as the burning of farms and the creation of the first concentration camps. In the midst of all this, in his small way, Sykes made trenches and positions defending the railway lines close by. He also used paid Kaffir labour – something that was not really allowed. According to Roger Adelson, this was something learned by Kitchener later.

In the summer of 1901 his responsibility had expanded to cover the defence of a line of stations. He had time to reflect on the conduct of the war, and he spotted the weakness in overall strategy. He wrote in one letter that, 'The art of war is as dead as the making of stained glass or true Gothic architecture.' In effect, throughout the campaign of that summer, against De Wet, several limitations of intelligence were exposed. One officer captured by De Wet, Molyneux Seele, recorded that he had been captured because his MI department had insisted that there were no Boers around for miles when, in fact, De Wet's own home (and his laager) was in the next valley. In this climate of incompetence, Sykes played a small and disciplined part in holding a line of communication. He was similar to Robert Baden-Powell in that his restless mind, while in a defensive role as an officer, simply keeping land, was roving into innovation and experiment. He came up with special camouflage for guns and limbers, for instance.

At the end of 1901 he was separated from his regiment and attached to the Royal Corps of Engineers at Honigspruit. Here he had one final taste of the war before contracting a terrible illness that temporarily deafened him. He was engaged in engineering work at Honigspruit, having impressed his commanders with the bridge and line defences. Here he had to re-plan the defence of a position so that it could be held by only fifty men. It seems that he accomplished this before illness struck.

Mark Sykes return home was intensely politicised. In the next few years he would be active travelling, writing and creating a network of contacts that would open up the world of politics and diplomacy to him. His biggest step forward came when he was made secretary to George Wyndham, Chief Secretary for Ireland. This was the beginning of the road that was to take him to diplomacy and espionage. Mark was Catholic, had no extreme political views on Irish questions, but had charm in abundance, was a skilful organiser and adept at communicating to audiences and listeners of all kinds and classes. He was also a man who had fought in South Africa, and was vociferous on some of the emerging issues from the ensuing debate on that war.

Mark married Edith Gorst, and as the demands of his work with Wyndham were not great, he got to spend some time with his new wife. He was also writing and could have easily become the literary man his mother wanted him to be. But the tail-end of the Great Game with Russia, and the other aspects of Middle Eastern politics, was calling him, so he asked to be assigned there. In 1905 his life as an attaché began – in Constantinople.

The work of an attaché was one that could relate to almost anyone in any context at the time, because the nature of intelligence throughout the nineteenth century had been such that definitions had been blurred regarding the nature of information passed and circulated. Just as the Tsar of Russia traditionally learned about British tactics from reading *The Times*, so the men in high military command would often learn important information by means of a whole range of sources, from diplomats to travellers and from newspaper correspondents to academics. So Mark Sykes found himself in this cultural network in Constantinople, at a time when the position of Russia just across the border was still in question. He mixed with staff from the army and navy, with politicians and industrial men, and of course private travellers. The Sultan at the time was Abdul Hamid, and it is necessary to recall here that Sykes was a man who aspired to play a part in helping states to govern themselves, and to be aided by the West. There was no time in his head for the myth of 'The White Man's Burden'. Hamid and Turkey were crucially important in the Realpolitik of the time and place: Germany was there too, training officers of the Turkish army and building railways. The safe, middle way in Turkey was to be patient, advise on and monitor progress.

The subject of Turkey as a buffer state between Russia and the Middle East was always there. On the actual frontier were the Kurds. That was where Sykes, along with Colonel Maunsell, began to be more involved with intelligence reports. He continued with that border intelligence by extending his interests into Anatolia. But for a while he had to content himself with literary work, as well as reporting, as his profession entailed. Perhaps his most vivid and significant report was done after a trip to the Persian frontier where he saw the results of neglect on the Turkish detachments assigned to the border. This was yet another instance of the central command hierarchy of a state being slack on important matters of boundaries and personnel.

There followed several years away from diplomacy, extended up to the outbreak of the First World War. Mark was elected as Unionist member for Central Hull in 1911. His first main speech to the House was, naturally, on foreign affairs. In his *Times* obituary, it was opined that his best speech was that given in December 1917 in Manchester, at a Zionist meeting just before the fall of Jerusalem.

But after busying himself raising a special battalion of Wagoners for the Yorkshire Regiment, destiny called: Kitchener knew about him and his special abilities. Mark Sykes was made a special emissary – first to Petrograd and later to Aden and Basra. The essential and inescapable fact was that Germany was claiming Turkey, after years of stealthy preparation. The Eastern Front of the First World War had repercussions in Middle Eastern politics as well as on the Balkans and Russia. In 1915 it was all beginning to look like a massive and complicated version of the 'Game of War' – a game officers had been playing in their spare time since the 1870s. One action in any one of a dozen countries could have consequences somewhere else. Men like Mark Sykes were naturally suited to working in that arena, with one ear to the war across the Mediterranean, and another south to the Arab tribes.

In November 1914 Britain declared war on Turkey. The Dardanelles expedition was prepared and Sykes was offered a post in Cairo, which at first he refused. But Sykes was becoming a part of the team of advisers to the War Cabinet, and soon after Kitchener spoke to him he was working with the War Office. He was in Kitchener's committee, assigned to be involved in the Turkish question. At the base of all this was Britain's concession that she would let Russia have Constantinople as long as Russia would allow Britain to continue with her claims on Persia. The committee, under Maurice de Bunsen, met and considered these issues, but military movements were beginning to take over, such as the involvement of the Indian Army in Mesopotamia (now Iraq). Sykes went to the Dardanelles to meet General Ian Hamilton, one of the main commanders there. He was now moving around the war zone, his task to write a full report on matters for General Calwell. Mark Sykes had moved much closer to that position in Cairo from which he was to begin his deepest involvement in the war and with the Arabs, Egypt and Zionism – all being interested parties in the balance of power centred on work at Cairo.

The scene was set for the work of the British agents in Cairo to form their networks, so that when Mark Sykes began setting up the Sykes-Picot Agreement, much of the information given him was checked and commented on by his ring of agents, in particular, Gilbert Clayton, who was Chief of Military Intelligence in Cairo, Reginald Storrs and also Gerald Fitzmaurice in Athens. One major event made the Cairo assignment, set up to work out an opposition to Turkish advances, even more important: the disaster at Gallipoli. In March 1915, the British and French navies attacked Turkish positions, but only small landings and beach-heads were won by British, French, Australian and New Zealand forces. This meant that thousands of men were trapped, held in isolated positions by the Turkish defence forces.

Sykes and the other British agents in Cairo, and T.E. Lawrence in his desert war against the Turks, found themselves intricately involved in the counter-resurgency against Turkey – a process that would entail sabotage, open battle and espionage across a theatre of war that was vast. Reginald Wingate, governing Sudan, made his position clear on the issue of Arab government. He wanted Sherif Hussain to be Caliph, and all efforts to be made by British elements to support him and try to bring about unity across Arabia. In late 1915, Mark Sykes had his own ideas, and his momentous work in Cairo was just about to begin. What was about to happen was, in the words of Polly Mohs, in her book *Military Intelligence and the Arab Revolt* (2008), 'the first modern intelligence war'. This was the aim of Sykes and Clayton, who gathered around them a group of agents who could not only use codes, translate obscure languages, encourage sabotage, ascertain what the enemy were up to, and supply information to both the HQ in Cairo and the War Office. The world in general knows only of Lawrence of Arabia from this group. His *Seven Pillars of Wisdom* has always given the old-fashioned battle campaign element of the agents' work the centre stage. But the minor players are slowly becoming more known in popular history. Their work was extraordinarily successful. As Andrew Roberts noted, when reviewing Moh's book:

> Lawrence, a rather weedy looking twenty-six year old subaltern, in 1914 might have seemed a strange person for the British Empire to trust with the delicate task of raising the Hejaz only two years later. Yet with the kind of intelligence Mohs explains that he and his fellow agents were constantly receiving from the Arab bureau, his astonishing achievements are now wholly explicable.

Chapter 8

The Arab Bureau and the Sykes-Picot Agreement

In recent years there has been extensive renewed interest in the Arab Bureau, and though there has been much written on this intelligence network, Mark Sykes's part in it has been, in my opinion, undervalued. The Arab bureau was conceived originally by Mark Sykes. The genesis was a plan to have a centre for propaganda and counteraction against the Turks from Cairo. He wrote a memo headed *Constitution and Foundation of the Arab Bureau*, and tested his ideas and thoughts on a number of associates. It was intended to be a nerve centre for intelligence with regard to all important elements of British rule, as it could affect (and be affected by) the process of power in the Middle East. That meant that India would be a part of the network, and, of course, the Admiralty as well as the War Office.

When the top brass met and considered this, the idea was adopted, but not with Sykes at the head. The panel of advisers chose an archaeologist and scholar who knew the area, but rather differently from Mark. This was D.G. Hogarth, based in Oxford. The bureau was born, and of course, Mark was still there as an integral part of the outfit. They were housed in the Grand Continental Hotel in Cairo, with offices in the neighbouring Savoy. Intelligence had been led by Sir Gilbert Clayton and his successor, Henry McMahon, and when Hogarth took over, working with Clayton, he had the rank of lieutenant commander. The work of Ronald Storrs, diplomat and adventurer, was included, and he composed a rhyme that listed all the main personnel in the bureau:

'Do you know
The Arab bureau?'

Asked Hogarth, and answered:
'Clayton is stability,
Cornwallis is practical
Dawnay syntactical.
Mackintosh hovers
And Fielding palavers.
Macindoe is easy
And Wordie not breezy.
Lawrence licentiate to dream and to dare.
And yours very faithfully bon a tout faire.'

The name of Mark Sykes is missing, and the reason for this is that he was the one person who worked at a level comprehending the bureau and the leaders of the wider, international personages who would be important in the work – such as the Arab leaders, the French, the Russians and indeed the Indian spy ring. The latter is not well known, but in fact, before the Arab Bureau was in place, a group of Indian spies working for the British were in Egypt, being sent there on a mission by Hakim Nuruddin, a doctor and court physician at Kashmir. Hakim worked with British political officers in the Raj from 1870, when he arranged for spies to travel to Tashkent and find out what diplomacy was going on regarding the Russians. In fact, William Robertson knew of their activities. Hakim worked with Amar Singh, who was working in secret with the British Resident in Kashmir. The administration of the Kashmiri lands was, in 1889, in the hands of Amar Singh, Ram Singh and the British. Then, in 1908, when the Zionist activists were openly against Turkish forces, a volatile situation developed which threatened the stability of the Suez Canal and the surrounding land. In 1912 Hakim sent his spies to Arabia; Mirza Mahmud led the group and was joined by others in Jedda. These men were communicating with the Sharif of Mecca at the same time as Mark Sykes. The Indians went under cover of being religious missionaries.

All this thickens the atmosphere in which Sykes began his work. But he never lost sight of the fundamental objective of securing Egypt. Some historians and biographers have misunderstood his attitudes and achievements, depicting him as a short-tempered aristocrat used to throwing his weight around and riddled with prejudice. As with Lawrence, he has been seen as a strong and eccentric individual who had his own vision for a settlement with the Arabs and other interested parties in Egypt. But the fact is that the Arab Bureau was very well organised and had a number of very talented people working in its ranks. Lawrence founded a journal, the *Arab Bulletin*, first in print in 1916, to give information on all aspects of the cultural and political context.

The setting for what was to become the Sykes–Picot Agreement of 1916 is best understood in terms of the progress of the First World War. By 1915, Britain was busy with troops and naval personnel in the Suez, the Dardanelles, Aden, Mesopotamia and Persia. After the failure of the landing in the Dardanelles, and the setbacks which happened in Mesopotamia, Lord Kitchener realised that a different policy was required to keep on top of the situation in Egypt. In short, if there were any more reverses in the field, Britain could lose the Suez Canal to Turkey. The Arab bureau therefore, with Lawrence as the principal man in the field, as it were, had the task of organising subversion, guerrilla war and the formation of fighting units from many different sources, to create a counterattack by multiple means. Sykes was a key player in this, as may be seen from his correspondence with London, and with a number of important figures in the bureau in the year 1915. On 4 October that year he wrote to Sir Robert Cecil at the Foreign Office about the formation of the Arab Bureau, presenting a critique of the whole situation, listing the failures in intelligence as they had previously been orchestrated. He put the emphasis on poor communication:

> This, let me say, is the fault of no individual but the result of our traditional way of letting various officers run their own shows. (1) The Dardanelles expedition is not in close touch with Egypt. (2) Egypt is not in touch with the Ibn Saad question which is run from Mesopotamia. (3) The Indian government regards the Mesopotamia question from a purely Indian point of view, and not as an imperial question. (4) The Persian littoral of the Gulf is divided between the Indian political and the Foreign Office. Now, this has grown up in the course of history.

Ibn Saad, or Ibn Saud, was a rival to Hussein, father of Feisal, later King of Iraq, and he had threatened to disintegrate any chance of a united Arab revolt by taking an army of 7,000 armed men with him to Mecca that year. In other words, the Arab unity and the work of achieving that, as told famously in Lawrence's classic, *Seven Pillars of Wisdom*, was becoming a central issue for the Arab Bureau as plans for a settlement and defeat of the Turks were in progress.

Sykes became more and more adept at providing information and intelligence advice as the bureau gathered momentum. He discussed the concept of the bureau with Percy Cox, the political officer in Baghdad, after suggesting that one man should take a lead role and have two advisers to work with him. Sykes then added, 'The existence of the bureau should be kept a secret and each member should have an ostensible appointment, as has our intelligence officer in Athens. On this last matter I should like to have your opinion a.s.a.p.'

At a Cabinet Meeting on 16 December 1915, what was to be the Sykes-Picot Agreement was conceived. At that meeting were Asquith, Kitchener, Lloyd George and Arthur Balfour. The 'evidence of Lieutenant-Colonel Mark Sykes Bart. MP was heard on the Arab question' at that meeting. He had been with the Mesopotamian field force for eight weeks previously. At that crucial meeting, Sykes wanted this special addendum to be printed: 'I am of the opinion that passive defence of Egypt, with its natural sequences, will necessitate the eventual despatch to India and Egypt of a larger number of troops than under the scheme of building up in Egypt now a force capable of offensive action.' This meant, in effect, that Sykes had a plan for creating a regiment to go quickly into action, recruited in India. Reading between the lines, it is not impossible that he had been in liaison with Hakim's spies.

At that meeting, there was a first statement of the map that would later define the Agreement. At that point, Sykes envisaged the stretch of land from Damascus in the north to an area south of Bethlehem being organised into four maps, the second map being land covering the Holy Places – Jerusalem with its focal religious centres of the Jewish, Islamic and Christian faiths. But on his return to Cairo, the everyday communications of the Arab Bureau continued. In his papers, for instance, there are many short and cryptic notes from agents, such as a note on one Ormsby Goss: 'I have now definitely ascertained that there is no intention of entrusting any mission to the gentleman named in this paper.' The voluminous files and papers in the Sykes archive give ample evidence that he was a vital member of not simply one but several rings, having connections in espionage as well as open, public diplomacy. Ronald Storrs, so often a part of the bureau's activities, reports a typical example of the kind of mission when he writes of going to take a large sum of cash to the Suez. He comments: 'In accordance with his Excellency the High Commissioner's instructions, I left Cairo at 6.15 p.m. on 28 May, 1916, accompanied by D.G. Hogarth and Captain Cornwallis, and taking with me £60,000 in gold.'

Sykes was working at the heart of an atmosphere buzzing with the excitement of conducting both a war of subversion and an intelligence support network for counter-activity, particularly on the destruction of

Turkish railway lines. The product of all of this was a series of Arab bureau reports, and in a typical example from April 1917, we have an intelligence report from the Hejaz, the area on the western fringe of Arabia, stretching from the Gulf of Aqaba to Jizan, and containing the holy places of Mecca and Medina. Part of this report summarises some of the results of Sykes's efforts to produce irregular forces against the Turks:

> The Arabs, on their side, have been unable, owing to transport and supply difficulties, to maintain forces near enough to the line to keep communications cut continuously. On April 11 we heard that two of Feisal's lieutenants, Mirzuk and Sharif Mastur, had destroyed 1,200 metres of permanent way north of Medain Salih station.

Behind this had been the creation of what was called a composite army – something first envisaged by Sykes and described in 1915. In June 1917, it was accounted for in these terms: 'It would be valuable if steps were taken to raise an Arab legion from prisoners of war in Syria and Egypt.' By 27 May, Major Wood had been busy on that and wrote to Sykes that the recruits were to be paid fifteen rupees a month, with £5 to be paid on termination. The reasons for the irregular outfit were summarised: they would provide a reason for Syrian and Arab unity, the force would give a rallying-point for deserters, and they could potentially be a force capable of being used anywhere in the Hejaz, and have no European troops in the ranks. Of course, they would almost certainly have had British N.C.O's, as that body of men were used for all kinds of duties, even as official escorts on certain undercover missions.

The Arab legion developed into something grander. Sykes listed some new aspects of the force at that time, including the stipulation that they were only raised to help the Arab cause against Turkey, that they had to be conceived under Anglo-French auspices, controlled by the British along with the King in the Hejaz, and were only to be in action in Arabic-speaking cultures. By 2 June 1917, there was a force ready to move, and there was an order from London to mobilise a complementary force: 'Please send Arab officers and men to Egypt without further explanation. They can decide on the arrival here ... and will take service with the Arab Legion.' In addition, the command at Baghdad wrote to say that officers and 117 men would be despatched to Bombay where more men were being raised. There were requests from various quarters for recruitment to take place in P.O.W. camps, and at the planning stage, Maurice Hankey, a secretary to the War Cabinet, was 'stirring up the right authorities about all the suggestions in your letter'.

At the centre of all Sykes' work in these years was the Sykes-Picot Agreement of May 1916. Mark had been liaising with Francois-Georges Picot, a diplomat of many years experience, in order to come to some agreement about the political geography of Arabia and the borderlands with Turkey and Russia, with the assumption that the allies would win the war and defeat the Turks, of course. Because of that fact, it needed to be secret. Unfortunately, the Russians found out about the deal, and enjoyed propaganda about the untrustworthy British, who had been carving up the Arabian land. France was involved because it had a long-standing claim on Syria, bordering on Arabia. The Maronites (a Syrian-Christian church) in Lebanon had been under French protection since 1860, and there had been a prominent French cultural and educational presence in Syria for many years.

The Sherif of Mecca allied with Britain in order to defeat the Turks and establish a new Arab state with himself at the head. Britain backed the independent Arab state in the 1916 Agreement. In addition, the zone with the Holy Places of the main religions had to be treated as a separate case, excluded from political and military control by any party. Russia agreed to the Arab state in principle, after reading the text. The map following the Agreement was composed of five zones:

The Blue Zone, to the north, came under complete French control.
The 'A' Zone, south of that, and covering Damascus, came under French influence again.
The 'B' Zone, under British influence, stretched from Egypt to Kirkuk close to the Persian border.
The Red Zone was basically Mesopotamia, with Baghdad and Basra.
The International Zone – where the Holy Places were placed – was effectively Jerusalem and environs.
Arabia was south of the two British zones.

Important details for Britain were mainly that she had the right to 'build, administer and be sole owner of a railway connecting Haifa with area (b) and would have a perpetual right to transport troops at any time.' Also, that there was to be a joint British and French accord that they would resist any third power acquiring land in this designated area.

Naturally, the Agreement has had any number of criticisms. The most immediate problem for Sykes was to reassure Hussein that France was not a threat to the aspirations of the Arab unity. The Agreement also left unanswered questions about Palestine, about the future of Mesopotamia and, of course, with no specific detail on the Holy Places Zone. Both Sykes and Picot left the topic of Palestine on the margins, with no clear idea of its political situation. It was simply designated a place for international administration. It was agreed at Whitehall, though, that there would have to be concessions to the French in order to make any progress.

With regard to the workings of intelligence, though, by 1916 there were all kinds of decisions made, and practical actions taken, that would streamline all the necessary work done by the Arab Bureau. As well as the bulletins issued giving topographical information, there were important achievements in progress, such as the interception of wireless signals between the Turkish HQ (in Damascus) and their men in Medina, under siege. There was also sabotage in all kinds of situations, and we know a lot about these, along with notions of a propaganda war from Sykes and others.

The threat of the Turco-German railway was considered very serious to all plans; intelligence reports to the War Cabinet were thorough and often detailed. Hejaz intelligence notes gave minute accounts of what was being done by the Turks to try to keep on top of the sabotage missions in which Lawrence was involved. One report noted: 'The Turks have organised railway repair patrols, and gangs of workers are remaking the line. None of the Arab raids has caused more than a very brief stoppage of either transport or telegraph connections.' An agent called Kemeid was the first to fully understand the real threat of the rail. He gained information from a German agent, and notes testify to the efficiency of the Arab Bureau's wide reach across a variety of contacts at the time.

There was also the diplomatic work for which Sykes had a real flair. One example of this is his ability to organise the work done in a range of key posts in the network. The status and function of the political officer in the French Commission is a good example. Sykes spelled out the role: 'The Chief Political Officer will act as adviser to the G.O.C. on political relations with native elements in the theatre of operations of the G.O.C. in Egypt, beyond the Egyptian frontier', and 'The Chief Political officer will keep the French commissioner apprised of any negotiations which the military or political officers with the Mesopotamian force may enter into communication with active elements in Area A.' Sykes was constantly switching roles and making new contacts while at the same time keeping all established contacts happy and busy.

One of the most impressive aspects of Sykes' spymastering is the sheer quantity of secondary information acquired and preserved in the records of his years in Cairo. He was, for more than a year after the Agreement with

Picot, still busy with all interested parties, including Zionists and French religious figures. As this was going on, he was also playing his part in selecting men for particular work or discussing candidates for intelligence work. In April 1917, for instance, a memo from the Foreign Office informed Mark that Billie Gore came to see a special person every Thursday with the 'Eastern Report'. The same writer confides that he 'Consulted CIGS about young Rodd as a liaison officer and he wanted Talnot's opinion as to his suitability, so we are telegraphing Wingate accordingly.' At that date Wingate had become governor-general of the Sudan, and in 1913 he had started a massive irrigation plan. He had Slatin still working with him, and of course, when war broke out, his opinion was valued in Whitehall on all matters of Middle Eastern intelligence and geopolitics. He played a vital part in the Arab Revolt by supplying Sharif Hussein with cash and supplies; he occupied the sultanate of Darfur in 1916 and, despite the shudders of war to the north, the Sudan remained excluded from the action. In the broader picture of the First World War, men in power were taking sides as either 'Westerners' or 'Easterners'. That is to say, as the battles in France on the Western Front intensified, the Eastern Front, in which the forces of Germany and the allies had the advantage of Turkey to the east for a range of support systems, became extremely volatile and complex, hence the need for intelligence to exploit previous knowledge of the terrain, such as Sykes had gathered on his travels and envoys. William Robertson was a 'Westerner' – wanting to keep all energies and resources on the Western Front, considering that if that were won, the Eastern questions could wait and be more easily settled in the face of that newly won power.

Sykes' work went on, and in May 1917 he put together his thoughts on the 'Arab question' for his superiors at home, and to pass on his opinion on the Emir Faisal's plans. His general view on policy was summarised like this:

a. Recognition of the principle of Arab racial independence in those Turkish territories which rightly belong to the various branches of the Arab race.
b. As a step towards the ultimate object of securing Arab unity.
c. 'The support of all friendly independent Arab chiefs and political organisations by the Entente, the promotion of mutual friendship and co-operation between them, and the settlements of all outstanding feuds and disagreements.

In May 1917, he wrote to Clayton on Feisal's plans, with plenty of good news, including a certainty that Feisal was raiding the railway between Damascus and Deraa, working from the land of the Jebel Druse, and that he was also raiding in Homs and Hama. Feisal had also formed a regular force by enlisting and enrolling deserters. A major part of Sykes' work in this context was in braising local tribesmen as allies. There is a somewhat idealistic and desperate tone to his notes in June that year when he says, 'Aden should be liquidated and the Turkish force at Lachej destroyed.'

We know a lot about the practicalities of military action as planned by Sykes and the officers in the field, and a good case study of this is the report by Pirie-Gordon concerning Ayas Bay. As the British expeditionary force in Mesopotamia was advancing up the River Tigris, a landing of forces at Ayas Bay would have been a definite threat to Turkish communications across Mesopotamia. Sykes was, as usual, involved, and Pirie-Gordon wrote to him with this in mind, although he also planned to form an offensive against the Baghdad Railway. He asserted that Ayas Bay was the only viable base of operations for such a plan, and that the landing facilities were good. He argued that the nearest point from the landing at Ayas Bay was near the road to Chelemli and another road to Dede Dagh, both around twenty miles away. The scheme was to land and make trenches at Bittern Point, then to use motorcyclist- and even cyclist-raiders. The Royal Cycle Corps had been used in Greece, for instance, and had been tried and tested recently. Pirie-Gordon wrote: 'Cyclist-raiders will be able to operate over a wide area and will do much to mystify the enemy and to cut his telegraph wires.' Pirie-Gordon even suggested the use of Ford cars with machine guns.

This invites a certain degree of scepticism, and conjures up images of Dad's Army, but in effect, the Arab Bureau was always interested in both propaganda and experimental warfare in an ancillary capacity. Pirie-Gordon knew that the Turks had kept up a coastal patrol along Alexandretta (the expected place of landing). In fact, an agent had been landed there already – a certain 'monocular Armenian, known to Mr Joseph Catoni, who was successfully landed and then removed from that area in February, 1915. It was planned that the Armenian would 'arrange with his friends to cut the wires extensively in all directions.'

The whole Ayas Bay business was meticulously considered, but it was destined not to happen. In enlightening the modern reader on how the intelligence staff around Sykes worked, it is a valuable case study. The agents knew that mines had been laid, and they planned a spot for an airfield for anti-submarine seaplanes. The element of desperation creeps in when we read that 'One of the tugs at Mersina is reported to be owned by a German-speaking Swiss, but the owner can have no present use for it as the port is blockaded.'

The information for Ayas Bay was detailed, and Sykes, with others and in between planning an attack on the Palestine Railway, worked out the actions at Ayas:

1   Arrival of naval party at Jeihan
2   Boat party up Jeiha River to Bebeli and motorcyclists set out
3   Armed Armenians from gun-boats
4   Landing of troops on western and central beaches at Ayas Bay
5   Landing of stores
6   Attack by sea and land on Karatach
7   Establishment of seaplane base
8   Advance to occupy Bebeli-Burnaz line and attack Missis
9   Land troops at Burnaz
10   Sea raids on Alexandretta

By 1918, Sykes turned to give attention to the domestic scene. He had been in Cairo, integral to the Arab Bureau and other related organisations, and a figure at the very heart of the War Cabinet functions, for three years. As a spymaster, he and his colleagues in Cairo had achieved astounding things, and he was understandably a 'sadder but wiser man'.

CHAPTER 9

ROBERTSON AND INTELLIGENCE
AFTER THE BOERS

At the death of Queen Victoria in 1901, military intelligence and espionage had changed radically since the years when the Great Game was at its peak and individual officers could range across vast unknown tracts of land in the East. The problem of Russia was still there, as was the Middle Eastern question. But another set of threats and uncertainties tormented the War Office by the first Edwardian years. These were the growth of the German navy, the Fenian bombings and anarchist trouble at home in England. The police had adapted to some of these things, slowly developing a sophisticated detective branch which had a special branch for Irish affairs and home security. But the army had to change as well.

The situation with our principal spymasters at that time was that Wingate and Slatin were in the Sudan, keeping it free from unrest and separatist movements; Ardagh had given evidence to the Elgin Commission as it compiled its report on intelligence in the Anglo-Boer War, and charges had been made. These were mainly that it failed to correctly assess the numerical strength of the Boers; it was ignorant of their armament, in particular their artillery; it had not understood the Boers' offensive plans on Natal; and that no warnings concerning these matters had been given to the government. These were responded to in the Statement of the Intelligence Division, and the important defence statements against the charges were that at the centre of the issue was the fact that the Free State and Transvaal were likely to join forces should a war have arisen. This statement made the point that opinions about that union were not in accord with intelligence information in 1896. Ardagh had written in that year that an assumption must be made that both states were hostile. He had written a memo for the War Office in 1899 making it absolutely clear that it was a 'practical certainty' that the Free State would officially join hands with Transvaal, should a war take place. Given that, there was no way that the intelligence personnel at that time could have ascertained the number of burghers in both states who would have done military service, nor any way the number actually bearing arms at the beginning of the war could have been calculated. With hindsight, we can see that it had not been in the mindset of the Intelligence Office at the time to indulge in the kind of espionage that would have meant undercover work within the Boer bureaucracy in order to try to ascertain statistics of the kind required.

Regarding the armaments of the enemy, intelligence described the 'Long Tom' guns in some notes published in 1898, but these notes had been obtained by the enemy and so lost all effect. The Intelligence Department had known that three of these large guns were in place at Langs Nek, where Britain suffered a severe defeat. But the most substantial defence for Ardagh was that his predictions about Boer movements and aspirations, made in 1899, were proven to be correct. Earlier, in 1896 and 1897, Ardagh had compiled and sent reports on *Transvaal Forces from a Military Point of View*, and several letters on specific topics. These and other materials made it clear, after the war, that there had been a large number of accurate and useful reports made in those years.

However, the debate went on and the mapping controversy, discussed in chapter five, added to the stress of all concerned in having to answer the criticisms. Ardagh left his post of Director of Military Intelligence in May 1901, but still remained involved in a number of matters such as the committee on submarine telegraphs. He was also active in the Red Cross movement, and in the decisions regarding the administration of the Suez Canal. He died in 1907 at Glynllivon. This was his final verdict on the intelligence work of the Boer War:

> I see no reasons whatever to admit any error in the statistics and predictions which we made, and their correctness has been tardily acknowledged in Parliament. The defence all through has been most creditable to the Boers, and has brought into prominence the great advantage which modern weapons confer in the defence in general. The man in possession is better off than he ever was before: as indeed Makefing and Kimberley have shown on our side.

That statement has the awful resonance of hard truth, when we consider the trench warfare that followed just a few years after his death. Much of the reverberations regarding intelligence around the year 1902–03 were concerned with the question of how to cope with military intelligence operations in the future, with lessons learned on how to rationalise intelligence in the domestic context. It was all to be sorted out by the War Office, with William Robertson in the new intelligence establishment, a man who had served in the South African conflict and knew the issues well. He was on intelligence duties at the War Office from 1902–07, and was part of a new organisation.

The War Office in general was reorganised in 1903 after a committee reported on new plans. The main reforms included a commission composed of a permanent secretary, two naval officers, two military officers, two Indian officers and one or more members from the colonies. On top of that there was to be an Army Council with a permanent under-secretary. Within the new Army Council there were four military members, and one of these had intelligence responsibilities. William Robertson worked there, with the Chief of the General Staff. The structure of the new Intelligence Division included two quartermaster-generals (Robertson and Altham – both Boer War veterans) and three sub-divisions: strategical and colonial defence, foreign and India, and executive, telegraphy and special duties.

Robertson was in the division responsible for the main European countries and America. The principal staff totalled forty-three, with Robertson as one of three assistant directors. Robertson came to be most concerned with Russia and France. He had a good working knowledge of French, and his work on the North West frontier had given him some knowledge of the Russian element in the Great Game. He was working with the two nations, however, at a time when peaceful resettlement in diplomacy was wanted by all concerned. Although Russia had expanded steadily eastwards over the past forty years, it was open knowledge that on the borderlands there was free and easy communication between British officers and their Russian counterparts. The explorer and soldier, Francis Younghusband, had been active in the borderlands of Russia for some time. Lord Curzon, Viceroy of India, wrote to Younghusband in 1904 that it was necessary to admit that Russian influence was everywhere in nations such as Tibet. He pointed out to Younghusband that the British frontier had been trespassed and that there were Russian guns in Lhasa. It seems clear, therefore, that Robertson was not entirely without a few worries regarding his responsibilities on Russian affairs.

In 1906 Robertson was Assistant Director of Operations, and most of his attention was given to collecting, preparing and communicating various items of information on boundaries and frontiers. But it cannot be underestimated now, with the gift of hindsight, how much the British mindset was one of preparation for war. The nation was intensely militaristic at every level, and diplomacy, together with the new alliances being planned across Europe, was making it clear that the theory of war, and therefore the necessity of intelligence information in every context, was essential. The days of leisurely aristocratic visits to shipyards were becoming a thing of the past, and new espionage networks were being established more widely than ever. Robertson had said, in a talk he gave, 'History ... shows in what hopeless position any nation may one day be if it neglects to make due preparation for war.' Robertson took up the old war game of Kriegspiel, looking into a hypothetical conflict, based on the 1870 war, involving France and Germany. This was merely a part of a whole cultural fascination with military theory. The academics were sounding off in the columns of *The Times* on the nature of war; journalists were making visits to the Middle East and India, passing opinions on the state of the army. The professionals, like Robertson, therefore had to be assertive and practical, as well as indulging his interests in Kriegspiel.

Victor Bonham-Carter, Robertson's first biographer, sums up Robertson's ability well: 'He was a man who always knew what he wanted when working up to any question. He went direct to the point.' If we add to that what he had learned in the Intelligence Branch, both at Simla and at home thirty years before, we may see that his ability for doing research (in many languages) and in classifying information, was combined with a zeal for directness and definition of terms in all communication. With this in mind, it must not be forgotten that Robertson and Altham were taking over at a time when the embarrassments and recriminations about the supposed failures of intelligence in the South African War had caused the entire concept of military intelligence to be called in question. Add to that the exigencies of a new naval intelligence, springing from the strange anomalies of Britain's former close diplomatic and indeed Royal links with the new Germany of Kaiser Wilhelm, and we have a very delicate situation, both in the problem of assuring the public about the competence of intelligence work in war and also in repairing our image overseas.

The Committee of Imperial Defence, in 1909, faced up to the possibility of there being a German spy ring in England, and that, combined with fears about the difficulties of coping with the immense costs involved in maintaining a home fleet and an imperial fleet, made domestic intelligence organisation a more pressing matter. Robertson was still very much concerned with international issues, and it was becoming increasingly obvious to the members of the department that there were interconnections beginning to emerge between both – the anarchists in London for instance, were there because of radical political change in Russia, and bombers from Ireland were similarly politicised with a mindset of being imperial subjects, oppressed and denigrated.

Robertson's memoirs make it clear that he saw the shortcomings of sources and material very quickly. He notes that there were some confidential handbooks, mainly done from newspapers, relating to the strength of foreign armies, but he saw these as merely elementary, and saw that more complete information was essential. But it has to be recalled that he was now working in a much larger outfit, and so there was more information coming through, and from different sources. He was always against amateurism, as one anecdote he wrote about shows:

> I remember a military attaché at one of the European capitals who, regarded by the other attaches as a favourable target for practical jokes, sent us a map, under every precaution of secrecy, in the way of sealing-wax and red tape, showing the peace distribution of a certain army which he stated had been given to him confidentially by a friend. Incredible as it may seem, the price of the map and the name of its continental distributor were printed at the bottom.

In the Anglo-Boer War, Robertson had been in the thick of the dissension over intelligence, as well as in the action. He notes that virtually every day there was a need to answer questions about armament and about economic factors such as cotes on coaling stations. It was gradually realised as the war progressed that Britain had been in a position too weak to have started that conflict with any real sense of certainty about resources and manpower. Robertson wrote that from the start, with an awareness of trouble brewing in the Transvaal, he and Altham, a man described by Boer War historian Thomas Pakenham as 'the short-sighted, elderly major who had written that Intelligence Department booklet, *Military Notes*' were to work together. We have conflicting views of Altham, as Robertson recalls him as a quick worker who had a good knowledge of the country. Pakenham depicts him as incompetent: he notes that Altham's booklet suggested that the enemy would make rapid raids and then admit defeat after one main battle. But Altham was still partnering Robertson in the new 1902 department, so someone in high office thought a lot about him.

Robertson had stayed in the Colonial Section after Altham was posted to join Sir George White in Natal. What happened, and this was a factor in the ultimate perceived failure of intelligence in this war, was that a number of parties offered advice and theories to the powers in the field, and these, in Robertson's words, were 'amateur prescriptions'. In other words, ideas and plans were broached in sedate meetings by men who had no real knowledge of how something could be done, in the face of a real war – one that was getting tougher every day, throughout 1899, as the *modus operandi* of both combatants changed.

Robertson makes a very important point with regard to intelligence work in that war. This was the preparation of reports to the War Cabinet, and indeed to Victoria herself. It was virtually impossible to find data on the numbers of enemy troops in their movements, and the same thing that had happened in the Crimea happened again: an at times reliance on war correspondents. He found himself explaining strategy and common sense with regard to the triple sieges of Mafeking, Ladysmith and Kimberly, as was the situation early in 1899. This throws light on what tended to happen with intelligence staff when explanations were needed by diplomats or by politicians at home. He argued against the view that Ladysmith should be relinquished so that the other two could be reinforced and retrieved.

In 1902, then, Robertson could look back with mixed feelings on his participation in the war. But one thing he and his old teacher, Henderson, did do that was a wonderful achievement was a ruse designed to give the Boers the wrong information about a point of attack. This was in February 1900, and the aim was to let the enemy think that the attack would be made at Norval's Point, a bridge held by the enemy, close to the British HQ based at Colesberg. Robertson and Henderson conducted a phoney war, and created false communications, with everything kept hush-hush and only a few officers being fully informed. It worked smoothly and would have been seen through fully had it not been for the G.O.C., Lord Roberts, who changed the overall plans for the area.

Robertson was fully aware, in 1901, that the Committee for Imperial Defence was being conceived, and his work was composite to that idea. The committee was properly formed in 1904, and a treasury minute of 4 May 1904 states that the purpose was to 'collect and co-ordinate … information bearing on the wide problem of Imperial Defence.' It had no executive functions, but its meetings and conclusions were of genuine value to both the War Office and the Admiralty. There is no doubt, then, that Sir William Robertson, in his third major period of participation in intelligence work, had been a crucially important player in three significant episodes in the growth of military intelligence between 1870 and 1905. He had seen service in the field at Chitral, with the Pamirs; he had been in

South Africa as a peripheral figure close to the Wolseley 'ring', and finally, by 1902, he was in the first Intelligence Branch of the new century. In fact, he was one of the few people who had witnessed the emergence of both internal and external intelligence work, and both on the fringes of Empire and on the domestic front.

Chapter 10

Epilogue: MI5 and Spies

What about the inheritance of men such as Robertson and Ardagh, who had operated on planes of sheer complexity, with a heady mixture of amateur and professional information sources, and a world of intelligence in which a truly streamlined, fully comprehensive department existed? What was the result of Robertson and Altham's days in the 1902 office? In short, fear and paranoia stepped in, and something radical was steadily achieved.

It is difficult to avoid sharing in Sir William Robertson's sense of a new beginning in his memoirs covering the first years of the new century when he writes of the new Intelligence Branch. To his mind, the organisation was to be in the hands of the great military men who had finally triumphed in South Africa, and who had been dealing with the affair in Chitral and with the last throes of trouble in the Sudan; men like Lord Roberts and Kitchener of Khartoum. But in fact there were influences bearing on the renewal of intelligence organisation and theory from much more universal sources.

This was due to radical changes in the balance of power and in the rise of the German Empire. The origins of what was to become first the special intelligence bureau, and later MI5, are in a meeting of a subcommittee of the Committee of Imperial Defence. Captain Vernon Kell, of the South Staffordshire Regiment, was on that panel, and he was one of many who heard a comment that day about a German spy in England. The man who related the tale of a spy called Steinhauer commented that the spy menace could not really be combated because of a shortage of men available who could be there to do such work in the domestic arena. It seems almost a piece of bumbling amateurism now, but a short discussion led to the suggested formation of a special unit to do what would be later called counter-espionage. Since the turn of the century, a war with Germany seemed more and more likely, and the committee, together with the cabinet, was aware that adaptations were going to be necessary. At this point no-one was really aware that Germany, via Admiral von Tirpitz and the German Admiralty, were accelerating the level and effectiveness of a German spy network, far more determinedly than desultory talk about Steinhauer might have suggested. Moreover, when the plan was approved, and it was agreed that there should be such a thing as a counter-espionage unit in England, it was soon realised that no-one had considered what kind of personnel would do such a thing.

A profound influence on this indecision and uncertainty about espionage was the nature of the military mindset in the imperial phase. The wars of the Empire, both large and small, had been in the hands of men who conceived of soldiering and battle as aspects of brave and honourable behaviour: a code of courage and army operations inextricably bound up with the concept of gentlemanly attitudes and respect for conservative values. Therefore, in that context, the idea of spying on enemy dockyards or gun placements was something outside the lines of thought of many. Germany had inherited the same values, entrenched in Prussian militarism, and both countries had to cope with the nature of counter-espionage. The notion of military intelligence in the field was a very different animal: it could be integrated into general army structures and absorbed without being seen as anything new and innovative. After all, Wolseley had proved that it was all a matter of having a staff who could ascertain information about the enemy and about the terrain involved in the theatre of war.

But there was so much literature and so much media coverage on the work done by spies that it was being accepted as a legitimate line of work for a soldier. Captain Kell was observed at that meeting as a likely candidate to lead the new branch. After the decision was approved, the two senior men in intelligence at the meeting, General Sir Fraser Davies and Colonel James Edmonds, turned their attention to Kell. Edmonds said, 'What about you, Kell?' And from that moment it was left to Kell to take a few days to think it over. He was accustomed to changes of responsibility, and, indeed, to location, in his army career, because his skill as a linguist and diplomat had made such moves possible. But this was totally different, and he mentioned some objections: mainly his lack of experience in that and in administration within the government structure. The panel still thought he would be suitable and he was given more time to consider.

The doyen of military theory, Edmonds, described the nature of the new post. It would be secret, and its actions covert. Although such work would entail a complete volte-face in his military career, even to the point of being in plain clothes, it attracted him and he made the decision to accept after his wife and family had expressed support. It was soon in process, beginning with an office within the bureaucratic corridors of government, and directed to liaise with Scotland Yard. The Yard had had its Special Branch (originally the Special Irish Branch during the Fenian troubles) since 1888, and had become increasingly cosmopolitan. They had been watching Lenin and Trotsky, for instance, since their arrival in London just after 1900, and Herbert Finch, a superbly efficient linguist, had proved that espionage was possible in a dramatic way by hiding in a cupboard to listen to Russian émigrés talking.

There was Kell, with no staff and a strong suggestion that he should work with the Yard, initially merely gathering any information he considered to be useful either at present or in the future, with Germany and German connections top of his list. He had the highly experienced Melville to work with, and though he did not realise it at the time, he was going to be a crucially important part of that new world of pre-war preparations and military revolution that was to be energised partly by the Official Secrets Act of 1911, but also by the Agadir Crisis of 1911 when a German gunboat off that Moroccan port forced politicians to resolve a dispute over what the British Army was to do in various parts of the world in the event of war with Germany. But for the time being, Kell's immediate concerns were to have some help, particularly in the clerical line.

He was working with the director of military operations as his line manager, who was Major-General Ewart then; Kell's demand for help was reluctantly listened to, and he was given a secretary, with the reminder that there was a limited budget behind his activities. But by 1910 everything had changed. With the support of Major-General Henry Wilson, Kell was seen as someone of increasing usefulness and importance, and cash began to come his way. His hard work had paid off. He was given more staff. First, Captain Stanley Clark, and then others, including Melville, who had been permanently drafted in from the Yard. The new department's priority was to be defined and understood. Their role and responsibilities had to be disseminated throughout all the arms of the services and diplomacy so that the establishment would become aware of their existence. Kell's men went to talk to staff in a range of departments covering the police and the ancillary services. Even such bodies as the coastguard and the port authorities would be important in what was to come.

After the expansion of the department and the increase in staff, a pattern of work began to emerge that was to become exactly what readers of spy stories would have expected: officers were detailed to trail and observe suspects at any place in the land where reports had been made. Spying really was becoming undercover, and impinging on traditional detective skills. Work done against anarchists and Fenians was proving to be very useful.

It is important at this juncture to understand something of Vernon Kell, the man who was at the centre of what was to become MI5. He was born in Great Yarmouth in 1873, and his father was a distinguished soldier who had seen service in the Zulu wars. On his mother's side he had Polish blood, as she was the daughter of a Polish count, and that fact, together with the private education he received before entering Sandhurst, probably explains why he was such a proficient linguist. He enlisted in the South Staffordshire Regiment (his father's) and his language skills and exceptional abilities in the more diplomatic duties of soldiering took him to postings in Russia and China, where he played his part in the Boxer Rebellion reprisals. His early years in a cosmopolitan milieu clearly became a profound asset as he grew older.

Back in England, it was as he began his service as a staff captain in the War Office that his destined career as a spymaster became possible. He had always had an element of restlessness and terrific ambition. When in Shanghai (and newly married) he had served with Colonel Dorward in Tientsin, and in that campaign Kell had been mentioned in Despatches. During the Boxer troubles, one aspect of his character came out. There was a rumour that the besieged troops in Peking had given in and the resistance failed. Kell did not give in to pressure to send reports to that effect, and his restraint was to prove right. There was no truth in the rumour. Obviously, his talents attracted senior staff, and he was assigned to General Lorne Campbell's staff in Tientsin as an intelligence officer.

Another valuable learning experience for young Kell came during an episode when he was posted to the remote Shanhaikuan, in northern China, close to the Russian border. Here he came to understand the importance of Manchuria to those two great powers: he was in close contact with a Russian officer called Ignatieff, and spent time usefully making notes on the nature of the Russian presence there. This was followed by some time in Moscow, where he added Russian to his language repertoire. When a serious illness struck him his travels ended and he was given the office job; but time spent travelling the world was to prove invaluable in his intelligence work at home.

As Kell established himself and his team in the War Office, developments in German espionage activities across Europe, in particular, to ascertain the real power and condition of the famous Royal Navy began to be felt. Statute law was changing with regard to protecting Britain's military establishment. There had been an Official Secrets Act in 1889 and it highlights an entirely new attitude to intelligence theory. Under that law, espionage was a version of high treason, and it stated that 'a foreigner convicted of espionage was liable to the same penalties as a native-born subject.' Much of the substance of that Act influenced the attitudes of the subcommittee on invasion – a group which had met no less than twenty-seven times between 1907 and 1908. What always appeared to be the basic reassurance of such groups was that British naval supremacy was beyond dispute and led to fears in the enemies of the land over the seas.

But in Royal Navy manoeuvres in 1908 there was a disturbing slowness and inefficiency with which the Territorial men had responded to a pretended German invasion and naturally this was all grist to the mill for those who considered a potential German threat of invasion to be something we could not combat. What was happening was the high command realised that the state needed to know what was happening in Germany regarding espionage. What was happening was that a section of the War Office with responsibility to know about Germany stated that there was an element of truth in the media panics about potential invasion. All this helped to initiate the beginnings of Kell's group. Therefore, even before Kell's new office and staff got to work, there had been a movement to strengthen the intelligence network, such as it was. The turning point was arguably with the appointment to Edmonds as Director of MO5, the first core personnel of what would become the true intelligence arm of the War Office.

At this point it is useful to recall that the part played by the Admiralty was always fruitful and the naval experience was constantly useful and constructive in these early preparations. After all, dockyards and naval technology had always been a priority for foreign powers. Now that Tirpitz and the other members of the German high command had decided that England was their real enemy, as opposed to France or Russia, the Royal Navy was their prime target in terms of gathering useful information regarding any future conflict. Before 1909, Edmonds, after much co-operation with the navy, had noted several acts of attempted espionage, notably forty-eight cases in 1908, and twenty-four in the first three months of 1909.

Admiral Alexander was Director of Naval Intelligence and he sat on the committee that appointed Kell. Knowledge of the German equivalent group was beginning to percolate into the consciousness of the men in power. At the centre of this were a group of dignitaries who were clearly trying to accelerate the move towards the creation of an intelligence community that would rival that of Germany. Their arguments were strengthened by world events, such as the assassination of Sir William Curzon-Wylie, aide-de-camp to Lord Morley, the Secretary of State for India, by a Punjabi student in Kensington. The pressure group included Winston Churchill, Lord Haldane and Ewart himself, Kell's superior and supporter. David Stafford has described Ewart as:

> A veteran of Tel-el-Kebir, Omdurman and the Boer War, since 1906 he had been in charge of strategic planning and intelligence. A sociable and well-connected Scot, he enjoyed a close relationship with Haldane, and they frequently dined together. Ewart was obsessed with espionage, both lamenting the lack of British spies abroad and deploring the presence of German spies in Britain. For much of the previous six months he had been laying plans for a new organisation.

That is, the group around the Committee for Imperial Defence had been waiting for the right time and right man to come along, and in Kell they found the leader they needed.

Churchill himself had been well aware of the need for the reform of intelligence within the army, certainly since the Boer War. He had been clamouring for reform before the end of that conflict, and in 1901 wrote that 'The whole Intelligence Service is starved for want of both money and brains.' In the House of Commons he confronted the estimates made by Sir John Broderick, the Secretary of State for War, on the costs of army reform, and he spelled out the advantages of reforming the Intelligence Branch. Lord Haldane's cousin, Aylmer, told Churchill that Germany had over 200 intelligence officers whereas England had around twenty. The pressure group needed a spokesman and it certainly had one in Churchill, who spoke of the need for 'an army of elasticity, so that comparatively small regular units in times of peace might be expanded into a great and powerful army in times of war.' He explained that for that to happen, what was needed was 'an efficient and well-staffed Intelligence Department.'

When it came to a diplomatic incident, such as the Agadir Crisis of 1911, other aspects of intelligence work became apparent. After visiting

London in May 1911, the Kaiser Wilhelm II stated that he intended to step in and claim a place in Morocco for Germany, responding to a revolt in Morocco in which tribesmen had forced French troops to move in and protect Tangiers. Germany thought the time was right to annexe a part of Morocco, and the Kaiser had a gunboat sent out there. Britain issued a challenge to that, embodied in a speech by Lloyd George in which he said, 'if a situation were to be forced upon us, in which peace could only be preserved by the surrender of the great and benevolent position Britain has won ... peace at that price would be intolerable for a great country like ours to endure'.

What this did do, in spite of Germany's withdrawal from confrontation, was create a cast of mind in the German naval command regarding future confrontation, and espionage was the first step in being prepared. The Kaiser supported a statement by Admiral von Heringen that a clash with Britain would be welcome, and German intelligence adapted to support this long-term aim. The man in charge, Tapken, started to plan actions that would lead to the Royal Navy being watched and monitored from close range, from within the land of Britain, with major ports as the first espionage targets.

In England, the writers of books on espionage were playing their part in the coming acceleration of the intelligence organisation. Erskine Childers' novel, *The Riddle of the Sands* (1903), concerns two yachtsmen who, while in the North Sea, accidentally come across naval war preparations at a place called Borkum. Childers envisaged a major plan of invasion, launched across the sea from Holland. Articles with titles such as *The Drama of the Missing Spy* and *Secrets of the French Foreign Office* were everywhere in the popular press, and, of course, the Dreyfus affair of 1894, followed by Emile Zola's famous essay, *J'Accuse*, in 1898, which opened up a whole new range of literature about spies and traitors in the popular media.

It was widely known that British sea power was still burgeoning, particularly when the development of the Dreadnought is considered. In 1905 Earl Cawdor became First Lord of the Admiralty; he had formerly been a major industrialist, and he was not First Lord for very long, but in his time in that position he and 'Jacky' Fisher had a stunning impact on the navy. Fisher suggested to Cawdor that the whole fleet should be redeployed. Cawdor relished the thought of being responsible for such an achievement, and however large the task, they both warmed to it. The main fleets were repositioned, with the Mediterranean Fleet based in Malta and the Channel Fleet at a range of home ports. As the Atlantic Fleet was to be in Gibraltar, there was a clear indication to Germany that

Britain was determined to retain a tight grip on key strategic positions for any confrontations that might occur – and the positioning of the fleets was in line with Napoleonic history, a fact of which the Germans would have been well aware.

Then Fisher set to work to create the Dreadnought – a new kind of battleship. The design for this advanced warship was done by Vittorio Cumberti who described and explained the potential of this innovation in sea power as if it were a creative as well as a warlike dream. In the standard work of Jane's *Fighting Ships for 1903* the template is there; clearly Fisher and Cawdor thought it was worth the investment. The accepted view was that turbine engines just would not work with very large ships, but whatever the points argued by all interested parties, the central fact that turbines would have to be used was a definite factor should plans go ahead. So ambitious was Fisher that he not only wanted the new ship to be built to his specifications, he wanted it ready inside a year – something thought impossible by many. But the first trials took place by the end of 1906. Results were impressive, in gun capabilities as well as in speed. The Dreadnought was made with the massive size of 17,900 tons; it could also fire huge shells of 850 pounds. The building of this new ship was a direct challenge to Germany. Could she equal that? She was certainly going to try, even widening the Kiel Canal, as the Germany corridor to the North Sea, in its current state, was not wide enough to accommodate something with the dimensions of a Dreadnought.

Of course, there was a lobby for peace, and so a restraining arm was applied, to the extent that Fisher and Cawdor's plans for building a series of Dreadnought ships were shelved for the time being. It was an indication that Britain was not war-mongering. A cynical view would be that all the great powers were playing for time, and that not only would more time give some space for building vehicles (and 'ironclads') and ships, but would also allow for the real contributions of intelligence activity to show through. There was the usual game of 'diplomatic chess', in which each government made promises not to build more murderous engines of war if the other would do likewise. But certainly the navy became the centre-stage interest; it was playing a vital role in the gradual militarism encroaching on all sides in British life and culture. The social historian, Anne Summers, has shown how this process happened and to just what extent the navy, by means of the Navy League, was prominent in these developments. The Navy League was founded in 1895, and its main objective was to press for an increase in the sheer manpower and strength of the Royal Navy. By 1914, the League had 100,000 members. Summers' research on the increasing militarism of the country leads to the presentation of huge figures of reservists and volunteers, and lends credence to Churchill's theory of fewer professional soldiers but with an Intelligence Section to apply logistics. Summers calculated the daunting arithmetical perspectives on the forces of the Empire at the end of the nineteenth century:

> The British suppression of an uprising of armed and mounted farmers required a war of three years, an expenditure of over £222 million and the deployment of 450,000 imperial troops. As the empire had only about 250,000 men in training, the numerical deficiencies had to be met by virtually denuding the defences of the empire and by seconding the volunteer hosts of Great Britain.

These figures help the modern reader to understand why militarism accelerated and went so deeply into the consciousness of Britain in the last decade of the Victorian years, and into the pre-First World War years. It partly explains the attention given to naval matters, also, as the notion of home defence became more urgent as it was observed that Cardwell's earlier reforms, which gave each regiment a home as well as an imperial force, were not really working as the Empire expanded.

In the pre-First World War years, not even the huge power of Russia, embracing almost a half of the globe, had an efficient intelligence system linked to its work in maintaining and policing the Empire stretching across far Asia. The army there had a section called the Military-Academic Committee, reporting directly to the War Minister. But in the war on the Manchurian Front intelligence measures failed. There was no real knowledge of Japan or of the militaristic philosophies and traditions of that state. According to David Schimmelpennick Van Der Oye, the failure was explained in terms of communication and a paucity of knowledge, something Britain at the time would have understood, licking its wounds after the debacle in South Africa:

> Despite its existence, intelligence was carried out neither systematically nor thoroughly. Aside from despatching quartermaster section subalterns and recruiting the occasional 'confidential', the committee did little to gauge enemy intentions and capabilities.

With this broader background in mind, the cultural and military climate around Vernon Kell begins to explain why the first steps in establishing his work and his responsibilities were so tentative. With hindsight, historians can see why it was inevitable that his work would be so hugely important in that uneasy Edwardian decade before war, on a European scale, became assured. Kell had no inheritance of previous working methods or, indeed, of consolidated records: he had to create these from nothing.

In this respect the early alliances and co-operations were vital; he did have one Special Branch colleague, Patrick Quinn, a superintendent. This collaboration cannot be underestimated. With Quinn to assist, Kell began to understand exactly how the criminal underworld worked and what networks were in place. The obvious parallels between espionage and standard detective work became clear. Naturally, there would be some characters under observation who may well have been involved in espionage but there was no clear offence for which the Special Branch could approach them. It was out of these hard lessons that Kell began to see what was needed, and he wrote copious reports for his superior, Ewart, outlining these difficulties. But, on the positive side, these difficulties were the impetus to opening up quite optimistic developments. Basically, the world of information-gathering had been too long open to the exploitation of what should have been secure locations, by 'gentlemen' and scientists merely wandering around taking notes. The 1889 Official Secrets Act was toothless in respect of acting on that kind of activity.

What was being learned in the dark and secret world of Bolshevism and Anarchism was also open to a revisionary inspection. Joseph Conrad's novel, *The Secret Agent* (1907), had dealt with the undercover world of terrorism, and the villain, Verloc, operated his nefarious business from the cover of a London shop. The novel instructed readers on the new phenomenon of the spy who was so mundane and seedy that he was capable of slipping unobtrusively into the everyday affairs of life: he could be the man in the doctor's waiting room or the man sitting opposite you on the omnibus. The character Vladimir looks at Verloc and thinks, 'This was then the famous and trusty secret agent, so secret that he was never designated otherwise but by the symbol of a triangle in the late Baron Stott-Wartenheim's official, semi-official and confidential correspondence…'

A significant step forward in Kell's work came after he learned of something that had happened in 1907. Quinn told Kell about a German naval officer of senior rank who had gone for a haircut in a German barbershop in London. Quinn was sure that the barber was a spy – a certain Karl Ernst. To take this up, as Kell wanted to do, would entail looking at Ernst's mail, and for that a go-ahead was needed from the postmaster-general. It was just the beginning of a new departure for British espionage. What happened was that a cache of letters was collected, signed by 'Fraulein Reimers' from

Potsdam. The correspondent turned out to be a major figure in German intelligence, Steinhauer, known to the British Foreign Section. This mail interception was extended across the land and it brought incredible results. A German officer called Helm, who had been living with an English girl in Portsmouth, was taken while in the process of drawing fortifications. Helm was with Hannah Wodehouse, who had had an affair with a friend of his previously, but she became suspicious of him and told the local army at the Royal Marines barracks. Surprisingly, the officer did not act, but two other officers saw Helm sketching. Helm was arrested and Kell's counter-espionage bureau was told of this.

Here we have a useful insight into Kell and his work. Helm was tried before the famous Rufus Isaacs (Lord Mansfield), but really there was no evidence of espionage. He was bound over to pay £250. But Kell was busy through this enquiry, contacting Miss Wodehouse and looking at Helm's luggage. He then sat in the courtroom during the hearing, in disguise, and even tracked Helm and a friend on the train journey to London, listening in to their conversation.

In Kell we have a man who had learned police detective measures, specifically in that aspect of detective work that has to cope with networks of criminals in ganglands within cities. He had had to learn to fade into the background when necessary, and also to talk and put on a performance when that had to be done. But whatever the case with Helm, it was a frightening episode, very much like a scene in a dramatic spy tale, even to the extent that poor Miss Wodehouse had received a threatening letter beginning with the words: 'Dare go into the witness box against Lieutenant Helm and you will be marked down for extermination.'

In her autobiography, Stella Rimington, former Director-General of MI5, summarises the turning-point in Kell's reign that led to MI5 – his stunningly successful work against the German espionage system in Britain:

One of Kell's helpers was travelling one day on a train in Scotland when quite by chance he heard two men in the same compartment talking German, a language he understood. One was telling the other about a letter he received from Potsdam asking questions about the British preparations for war. The letter gave addresses in Potsdam to which Holstein was supposed to send his information.

As Rimington adds, 'No intelligence system worth its salt would make such a mistake in tradecraft nowadays'. Kell got to work, and by the outbreak of war, the Germans were brought in. On the day war was declared, twenty-one key spies were arrested and tried. Some were hanged. Thomas Pierrepoint, for instance, hanged Robert Rosenthal on 15 July 1915, after intercepted coded telegrams sent by Rosenthal to his spymaster in Holland led to his arrest. Rosenthal then did what so many spies have done since: he thought that naming a spy in Britain might save his neck, even writing to Lord Kitchener to spill the information. Indeed, he named a man called Melton Feder. Nevertheless, he was hanged – the only spy to be hanged, as the others faced firing squads.

Vernon Kell's achievement is primarily that he established the modus operandi of internal security operations. In his time in office, he had to concentrate on tracking spies, preventing their entry to Britain, and, in fact, to apply detective methods to find them once they were here. He defined counter-espionage. There have been criticisms of him, and these have been well expressed by Nigel West in his book on MI5: 'a widely held assumption is connected with this: that old Sir Vernon Kell was quite unsuited to head a counter-intelligence organisation, and that his methods were, to put it bluntly, quaint.' West's defence is that while Kell was old fashioned and paternal, the 'MI5 was never accused of behaving like the Gestapo.'

The momentous date of Monday 23 August 1909, when the Special Intelligence Bureau came into being, will always be the birth of what everyone calls MI5. Kell was to remain at the helm until 1940, and he died just two years later. It is difficult to underestimate Churchill's part in that creation. He was also fighting for similar changes in the context of the navy. As he wrote in 1911: 'The lack of secrecy which prevails in this country with regard to naval matters, and the levity with which disclosures are regarded, appear to me to amount to a very considerable national evil.' He had backed Kell in the matter of making warrants easier and quicker to obtain when there was a spy in sight about to be arrested. He saw that Kell's work intercepting mails was producing some major results – and also significant implications for future undercover work. Kell even gave the Home Office a form for alien registration, and Churchill also saw the immense value of that.

By the time that the first spy arrests were taking place, Kell's department had expanded considerably, and he then had the essential back-up of clerical assistance and a more significant recognition and respect from his peers. Even the scaremongers, who had been advocating all kinds of national defence measures involving volunteers and police, had to admit that the secret services were giving results. Even Lord Roberts, who had been working with the novelist William Le Queux on hypothetical measures to cope with a German invasion, had to admit that a new age in intelligence had arrived. The next concern, as Churchill was well aware, was to bring naval intelligence in line. Sir George Aston, in his memoirs, includes some reflections on naval intelligence at the end of Victoria's reign, and he has plenty of anecdotes about the rather lax attitudes in this respect, such as this: 'An Admiralty messenger got into serious trouble. One of their Lordships went out to luncheon, leaving a drawer of his writing-table not quite closed There was an attachment which rang a bell in the next room, which was occupied by a private secretary, if the drawer was opened. Directly after the admiral left his room, the bell rang, and the private secretary came in and found the messenger at the drawer.' On a more general level, Aston makes it clear that there was no real comparison with Kell's work, even when war broke out, but then, limitations could be expected, as naval intelligence is a concept that has to have applications across vast areas of the world, and Aston's notes about the navy in 1914 knowing nothing about German wireless stations in the Pacific have to be taken with some healthy scepticism.

The overall picture of intelligence work before Kell arrived, and before the office led by Ewart was really in full swing, is that Britain was caught between differing conceptions of what home security meant, as well as what exactly should happen in communication between field intelligence and theoretical texts written by men such as Sir John Ardagh. The military theorists could see what was needed, but in the 1890s the gap between the theorists and the practical soldiers in the field was immense. When criticisms of the intelligence information used in the Boer War were all over the daily newspapers, it was very hard for anyone in the high command to take up a stance regarding the failures of that war with any real objectivity. Churchill had been in amongst it all, and he had seen the nature of the new tactics of winning battles by means of what Steevens, the journalist and author of *With Kitchener to Khartoum*, had called 'Machine warfare' led by the Kitcheners of the army. He could see just how entrenched the attitudes in the officer class regarding a reliance on traditional values and priorities were. To create a new intelligence department took vision and courage; it also meant that new breeds of officer would be required: men who would happily see military efficiency as something that could work alongside such august and civilian institutions as the Post Office. Fortunately for Britain, the top brass in the Metropolitan Police, since their creation in 1829, had been military men, since the very first Commissioner, Sir Charles Rowan, who had fought with Wellington at Waterloo.

The new world of espionage in the twentieth century was to be, as Kell soon learned, a milieu in which a soldier was as likely to need some acting skills and an ability to wear plain clothes as to gallop on a horse. There were fights to be won with enemies who were walking the streets of London, and Kell had found the tactics to combat the enemy.

Of course, at the heart of Kell's first successful operation, there was mail interception: considered by some to be an infringement of liberty. But at that very moment when he was developing such activities, the Official Secrets Act of 1911 was drawing out interesting debate in the general populace on that score. Everyday events were changing minds: notably in the stories of the lives and adventures of real spies. One writer to *The Times* described a spy of the distant past in this way: 'Karl Ludwig Schulmeister, whom the Germans called Napoleon's Hauptspion (top spy) was indefatigable in procuring, at great personal risk, useful military information. Perhaps he is not the only specialist in this line of military activity…' The last few words say a great deal: the implication is that, in 1910 when that letter was written, spying was thought of as a military activity and past masters in the art were beginning to be heroic rather than despicable.

As Kell carried on his work during the First World War, the Directorate of Military Intelligence began to employ women. At first it was a case of using them as typists, but as time went on, this massive arm of intelligence work, with a staff of 6,000 by 1918, used women for all kinds of work. MI5 itself employed many women. Kell had four women on his staff when war broke out, and by the end of the war women were working overseas as well as in London, being most numerous in H Branch, the section in control of records.

In the field, there were women working in intelligence networks in occupied territories, notably for the organisation in Belgium known as La Dame Blanche. At the War Office Captain Henry Landau was the pivotal control and liaison man working with the Belgian people. Women began work as couriers and observers amongst other roles, and, of course, everyone knew that if caught they would face a firing squad. Field intelligence was just as dangerous as it had been for the Kaffir spies in the Boer War, but at least communications were more sophisticated by 1914. Cryptography was becoming more advanced and technology was influencing the work of agents as never before.

As Tammy Proctor has said, with regard to women's work in Belgium: 'In a larger sense, wartime intelligence networks such as La Dame Blanche helped define the twentieth century development of the concepts of espionage, resistance, clandestine activities and military intelligence.'

But as these general changes were taking place, and Whitehall was becoming excited by the prospect of internal warfare done invisibly and with high drama, as well as tedious police work, the press and media along with literature and film, were advancing the cause of the spy as an international man of mystery. The media had to handle mundane tales such as that of the Swede Olsson, caught on Grimsby docks talking too freely about his ship-watching, but on the other hand they had characters like Helm and Steinhauer who really were 'the enemy within.' Espionage, as soon as Vernon Kell walked into his new office and surveyed his shelves and filing cabinets, was here to stay. The drama and adventure was sure to happen as codes and writing in invisible ink began to be part of the trappings of the work done by the profession.

To anyone observing the situation of intelligence in the field and in espionage and diplomacy, the creation of MI5 had been miraculous. In no small part, the changes and the new sophistication in espionage was due to a long-standing habit of amateurism which had transmuted into something strangely efficient. The century of using intelligence systems across whole wars and diplomatic domains as piecemeal and often fortuitous, was gathering far more than the sum of its parts. Even into the twentieth century the part-timers and amateurs still had a part to play. Sir George Aston's remarks in his book, *Secret Service*, about the idea of intelligence first planted in the 1870s: 'In 1875 "Intelligence" rose steadily in importance. The idea began to be grasped that a War Office was intended to aid in the conduct of warfare and that the necessary preparations, as the Germans had shown in 1870, must, of course, be carried out in time of peace.' From the time Intelligence officers were housed in Queen Anne's Gate, near St James' Park, in 1884, the first step to true specialization had been taken.

Following on from that momentous move, the men whose lives have been recounted here illustrate the principal dimensions of that imperial enterprise – to try to encompass the massive tracts of land on the pink-painted map of the globe, and to do so by understanding the interrelatedness of all information. Robertson's first grasp of the importance of filing, indexing and classifying was exactly the most constructive first step to take. When the links began to be made between the Special Branch of Scotland Yard in the early Edwardian years, all this communication and liaison was to be tested, by anarchist events and later by the need to intercept the letters of German spies based in England.

The road from the first officers venturing into Persia and Afghanistan in the 1830s to the bureaucracy and white-collar intellectualism of the first

MI5 men reflects the nature of the part played by essential information on the enemy in all areas of the Empire. Each of the men figuring here shows, in his career, a specific aspect of that journey to utter professionalism: Robertson was a hardy soldier with the right common sense and instinct for order; Wingate was a linguist and a thinker. Slatin, the adventurer, far from home; Ardagh, the organiser, fond of method and system; and Mark Sykes, a diplomat placed oddly between two worlds, sympathetic to the Arabs and Egyptians, yet fully aware of the machinations of espionage.

As Peter Hopkirk wrote in *The Great Game*, Britain and Russia found themselves fighting as allies in 1914. He wrote: 'For the first time, instead of glowering at one another across the mountains and the deserts of innermost Asia, Sepoy and Cossack fought together.' Indeed, as Britain was looking for spies on the domestic front, and a new secret service mentality was engendered, even the notion of military field intelligence was beginning to change. The world of immediate concern to the likes of Churchill, Kell and Haldane was one of increasing specialisation and of technology being applied to espionage. Gradually, as the long nineteenth century came to a close, in the peaceful summer of 1914 all the signs of an alliance with France and an enmity towards Germany were coming together in what was destined to be a new kind of war, on a scale previously unimagined.

The role of espionage in that war was to be quite marginal in some ways, but nevertheless, MI5 was there, increasingly claiming a major role in that new world. The idea of the Great Game was bound to recede into the realm of imperial adventure. In fact, one could argue that even in the major events of the Raj years, such as the Afghan Wars, the Mutiny and the wars in Chitral and the North West Frontier, there had always been something that emanated from a heady mix of paranoia and Realpolitik. The distant machinations of British diplomacy, sending individuals into war zones and buffer zones, in order to maintain a flow of military information was still there and was always going to be there, but it gradually lost its sense of being part of a context of adventure and of personal heroism and endeavour. Sir Francis Younghusband, leading an expedition into Tibet in the first years of the new century, has come to represent that former high adventure in the Great Game. Since then, the lengthy and large-scale conflict that was a milieu somewhere between the fictional narrative of *Kim* and the real deeds of officers who actually did give their lives for high diplomacy and Russophobia, has declined.

Yet in the popular media that game persists. In the *Flashman* novels of George Macdonald Fraser, for instance, the element of gentlemanly play and risk has been isolated as the stuff of self-conscious military fiction. Hollywood may have mostly ignored that material, but the myth of imperial military enterprise and courage never goes away, its stories being revisited regularly in the popular magazines of military history. Regarding the confrontations figuring in these pages, the most informative male romance on the wars in the Sudan is arguably *The Four Feathers*, by A.E.W. Mason, in which the imperial warrior ideal is openly celebrated, as in the character of Durrance: 'He was a soldier of a type not so rare as the makers of war stories wish their readers to believe.' The acculturation of the officer hero on the fringes of empire was even written about with self-regarding humour, in that description, and the myth owes its life mainly to the officer spies of the Great Game.

In terms of what the early twenty-first century sees as espionage, the stage on which the likes of Connolly, Sykes and Younghusband acted, has faded into a partially-understood time when all kinds of bias and denigration of ethnic groups went hand-in-hand with concepts of the 'whites' and the 'others'. That is, the modern media-driven world of metanarrative sees the British Empire as something of a curiosity, and consequently the deeds of derring-do, by brave and often eccentric officers engaging in military intelligence in some distant desert or mountain range, appear to be anachronistic oddities.

However, in the main spine of the narrative history of how the Great Game and the beginnings of work by Special Branch staff at home led to the more recent notion of the spy, the Victorian years have much to teach us today. Mainly, those lessons are about how individuals can come to play parts in much bigger pictures. A writer was once asked if she wrote about political ideas. She replied that she wrote about people, and that ultimately people made the political ideas, so it came down to the same thing in the end. Arguably, the same line of thought applies to the work of strong personalities such as Baden-Powell and Wolseley. Their intuitions as well as their obsessions led to new ways of thinking about field intelligence and, in strange but powerful ways, these ideas had an impact in the more central ideologies of their time.

Military intelligence in both the field and at home, in both transparent, obvious activities and in covert operations, has always been a force in the story of the British Army and indeed of the police force. I hope that this introductory history has opened up questions about how the Empire worked and to what extent it relied on marginal figures who insisted on going their own way in life, and eventually played a role in establishing the secret services we have today. Gentlemanly amateurs have often been principal players in the theatre of British history, and never more so than in the Great Game in which Britain, Russia and a cluster of other states made both offensive and defensive gambits for a century or more.

DESTINATIONS

To complete the story, we will end with a short account of the final stages of the careers of the spymasters featured here.

William Robertson

In 1910, Robertson took up the post of Commandant of the Staff College he so much admired. After that he was director of military training at the War Office. Then in the First World War he became chief general staff officer, with the responsibility of Home Defence. He was actively involved in the Western Front, being given the post of quartermaster-general of the British Expeditionary Force. In the first battles, into 1915, Robertson's responsibility was to control supplies. After becoming a lieutenant-general, in 1915, there were disagreements at a high level, leading to his opponents asking him to leave the War Office. The man who replaced him, Sir Henry Wilson, was assassinated in London.

Back in England he took command of the Eastern Front, and thus he was marginally involved in Sykes's work, insofar as he had to consider the consequences of actions against the Turks. But after being made Field Marshall, he achieved the unique position of being the first ranker ever to gain the highest rank in the army.

He died on 12 February 1933, in London. His name certainly lives on in his native Lincolnshire, in the shape of a school in his birthplace of Welbourn, near Lincoln.

Rudolf Slatin

After Omdurman, Slatin was knighted by the Queen. He was made a brigadier and then inspector-general of the Sudan. He worked with his friend, Wingate, in rebuilding the nation. Although he was still in the Austrian army, as a lieutenant, he rose to be major-general in Britain. Then his Sudan administration ended in 1914.

When his days of fame were over, he retired back home, becoming active in the Scout movement in Austria. In 1918 he worked to help the Viennese during their hard times when people were very short of food. His wife died in 1923, and Rudolf then lived in Merino. He died on 4 October 1932, of cancer. He has been memorialised in Khartoum, not as famous as 'Chinese Gordon' in the history of that city, but still a major figure.

Reginald Wingate

During the Arab Revolt, a great deal was asked of Wingate. Not only did he have the Sudan to consider, but north of his borders Lawrence was active with the revolt, and all kinds of unthinkable possibilities loomed if any natives in the Sudan decided to join other causes. In 1919 Wingate was in Paris, speaking out for Egyptian representation, but the powerful Lord Curzon was opposed to him, and this caused major problems in Cairo, including a few murders. That was the end of Wingate's time in Egypt.

He was a general on leaving the army, and then turned his attention to other matters, including being a director on the boards of a number of companies, as well as becoming governor of the Gordon College in Khartoum. He had the tragic experience of having a child die in infancy and then losing a son in action in France. Wingate lived to be ninety-two, dying in 1953.

Sir John Ardagh

It was said of Ardagh in his *Times* obituary that 'he habitually overtaxed his strength for the public'. Even before his retirement, he served as a delegate at the first Peace Conference at The Hague in 1899. In 1906–07 he was active in the Red Cross movement. There had been a Dutch Red Cross ambulance on one occasion, in 1900, at Elandsfontein, and Kitchener had refused to let another flag fly on his campaign in South Africa, so he had had the flag taken down. The Dutch doctor considered that to be a breech of the Geneva Convention. Ardagh saw that there had become uncertainties as to what constituted the terms of the Convention, and in 1906 he played a part in revising that document.

He was then a Director of the Suez Canal Company. Every year he made a point of travelling up the Nile to Aswan, and enjoyed mixing with the other representatives, French and English.

Ardagh died in 1907, and his wife stated in her biography that the cause of his death was 'the effects of overwork'. It was partly thanks to his wife's biography of him that the responses he gave to the criticism of his work in the Anglo-Boer War were more widely known, beyond the military personnel and politicians who had been informed of his responses to charges.

Sir Mark Sykes

After being so fully occupied in Cairo, and elsewhere, for many years, after 1918 Sykes was much involved in the Zionist cause for the international zone of his Agreement. He gave a special lunch to Armenians, Syrians and Zionists at Buckingham Gate in 1918, and then he went back to organise the French-Syrian entente, going to Paris en route to perform a diplomat's task of nurturing good liaisons between those people. He was designing an arrangement whereby France would have Armenia and Britain would have the oil lands of Mosul. But finally he reached the Middle East again, met General Allenby, who was then in charge of Cairo, and after that he dashed across several nations trying to help where he could in maintaining good relations. At one point he found out that some Armenians were being held captive by the Kurds, and he immediately went on his way there to help.

On his last mission, he had been based in Paris and had gone to London to be with his wife before returning. A message from military intelligence was sent to him while he was there for a peace conference. He had his own ideas for a successful Middle East settlement. But he was not to see them through. He collapsed, and the next day was too weak to leave his bed. His influenza became pneumonia, and he died on 16 February 1919.

Others in the Background

Such is the scope and complexity of the history of British military intelligence in late Victorian and Edwardian wars and diplomacy that the selection of the principal subjects of this book was done to show representative types. This list gives some idea of the secondary figures in the story, though dozens more could have been included.

Gertrude Bell

A graduate of Oxford, Bell travelled extensively in Arabia and moved freely among all classes and groups. She later became an influential figure in the creation of Iraq. But in the years around the turn of the century, Bell met and worked with the Arab Bureau. She was born in 1868 in Washington, County Durham, and was the first woman to hold a first-class degree in modern history. She was an excellent linguist, learning from people as well as from books, writing her first travel book in 1897. She became an archaeologist, but was also involved in espionage, and maintained liaisons with various diplomats and heads of the Bureau.

Henry Brackenbury

Brackenbury was with Wolseley early in his career, and played a central role in the various developments in the establishment of the Intelligence Branch from 1870. He was born in Lincolnshire in 1837, educated at Eton and at the Royal Military Academy at Woolwich. He was in India in 1857–58, and as well as working with Wolseley in the Ashanti War of 1873–74, was still involved in running intelligence work in the Anglo-Boer War. He retired in 1904, and died in France in 1914. Despite criticisms, his performance was always impressive in theatres of war: a learned and sociable man, he had a large network of friends and contacts, and balanced practicality in field intelligence to a love of abstractions in the area of strategy.

Gilbert Clayton

Clayton was with Kitchener in the Sudan campaign, and then became Wingate's secretary, before becoming the Sudan agent in Cairo and eventually Head of Intelligence at the Bureau. In 1917 he was chief political officer to General Allenby, and then adviser to the new Ministry of the Interior in Egypt, from 1919 to 1922. He was close to Sykes's work, and often advised him, though they disagreed on some matters. His attitudes were liberal: he backed a move to support the loyalty of the Supreme Muslim Council, and also helped with frontier negotiations in the Arab world.

David Hogarth

He was first in Egypt in 1915, and became the first Director of the Arab

Bureau in 1916. He was an academic archaeologist who played a major role in allowing Lawrence to be active in the Arab Revolt. He died in 1927.

George Henderson

He was the likeable 'Hendy' to William Robertson at the Staff College. Born in Jersey in 1854, Henderson went to Oxford and then Sandhurst. He first served in India and then Egypt. After writing *The Campaign of Fredericksberg*, in 1889, he was seen as a theorist and teacher, and was professor of military history at the Staff College. He saw active service in the Anglo–Boer War as director of intelligence. He died in 1903, in the process of writing a history of the war in South Africa. Maurice, with Brackenbury's help, finished that book for his old friend. Henderson and Brackenbury had a lasting influence over Robertson and his contemporaries.

John Maurice (General Sir John)

Another Wolseley 'ring' officer, Maurice was on the Ashanti campaign, and had a speciality of providing immense amounts of information in compendium form. He won his reputation in the 1870s, while serving in the Anglo–Boer War, and was one of the official historians of that debacle, writing *The History of the War in South Africa* (published between 1906 and 1910). Maurice was representative of the new breed of officer nurtured by Wolseley, who was himself very much aware of the reformations needed in field intelligence.

Ronald Storrs

Storrs was a diplomat who moved easily in virtually all political circles around the Middle East. He read classics at Cambridge, and took an initial post as secretary to Kitchener during the last decade of the nineteenth century. Immediately after, during the Arab Revolt, he worked as an agent for the Hashamites (in Jordan), and some of this involved working with Lawrence, who once called him 'Ruhi the Ingenious, more like a mandrake than a man'. Storrs appraised Lawrence in a biographical summary published in 1949: 'The secret of Lawrence's ascendancy is that with the Arabs … he lived with them, ate the ranks' food, wore their clothes…' He was later the first military governor in Jerusalem, as Allenby was settling in there. He was then a force in the development of Palestine, and always had wider cultural interests as well as professional ones in diplomacy. His memoirs are an excellent source for many on the side-issue of the Arab Bureau and the wider circle of negotiations.

BIBLIOGRAPHY

Main Sources

For William Robertson, his own memoirs have been most valuable: *From Private to Field-Marshall*, (Constable, London, 1921). Also, Victor Bonham-Carter's biography, *Soldier True*, (Constable, London, 1963), has been essential reading. Susan, Countess of Malmesbury, wrote her biography of her husband, John Ardagh, *The Life of Major-General Sir John Ardagh*, (John Murray, London, 1909), and this has a very detailed account of Ardagh's career in all phases. For Slatin, his own *Fire and Sword in the Sudan* (Arnold, London, 1914) is a profoundly important source. Wingate's life has been written in most detail by Ronald Wingate: *Wingate of the Sudan* (John Murray, London, 1955). Wingate's own book, *Mahdism and the Egyptian Sudan* (1891), most recently reissued by Frank Cass in 1968, is a detailed account of the whole Mahdist history at the time.

My primary source for Sir Mark Sykes has been the archive at the University of Hull: *The papers of Sir Mark Sykes 1879–1919*, with special reference to the Sykes-Picot Agreement and the Middle East. Of special relevance have been items DDSY2/4, DDSY2/5 and his projects, covered by DDSY2/6. Shane Leslie's book, *Mark Sykes, His Life and Letters*, (Cassell, London, 1923), has been invaluable as the first appraisal. Following that, Roger Adelson's *Mark Sykes: Portrait of an Amateur*, (Cape, London, 1975), is a first-class account of the main events. More recently, in 2005, Christopher Simon Sykes, Mark's grandson, wrote the whole story of the Sykes family and Sledmere in *The Big House*, (Harper, London, 2005).

Also very useful are the collected Arab Bulletins of 1916–1919, edited by T.E. Lawrence and D.G. Hogarth (Archive Editions, 1986). Of course, the other primary source underpinning much of chapter eight is T.E. Lawrence's classic, *Seven Pillars of Wisdom*, (Penguin edition, London, 2000). The debate in some quarters regarding Lawrence is to what extent he was actually a significant role in the Arab Revolt? Recent thinking places Lawrence firmly in relation to the Arab Bureau, under the supposition that the bureau really orchestrated things.

Bibliographical Survey

Interest in the Arab Bureau has burgeoned in the last few years. Together with that renewed curiosity is a realisation that there are plenty of sources for espionage in the years 1900–1918 still not fully subjected to scrutiny and commentary. An example is *Setting the Desert on Fire*, by James Barr, who looked at the 'secret war' discussed in the foregoing chapter on Sykes. Although there are ample secondary sources, largely in biographical material, what has happened is that popular biographies (such as *The Life of Gertrude Bell* written by Georgina Howell) have tended to offer distorted portraits of some of the main participants. Barr went back to the archives, found papers by some of the lesser-known figures, and added depth and substance to the story.

In 2008 this revisionary enquiry continued unabated. Polly A. Moh's concentration on the methods and networks around the Arab Bureau in *Military Intelligence and the Arab Revolt* (see bibliography below), has made it clear that in spite of the fact that the Bureau may have been working without links to India, it achieved quite incredible feats of propaganda and subversion. There are materials that suggest that the Indian liaison was often in touch with the Indian army, and as I have noticed in passing, there were splinter groups based in India which played a role in things Middle Eastern, albeit without official backing. Certainly Mark Sykes forged links with the Indian political officers, using his agent in Baghdad where necessary.

For the war in the Sudan and the Mahdi, again, interest has been maintained, notably in the writings of Michael Asher, whose *Khartoum, the Ultimate Imperial Adventure*, has stirred up the dramatic history of those desert encounters once again. Interest in Kitchener has always been maintained, while, surprisingly, Garnet Wolseley has been ignored, at least in relative terms. The same applies to Reginald Wingate, who will perhaps attract more biographers in the future.

Of all the men whose stories have been told here, William Robertson has arguably been the most neglected in the pre-First World War years. That has been my main aim here: to persuade readers to look again at the remarkable man who was involved in so many campaigns and did so well in so many responsible positions. The context of his time in India has been widely written about, of course, notably by Charles Allen, Jules Stewart and naturally, Peter Hopkirk.

The same applies to Sir John Ardagh, perhaps destined to be a footnote in the literature of the Anglo–Boer War. In all of Thomas Pakenham's magisterial accounts of that war, Ardagh merits two brief mentions in the 650 pages. In all historiography, one expects gaps, lacunae, neglect and the process of selection and rejection as modes and fashions in history change. But in the matter of what was Mesopotamia, and is now Iraq, is surely going to preset compelling historical parallels from imperial history with the situation today. The same applies to Afghanistan.

The Middle East, during the Edwardian years, has attracted a good deal of attention and writing covering the wider sweep of Islamic history, which has helped explain to readers who only know European history the complexities of the situations that Wingate, Slatin and Sykes dealt with. There has been a need for historical surveys of that cluster of nations around Egypt for some years, and works such as Peter Mansfield's provide that (see below). Much that is valuable in that context appears in learned journals, of course. In addition, much of the vast number of works on General Gordon, published between his death and 1900, introduce minor and secondary figures involved in military intelligence. The majority of these discuss such people as Captain Burnaby, who died heroically at Abu-Klea, after which one writer commented that 'He found the soldier's death he had always sighed for.'

The influence of the Franco-Prussian War of 1870–71 cannot be underestimated, and as a source of impact on the officer elite, sources such as *The Journal of the Household Brigade* are essential. The 1871 issue, published by Clowes, London, is a mine of information on the profound interest in matters German in the officer class at that time. In the years between the end of the Crimean War (1856) and the 1870s, there was a popular demand for education about military matters, even reaching such domestic journals as *Home Friend*, in which, for instance, we find a detailed account of 'Field Fortification and Siege Work' (in the 1858 number). The militaristic Britain of the end of the century had had plenty of preparation in being informed on every aspect of military life in the earlier years of the century. When the young officers of 1900 played the Kriegspiel game, they were repeating the activities of the 1870s: the learning curve from other nations was a long one.

It is understandable, with the wisdom of historical process behind us, to see that change in the Victorian army was necessarily slow and suspicious. Many writers have blamed the high command for exacerbating this. Notably, accusations have been levelled at the Duke of Cambridge, firmly planted in the security of the Royal Family, but there were more profound causes of apathy and complacency. Recent writing on the growth of reform has now been voluminous and perhaps all that needs to be said has been said.

Finally, it has to be recalled that, particularly since the famous war correspondent William Howard Russell observed the action at Balaclava in the Crimean War, and then went to Indian after the Mutiny to report and keep a journal, war reportage has had a certain relationship with military intelligence. Russell's *My Diary in India*, (Routledge, London, 1860), is an important source text for this. Reference has already been made to G.W. Steevens who went with Kitchener to the Sudan and witnessed events at Omdurman. But in the Anglo–Boer War and in the spy mania preceding the First World War, and, indeed, in the Middle East, there was still such a heavy volume of press reportage that amateurism seemed to many to have a place. The clearest example is in India. So many civil servants, as well as military personnel, had served their time in various parts of India that, on retirement, some provided memoirs, often with strong opinions on what should be done that was not being done. Similarly, the end of the nineteenth century was a great age of adventurous travel, and the experiences of intrepid gentlemen and ladies who ventured into deserts and into dangerous places were sometimes useful and sometimes merely trivial. But they were often useful in small matters or in adding detail to what was already known.

Primary Sources

Books

Aston, Sir George, *Secret Service*, (Faber and Faber, London, 1930)

Brackenbury, Capt. H., *The Tactics of the Three Arms as Modified to Meet the requirements of the Present Day*, (Mitchell, London, 1873)

Briggs, Sir John Henry, *Naval Administrations 1827–1892*, (Sampson Low, Marston and Company, London, 1897)

Churchill, Winston, *My Early Life*, (Collins, London, 1930)

Clausewitz, Carl von, *On War* (1832), (Wordsworth edition, edited by Tom Griffith, Wordsworth, London, 1997)

Cromer, Earl of, *Modern Egypt*, (Macmillan, London, 1908)

Duke, Joshua, *Recollections of the Kabul Campaign*, (W.H. Allen, London, 1883)

Earl of Birkenhead, *Famous Trials*, (Hutchinson, London, 1930)

Everitt, Nicholas, *British Secret Service During the Great War*, (Hutchinson, London, 1920)

Forbes, Archibald et alias, *Battles of the Nineteenth Century*, (Cassell, London, 1902)

Gordon, Major-General C.G., *The Journals*, (Kegan Paul and Trench, London, 1885)

Hackwood, F.W., *The Life of Lord Kitchener*, (Collins, London, 1902)

Hopkirk, Peter, (Ed.) Frederick Burnaby: *A Ride to Khiva*, (OUP, Oxford, 1997)

Humphries, Sir Travers, *A Book of Trials*, (Pan, London, 1956)

Jackson, H.C., *Osman Digna*, (Ed. Reginald Wingate, Methuen, London, 1910)

Kinglake, Alexander, *Eothen*, (Nelson, London, 1930)

Kipling, Rudyard, *Kim*, (Cassell's Magazine, London, 1901)

Kipling, Rudyard, *Plain Tales from the Hills*, (Thacker, Calcutta, 1889)

Le Caron, Major Henri, *Twenty-Five Years in The Secret Service*, (Heinemann, London, 1893)

Le Queux, William, *The Invasion of 1910*, (Eveleigh Nash, London, 1906)

McDonagh, Michael, *In London During the Great War*, (Eyre and Spottiswoode, London, 1935)

Malmesbury, Susan, Countess of, *The Life of Major-General Sir John Ardagh* (by his wife), (John Murray, London, 1909)

Maurice, Maj-Gen. J.F., *History of the War in South Africa*, (Hurst and Blackett, London, 1906–1910)

Ohrwalder, Joseph, *Ten years' captivity in the Madhi's Camp 1882–1892*, (Arnold, London, 1892)

Prior, Melton, *Campaigns of a War Correspondent*, (Arnold, London, 1912)

Robertson, Sir William, *From Private to Field-Marshall*, (Constable, London, 1921)

Russell, William Howard, *My Diary in India*, (Routledge Warne, London, 1860)

Russell, William Howard, *Despatches from the Crimea*, (Ed. Nicolas Bentley, Panther, London, 1970)

Steevens, G.W., *With Kitchener to Khartoum*, (Blackwood, Edinburgh, 1898)

Temple, Sir Richard, *Lord Lawrence*, (Macmillan, London, 1889)

Trotter, Captain Lionel, *The Life of John Nicholson,* (Nelson, London, 1904)

White, Arnold, *The Hidden Hand*, (Grant Richards, London, 1917)

Wilkinson, H. Spenser, *Thirty-Five Years 1874–1909*, (Constable, London, 1933)

Wolseley, Field Marshall, *The Story of a Soldier's Life*, (Constable, London, 1902)

Secondary Sources

Books

(a) Reference

Beales, Derek, *From Castlereagh to Gladstone 1815–1885*, (Nelson, London, 1969)

Browne, Douglas G., *The Rise of Scotland Yard*, (Harrap, London, 1956)

Cannon, John, *Oxford Dictionary of British History*, (OUP, Oxford, 2001)

Cook, Chris, *The Routledge Companion to Britain in the Nineteenth Century*, (Routledge, London, 2005)

Holmes, Richard (Ed.), *The Oxford Companion to Military History*, (OUP, Oxford, 2001)

Seth, Ronald, *Encyclopaedia of Espionage*, (NEL, London, 1972)

Talbot-Booth, E.C., *The British Army*, (Sampson Low, London, 1937)

Townson, Duncan, *The New penguin Dictionary of Modern History 1789–1945*, (Penguin, London, 1995)

(b) General

Alexander, Michael, *The True Blue: the life and adventures of Colonel Fred Burnaby*, (Hart-Davis, London, 1957)

Allen, Charles, *Duel in the Snow*, (John Murray, London, 2004)

Allen, Charles, *Soldier Sahibs*, (Abacus, London, 2000)

Andrew, Christopher, *Secret Service*, (Sceptre, London, 1985)

Anon. *Fifty Amazing Secret Service Dramas*, (Odhams Press, London, 1920)

Armstrong, Karen, *Islam, A Short History*, (Phoenix, London, 2001)

Arthur, Max, *Symbol of Courage: The men behind the medal*, (Pan, London, 2004)

Asher, Michael, *Khartoum: The ultimate imperial adventure*, (Penguin, London, 2005)

Barnett, Correlli, *Britain and Her Army*, (Cassell, London, 1970)

Barr, James, *Setting the Desert on Fire: T.E. Lawrence and Britain's secret war in Arabia 1916–1918*, (Bloomsbury, London, 2006)

Bassford, Christopher, *Clausewitz in English: The Reception of Clausewitz in Britain and America 1815–1945*, (OUP, New York, 1994)

Baxter, Ian A., *Baxter's Guide: Biographical Sources in the India Office Records*, (British Library, London, 2004)

Beckett, Ian, *The Victorians at War*, (Hambledon Continuum, London, 2003)

Bennett, E.N. *The Downfall of the Devishes: being a sketch of the final Sudan Campaign of 1898*, (Methuen, London, 1898)

Boar, Roger, and Blundell, Nigel, *Spies and Spymasters*, (Octopus, London, 1984)

Boghardt, Thomas, *Spies of the Kaiser: German covert operations in Great Britain during the First World War era*, (Palgrave, Basingstoke, 2004)

Brendon, Piers, *Eminent Edwardians*, (Penguin, London, 1979)

Brighton, Terry, *Hell Riders*, (Penguin, London, 2005)

Campbell, Christie, *Fenian Fire: the British Government plot to assassinate Queen*

Victoria, (HarperCollins, London, 2002)

Carver, Field Marshall Lord, *The National Army Museum Book of the Turkish Front 1914–18*, (Macmillan, London, 2003)

Chambers, Frank P., *The War Behind the War 1914–18*, (Macmillan, London, 1939)

Charques, Richard, *The Twilight of Imperial Russia,* (Oxford University Press, Oxford, 1958)

Clayton, Anthony, *The British Officer: leading the army from 1660 to the Present day*, (Pearson Longman, Harlow, 2006)

Cook, Andrew, *Ace of Spies: The true story of Sidney Reilly*, (Tempus, 2002)

Coulson, Major Thomas, *Mata Hari: courtesan and spy*, (Hutchinson, London, 1939)

Cromb, James, *The Highland Brigade: its battles and its heroes*, (Eneas Mackay, Stirling, 1902)

Dash, Mike, *Thug: The true story of India's murderous cult*, (Granta, London, 2005)

David, Saul, *The Indian Mutiny*, (Penguin, London, 2002)

David, Saul, *Military Blunders*, (Robinson, London, 1997)

David, Saul, *Zulu: the heroism and tragedy of the Zulu War of 1879*, (Penguin, London, 2005)

Davidson, Apollon and Filatova, Irina, *The Russians and the Anglo-Boer War,* (Human and Rousseau, Cape Town, 1998)

Deacon, Richard, *British Secret Service*, (Grafton, London, 1991)

Deacon, Richard, *A History of the Russian Secret Service,* (Grafton, London, 1987)

Deane, Edmund, *British Campaigns in the Nearer East*, (Constable, London, 1919)

Downer, Martin, *The Queen's Knight: the extraordinary life of Queen Victoria's most trusted confidant*, (Transworld, London, 2007)

Duckers, Peter, *The British-Indian Army 1860–1894*, (Shire, Princes Risborough, 2003)

Edwardes, Michael, *Raj*, (Pan, London, 1967)

Farwell, Byron, *The Great Boer War*, (Cassell, London, 1977)

Ferris, John Robert, *Intelligence and Strategy: Selected Essays*, (Routledge, London, 2005)

Fishlock, Trevor, *Conquerors of Time*, (John Murray, London, 2004)

Foot, M.D.R., *Secret Lives*, (OUP, Oxford, 2002)

Fremont-Barnes, Gregory, *The Boer War 1899–1902*, (Osprey, London, 2003)

French, Patrick, *Younghusband: the last great imperial adventurer*, (Harper, 2004)

French, Yvonne, *News from the Past*, (Gollancz, London, 1960)

Gall, Lothar, *Bismarck: The White Revolutionary*, (Unwin Hyman, London, 1986)

Gooch, John, *The Plans of War: The General Staff and British Military Strategy 1900–1916*, (Routledge, London, 1974)

Greaves, Adrian, *Rorke's Drift*, (Cassell, London, 2002)

Guttsman, W.L., *The British Political Elite*, (MacGibbon and Kee, 1965)

Haldane, Lord Richard, *Autobiography*, (Hodder and Stoughtin, London, 1929)

Hamilton, C.I., *Anglo-French Naval Rivalry 1840–1870*, (OUP, Oxford, 1993)

Harris, Stephen M., *British Military Intelligence in the Crimean War 1854–1856*, (Frank Cass, London, 1999)

Haswell, Jock, *The British Army: A Concise History*, (Thames and Hudson, 1975)

Hattersley, Roy, *The Edwardians*, (Abacus, London, 2004)

Haythornethwaite, Philip J., *The Armies of Wellington*, (Brockhampton Press, London, 1998)

Hayward, James, *Myths and Legends of the First World War*, (Sutton, Stroud, 2002)

Herman, Michael, *Intelligence Power in Peace and War*, (Royal Institute Of International Affairs, Cambridge, CUP, 2000)

Hernon, Ian, *Britain's Forgotten Wars: colonial campaigns of the 19th century*, (Sutton, Stroud, 2001)

Holmes, Richard, *Sahib: The British Soldier in India*, (HarperCollins, London, 2005)

Holt, P.M., *The Mahdist State in the Sudan – A Study of its Origins*, (OUP, Oxford, 1958)

Hopkirk, Peter, *The Great Game*, (OUP, Oxford, 1977)

Hopkirk, Peter, *Foreign Devils on the Silk Road*, (OUP, Oxford, 1980)

Hopkirk, Peter, *Quest for Kim: In search of Kipling's Great Game*, (John Murray, London, 1996)

Howard, Michael, *The Franco-Prussian War*, (OUP, Oxford, 1961)

Howard, Michael, *War in European History*, (OUP, Oxford, 1996)

Howell, Georgina, *Daughter of the Desert: the remarkable life of Gertrude Bell*, (Macmillan, London, 2006)

Ind, Colonel Allison, *A History of Modern Espionage*, (Hodder and Stoughton, London, 1963)

James, Lawrence, *Raj: the making of British India*, (Little Brown, London, 1997)

Jeal, Tim, *Baden-Powell*, (Pimlico, London, 1991)

Jenkins, Roy, *Churchill*, (Pan Books, London, 2001)

Johnson, Robert, *Spying for Empire: The Great Game in Central and South Asia*, (Greenhill Books, London, 2006)

Judd, Denis, *Someone Has Blundered: calamities of the British army in the Victorian Age*, (Arthur Barker, London, 1983)

Kayser, Jacques, *The Dreyfus Affair*, (Heinemann, London, 1931)

Keay, John, *The Great Arc*, (HarperCollins, London, 2000)

Keay, John, *The Honourable Company*, (HarperCollins, London, 1993)

Keegan, John, *Intelligence in War : knowledge of the enemy from Napoleon to Al-Qaeda*, (Pimlico, London, 2004)

Kennedy, P., *The Realities behind Diplomacy*, (Fontana, London, 1981)

Kipling, Rudyard, *A Choice of Kipling's Verse*, (Faber, London, 1983)

Knight, Ian, *The National Army Museum Book of the Zulu War*, (Pan Grand Strategy Series, London, 2003)

Koch, H.W. (ed), *The Origins of the First World War: Great Power Rivalry And German War Aims*, (Macmillan, London, 1972)

Laband, John P.C. (Ed.), *Lord Chelmsford's Zululand Campaign 1878–1879,* (Sutton, for the Army Records Society, Stroud, 1994)

Laffin, John, *Tommy Atkins: the story of the English soldier*, (Sutton, Stroud, 2004)

Lee, Stephen J., *Aspects of European History 1789–1980*, (Methuen, London, 1982)

Lehmann, Joseph, *All Sir Garnet: A Life of Field-Marshall Lord Wolseley*, (Jonathan Cape, 1964)

Makki, Shibeika, *The Independent Sudan: British Policy in the Sudan 1882–1902*, (Arnold, London, 1952)

Mansfield, Peter, *A History of the Middle East*, (Penguin, London, 2003)

Marais, J.S., *The Fall of Kruger's Republic*, (OUP, Oxford, 1961)

Marwick, Arthur, *The Deluge: British Society and the First World War*, (Little Brown, Boston, 1960)

Massie, Robert K., *Dreadnought: Britain, Germany and the Coming of the Great War*, (Pimlico, London, 2004)

Maxwell, Leigh, *The Ashanti Ring*, (London, 1985)

Moh, Polly A., *Military Intelligence and the Arab Revolt*, (Routledge, London, 2008)

Morris, Donald, R., *The Washing of the Spears*, (Cape, London, 1965)

Morris, Jan, *Heaven's Command: an imperial progress*, (Faber, London, 1998)

Moss, Alan and Skinner, Keith, *The Scotland Yard Files*, (The National Archives, London, 2006)

Nasson, Bill, *Britannia's Empire,* (Tempus, Stroud, 2004)

Nutting, Anthony, *Gordon: Martyr and Misfit,* (Constable, 1966)

O'Brion, Leon, *Fenian Fever: An Anglo-American dilemma*, (Chatto and Windus, London, 1971)

Pakenham, Thomas, *The Boer War*, (Abacus, London, 1992)

Panayi, Panikos, *The Enemy in Our Midst: Germans in Britain During the First World War*, (Berg, Oxford, 1991)

Pollock, John, *Kitchener*, (Constable, London, 1998)

Ponsonby, Arthur, *Falsehood in Wartime*, (Allen and Unwin, London, 1928)

Punch Library: Mr Punch on the Warpath, (Educational Book Co., London, 1909)

Proctor, Tammy M., *Female Intelligence: Women and espionage in the First World War*, (New York University Press, New York, 2003)

Rayner, (Ed.) and Stapley, Ron, *Debunking History,* (Sutton, Stroud, 2002)

Rice, Edward, *Captain Sir Richard Francis Burton*, (Da Capo, Cambridge Mass., 1990)

Richelson, Jeffrey T., *A Century of Spies: intelligence in the twentieth century*, (OUP, Oxford, 1995)

Rimington, Stella, *Open Secret*, (Hutchinson, London, 2001)

Royle, Trevor, *Crimea: The Great Crimean War 1854–1856*, (Abacus, London, 2003)

Royle, Trevor, *War Report: the war correspondent's view of battle from the Crimea to the Falklands*, (Mainstream Publishing, 1987)

Scott, Brough, *Galloper Jack: a grandson's search for a forgotten hero*, (Macmillan, London, 2003)

Singh, Simon, *The Code Book: the secret history of codes and code-breaking*, (Fourth estate, London, 2000)

Spear, Percival, *A History of India Volume 2*, (Penguin, London, 1965)

Spiers, Edward M., *The Late Victorian Army 1868–1902*, (Manchester University Press, Manchester, 1992)

Stafford, David, *Churchill and the Secret Service*, (John Murray, London, 1997)

Stevenson, David, *1914–1918. The History of the First World War*, (Penguin, London, 2005)

Stewart, Jules, *Spying for the Raj: the Pundits and the mapping of the Himalaya*, (Sutton, Stroud, 2006)

Sweetman, John, *The Crimean War*, (Osprey, London, 2001)

Taylor, A.J.P., *Essays in English History*, (Penguin, London, 1976)

Taylor, Stephen, *Shaka's Children: a history of the Zulu people*, (HarperCollins, 1995)

Teed, Peter and Clark, Michael, *Portraits and Documents: Later Nineteenth Century 1868–1919*, (Hutchinson, London, 1969)

Warwick, Peter, *The South African War*, (Longman, London, 1980)

West, Nigel, *MI5*, (Grafton, London, 1985)

White R.J., *Waterloo to Peterloo*, (Penguin, London, 1957)

Wilkinson-Latham, R., *From Our Special Correspondent: Victorian War Correspondents and Their Campaigns*, (Hodder& Stoughton, London, 1979)

Wynn, Antony, *Persia in the Great Game: Sir Percy Sykes, explorer, consul, soldier, Spy*, (John Murray, London, 2003)

Young, Kenneth, *Arthur James Balfour*, (G. Bell, London, 1963)

Ziegler, P., *Omdurman*, (Collins, London, 1973)

Periodicals
Atheneum, The, 1903
The English Historical Review
Historian: The Historical Association
History: The Historical Association
History Today
History Workshop
Home Friend, 1858
Intelligence and National Security, Frank Cass, London
Irish Historical Studies
Journal of the Household Brigade, 1871, Ed. I.E.A. Dolby, published by subscribers
Journal of Imperial and Commonwealth History, Routledge, London
Journal of the Society for Army Historical Research, Vol. 84 no. 337, spring, 2006
Military History, Leesburg, VA, USA
Military Illustrated, Ed. Tim Newark, London
Punch
Illustrated London News
Social History
Strand Magazine

Non-Book Materials
The Boer War, Eagle Rock Video, London, 2002
South African Military History Society Military History Journal online – http:/rapidttp. com/milhist/vol103di.html
Codes and Ciphers in History: www.Smithsrisca.demon.co.uk
IDC Publishers: British Intelligence on Afghanistan and its Frontiers: microfiche library. See, *www.idc.n*
Oxford journals online: www.Oxfordjournals.org
SIB History: www.Lhooper/sib-history.htm
South Australians at war: Ned Kelly in Khaki: www.slsa.sa.gov.au/saatwar
The Times Digital Archive

INDEX

Aberdeen, Lord 19
Abbott, Captain James 15
Adelphi Terrace 21
Adelson, Roger 133
Afghanistan 51, 58, 83
Afghan Wars 42, 67
Agadir crisis 159
Aldeshot 65
Ali, Mohammed 56
Ali, Wad Helu 106
Allen, Charles 17
Alma, battle of 32
Altham, Colonel 153
Anatolia 136
Anglo-Boer War 25
Aral Sea 58
Arab Bureau 139-148
Arabi 89, 113-4
Arab legion 143
Ardagh, Sir John 11, 74, 111-130
  at Staff College 112
  in Turkey 112-3
  in Egypt 112-3
  at Tel el Kebir 114-5
  Durr light lamp 120
  Director of Military
    Intelligence Branch 120
  *Military Notes on the Dutch Republic of
  South Africa* 120,
    last work, 150
  biographical summary 176

Army Regulation Bill (1874)
  75
Army Council 124
Asher, Michael 108
Ashanti Campaign 27, 77
Asquith, Herbert 142
Aston, Sir George 17, 26
  Secret Service 76, 78, 86,
    116, 129
Auckland, Lord 22, 58
Ayas Bay 147-8
Baden-Powell, Robert 10, 12, 23, 68, 135
Baker, Lieutenant-Colonel *Memoir on the
  Northern
    Frontier of Greece* 41
Balaclava 35
Bala Hissar 58, 67
Baring, Evelyn 89
Barkly Bridge 134
Barnet, Correlli 74
Bayly, C.A. 43
Beach, Hicks 126
Beach, Thomas 20
Bell, Gertrude 178
Belloc, Hilaire 105
Bentley, Nicolas 39
Berlin Conference 98
Bismarck, Otto von 49
Bloch, Ivan *La Guerre Future* 109
Board of Admiralty 124
Boeckenhoutskloof 123

Boer War (also Anglo–Boer War) 48, 74, 88, 116, 117-20, 134-6, 149-150
Bokhara 18, 56
Bonham-Carter, Victor 152
Boxer Rebellion 160
Brackenbury, Sir Richard 28, 76, 81
    biographical summary 178
Briggs, Sir John Henry 39
British Expeditionary Force 30
British Guiana 14
British High Commission 100
Broadwood, Colonel 107
Browne, Professor E.G. 133
Brudenell, James 65
Buller, Redvers 118, 127
Bunsen, Maurice de 136
Burckhart-Barker, W. *Notes on a Journey to the Source of the River Orontes* 41
Burnaby, Frederick 58-9
    On Horseback Through Asia Minor 62
Burnes, Alexander 55, 56-7
Burton, Sir Richard 30, 31
Cairo 137, 138, 139
Calwell, General 137
Cambridge, Duke of 34
Campbell, Sir Colin 38
Campbell-Bannerman, Henry 79
Canada 14
Cardigan, Earl of 35
Cardwell, Edward 27, 65, 75, 77
Carmichael-Smyth,
Catoni, Joseph 147
Colonel George 45
Caspian Sea 57
Caron, Major Henri le 20
Cattley, Charles 28-9, 36-7
Cawdor, Earl 163
Cecil, Sir Robert 141
Chelmsford, Lord 22
Chemkent 59
Chernaya Pass 37
Childers, Erskine 101
    The Riddle of the Sands 163
    Chitral 172
Churchill, Winston 85, 119-120, 127-8, 162
Clarendon, Earl of 36
Clarke, Sir George Sydenham 124
Clausewitz, Carl von *On War* 16
Clayton, Sir Gilbert 139

biographical summary 178
Committee of Imperial
Conrad, Joseph, *The Secret Agent* 166
Congo Free State 116
Congress of Berlin 112
Conolly, Arthur 52
Connaught Rangers 133
Constantinople 56, 112, 136, 140
Council of India 85
Cox, Percy 141
Crimean War 9, 19, 28-31
Cromer, Lord 89, 109
Curzon-Wylie, Sir William 162
Daily Graphic 71
Dalhousie, Lord 42
Dardanelles expedition 136
Dar Fur 92
David, Saul 22, 41
Davies, Sir Fraser 159
Delhi 43
De Windt, Harry 82
Directorate of Military Intelligence 170
Dongola 90
Dost Mohammed 19, 55, 57
Douglas, Sir Howard 40
Downer, Martin 13
Doyle, Sir Arthur 13
Dreadnought 164
Dreyfus affair 163
East India Company 31, 43, 55, 100
Edmonds, General J.E. 122, 158
Elgin Commission 149
El Obeid 91
Elphinstone, Sir Howard 13
Enlistment Act (1870) 75
Eshowe campaign 20
Euphrates 62
Evans, Lacy 52
Everest, Colonel 19
Ewart, Major-General 158
Feder, Milton 168
Feisal 141
Fenians 50
Fisher, Lord 164
Foreign Office 56, 146
Fort George 47
'Forward School' 84
Franco-Prussian War 12, 17, 66, 115
Frere, Bartle 85
Friedrich-Wilhelm IV 49
Frontier Force 104

Gairdener, Lieutenant-Colonel 45
Gallipoli 137
Game of War (*Kriegspiel*) 26, 152
Gazetteer and Military Report on Afghanistan
  67
Gerard, James 55
Gezira 108
Gibraltar 163
Gilgit 70
Gladstone, W.E. 59
Gordon, General 90-1
Gorst, Edith
Gortchakoff 59
Graham, General 114-5
'Great Game' 20-1, 50-1, 60-1, 85, 109
Grenadier Guards 105
Grierson, Major-General 125
Gulf of Aqaba 143
Gwalior 44
Haddendowa tribe 114
Haddington, Earl of 39
Haggard, H. Rider 13, 99
  King Solomon's Mines 99
  Hakim 140
Hamley, Sir Edward 71
Hampshire Telegraph 40
Hamilton, Colonel Ian 123
Hamilton, Lieutenant 68
Hankey, Maurice 143
Hartington Commission 77
Haynes, Alan 23
Helm, Lieutenant 167
Henderson, G.F.C. 72, 79, 119
  biographical summary 179
Herat 15, 56
Hernon, Ian 9, 87
Hickman, Colonel 123
Hicks, General 90
Hildyard, Colonel 72, 127
Hills, E.H. 123
HMS *Salamis* 113
Hogarth, D.G. 139, 142
  biographical summary 179
Holmes, Richard 101
Hopkirk, Peter 14, 53, 62
  The Great Game 172
Hughes-Wilson, John 50
Ibn Saud 141
Illustrated London News 29
Indian Mutiny 46
Intelligence Branch 69, 74

Isaacs, Rufus 167
Jackson, H.C. 106
James, Lawrence 52
Jane's Fighting Ships 164
Jebel Druse 146
Jedda 140
Jervis, Thomas Best 19, 25
Jhansi, Ranee of 42
Journal of the Household Brigade 26
Kabul 55, 67
Kaiser Wilhelm 152
Kaffir War 18
Kandahar 69
Karachi 50
Karakum desert 53
Kashmir 68
Kaye, Sir John 86
Keegan, John 9, 18
Kell, Vernon 127-8, 158, 162-3, 167
Kemeid 145
Khalifa Abdullahi 96, 102
Khan, Abdul Hamid 85
Khan, Ahsanullah 42
Khan, Ayub 54
Khartoum 79
Khiva 18, 63
Khyber Pass 55
Kinglake, A.W. 31
  Eothen, 32
Kipling, Rudyard
  Kim 15, 50
  Tommy 29
Kitchener, Lord 10, 73, 98, 101-2, 141
Kock, General 118
Kofi 77
'La Dame Blanche' 170
Lal 55
Lang's Nek 22
Lahore 54
Lawrence, Henry 17, 53-4, 63
Lawrence T.E. 132, 138
  Seven Pillars of Wisdom 138, 140, 145
Lehmann, Joseph 27
Le Queux, William 13, 169
Light Brigade 36
Lloyd, Colonel 36
Lloyd george 163
Long Tom guns 150
Lucan, Lord 34
Luxor 95
Mafeking 118

Majuba Hill 119
Mall, Jat 42
Mahdi, the 80, 90-91, 103
Malakand 84, 86
Mason, A.E.W. 99
  The Four Feathers 99, 173
Masson, Charles 19, 57
Maunsell, Colonel 136
Maurice, Sir John 28
  History of the 1882 Campaigns in Egypt 79
  biographical summary 179
Maxim, Hiram 105
Mecca 144
Meerut 45
Melville, Sir William 21, 159
Menelek 104
Metropolitan Police 169
Meyer, Lucas 118
Mesopotamia (Iraq) 137, 147
MI5 125, 158, 167, 168
  H Section 125
Milutin, General 60
Mirza Mahmood 140
MO5 161
Mohs, Polly 138
Montgomerie, Thomas 52
Montgomery, Sir Robert 85
Morant, Harry 119
Morris, Jan 21
Moscow 15
Mysore 43
Napoleon 14, 94, 170
Napleon III 32
Napoleonic War 25
Natal 118
National Defence Act (1888) 115
Nesselrode, G. 34
Nicholas I, Tsar 33, 57
Nicholson, Sir William 126
Norvals' Point 154
Nuba mountains 91
O'Connor, Feargus 18
Official Secrets Act (1911) 159
Omdurman, battle of 10, 101-109
Orange Free State 119
Orenburg 61
Osman Digna 106, 114
Ottoman Empire 32
Oye, David Schimmelpennick Van Der 165

Pakenham, Thomas 153
Palermerston, Lord 22
Palestine railway 148
Palin, Mildred 71
Pamirs 70, 81
Panmure, Lord 25
Pan-Slavists 33, 63
Parr, Colonel 100
Pay Corps and Remount Department 115
Petrograd 137
Picot, Francois-Georges 144
Pirie-Gordon, Captain 147
Political and Secret Department 86
Proctor, Tammy 124
Prussia 49, 72, 115
Punjab 51, 57
Purniya 43
Queen Anne's Gate 117, 122, 171
Quinn, Patrick 166
Raglan, Lord 29
Rawlinson, Sir Henry 85
  Field Service Regulations 127
Rice, Edward 30
Rimington, Stella 166
Roberts, Andrew 138
Roberts, Sir Frederick 67
Roberts, Lord 73, 118-9, 125, 154
Robertson, William 11, 26, 31, 65-88
  DSO 71
  At Staff College 72-3
  Simla 81-2 Chitral expedition 83 Chief of Staff 88
  In new Intelligence Division, 151
  Biographical summary, 175
Roerdanz, Major 26
Rorke's Drift 106
Rose, Colonel Hugh 33
Rowan, Sir Charles 169
Royal Corps of Engineers 135
Royal Cycle Corps 147
Royal Navy 160-1
Russell, William Howard 33, 39
Russian army 58-60
Russian Empire 51
Russo-Turkish War (1877-8) 109
Sahib, Nana 42
Scind 44
Scotland Yard 159
Secret Intelligence department 36
Seely, Jack 48
Sepoy Mutiny 21

Sevastopol, battle of 35
Seymour, Sir Hamilton 32
Sharif Hussein 146
Shipka Pass 112
Shujah, Shah 55
Sikh War (Ist) 54
Simla 67
Singh, Nain 46
Singh, Ranjit 56, 58
Slatin, Rudolf 10, 11, 91-98, 103-4
   Fire and Sword in the Sudan 93
   Imprisonment 94-5
   Sledmere House 130
   biographical summary 176
Sleeman, Colonel 44, 100
Spectator 63
Special Branch 171, 173
Spion Kop 118, 128
Staff College 26, 71, 72
Stacy, Brigadeer 45
Stanhope, Edward 115
Steevens, G.W. 10, 169
   In India 46
   With Kitchener to Khartoum 46, 102
Steinhauer, Gustav 157, 171
Stieber, Wilhelm 20, 49, 76
Storrs, Ronald 130, 137, 139
   biographical summary 179
Sudan 73, 146
Suez Canal Company 89
Sweny, Eugene 40
Sykes, Christopher 130, 133
   The Big House 133
Sykes, Mark 11, 31, 109, 130-148
   early life 130
   character 131-2
   with Jebel Druse 132
   at Jesus College 132
   early travels 133-4
   secretary to George
   MP for Hull 136
   Wyndham 135
   Turkish railways warfare 143
   -biographical summary 177
Sykes, Sir Tatton 132
Sykes-Picot Agreement 130, 137, 139-148
   zones 144
Sykes, Percy 86, 132
Tactique Maritime 40
Tel el Kebir 79

Third Section (Russian secret service) 48
Tashkent 59, 67
Tchernayev, General 59
Thornhill, Mark 45
Thornycroft, Colonel 128
Tigris 62
Tissot, James 63
Topographical and Statistical Office 20, 25
Towfik Pasha 92
Transvaal 149
Treaty of Burampoor 44
Trotsy, Leon 159
Turkey 33
Turkestan 52
Victoria, Queen 24, 38, 47, 101
Vitkevich 57
Wade, Claude 19
Walla, Dada 44
Walsingham, Francis 23
War Office 10, 18, 74, 137, 150
   cabinet for war 137
Waterloo, battle of 9, 26
Watson, Jimmy 104
Wellington, Duke of 25, 38
West, Nigel 168
Wet, Piet de 134-5
White, Sir George 72, 84
Wilcox, Craig 119
Wilmott, Louise 16
Wilson, Lieutentant Colonel 127, 159
Wingate, Reginald 10, 90, 92-98, 103-5
   Mahdism and the Egyptian Sudan 90
   early life 95-6
   wt Omdurman 107-8
   use of agents 97-8
   Battle of Toski 98
   friendship with Slatin 99-100
   biographical summary 176
Woerth 73
Wolseley, Sir Garnet 10, 26, 68, 77-8, 102
'Wolseley Set' 27
Wood, Evelyn 96, 102
Woodgate, General 128
Wyndham, George 119, 135-6
Yarkand valley 70
Younghusband, Francis 23, 132
Zionism 137, 145-6
Zobeir Pasha 99
Zulus 9, 10
Zulu War 128, 160